DALLAS COWBOYS

The Legends of America's Team

SECOND EDITION

BY JIM REEVES

BERKELEY PLACE BOOKS

DEDICATION

To my Mom, who taught me to love words ...
To Karen, who helped me to hear them sing ...

Dallas Cowboys: The Legends of America's Team 2nd Edition
By Jim Reeves
Cover illustrator: Mark Hoffer
Editor & book designer: Tom Johanningmeier
Book cover design: Kari Crane

© Copyright 2016, 2017 by Jim Reeves

First edition, 2016
10 9 8 7 6 5 4

Second edition, 2017
10 9 8 7 6 5 4 3 2 1

All rights reserved. No portion of this book may be reproduced mechanically, electronically or by any other means, including photocopying or scanning without the written permission of the publisher.

Bulk sales of books from Berkeley Place Books are available at special discounts for fundraising, promotions and premiums.

Berkeley Place Books
An imprint of Great Texas Line Press
Post Office Box 11105
Fort Worth, Texas 76110
817-922-8929 / FAX 817-926-0420

Printed in USA by Versa Press, East Peoria, Ill.

Library of Congress Cataloging-in-Publication Data
Reeves, Jim, 1946—
Dallas Cowboys: The Legends of America's Team 2nd Edition / by Jim Reeves.
   p. cm.
Includes index
ISBN 978-1-892588-609 (paperback, revised second edition)
1.Dallas Cowboys 2. National Football League 3. Football 4. Jerry Jones 5. Tom Landry 6. Roger Staubach 7. Troy Aikman 8. Dak Prescott I. Title.

Contents

Prologue	5
The Architects	
Clint Murchison Jr.	8
H.r. "Bum" Bright	11
Jerry Jones	14
Tex Schramm	23
Gil Brandt	27
The Coaches	
Tom Landry	30
Jimmy Johnson	33
Barry Switzer	40
Chan Gailey	41
Dave Campo	42
Bill Parcells	43
Wade Phillips	45
Jason Garrett	46
The Quarterbacks	
Don Meredith	49
Roger Staubach	53
Danny White	59
Troy Aikman	62
Tony Romo	66

The Running Backs
- Don Perkins — 70
- Calvin Hill/Duane Thomas — 71
- Tony Dorsett — 73
- Emmitt Smith — 76

The Wide Receivers
- Bob Hayes — 78
- Drew Pearson — 80
- Michael Irvin — 83
- Dez Bryant — 86

The Tight Ends
- Before Billy Joe — 89
- Billy Joe Dupree — 92
- Doug Cosbie — 93
- Jay Novacek — 95
- Jason Witten — 98

The Linemen And Defense
- Upon This Rock ... — 101

Championship Games
- The Ice Bowl — 109
- Super Bowl V — 117
- Super Bowl VI — 121
- Super Bowl X — 125
- Super Bowl XII — 132
- Super Bowl XIII — 137
- "The Catch" — 141
- Super Bowl XXVII — 146
- Super Bowl XXVIII — 151
- Super Bowl XXX — 157

The Breakup — 171
Keeping Up With The Joneses — 177
Finish The Fight — 183
Acknowledgements — 194
Index — 196

Prologue

The phone rang in my hotel room at Atlanta's Crowne Plaza Hotel sometime around 4:30 in the morning. Some eight hours earlier, on Jan. 30, 1994, the Dallas Cowboys had romped to their second straight Super Bowl title behind game MVP Emmitt Smith, who had rushed for 132 yards and two second half touchdowns. The hapless victims – again – were the Buffalo Bills, 30-13. What Troy Aikman had done through the air a year earlier in a 52-17 rout at the Rose Bowl, Smith had done on the ground this time around. The (counterfeit) Bills lost their fourth straight Super Bowl.

I'd filed my column for the *Fort Worth Star-Telegram*, partied with hundreds of others to the music of Jerry Lee Lewis sound-alike Jason D. Williams at Jerry Jones' massive postgame soirée, had a few nightcaps with Dale Hansen and met country singer Clint Black at Aikman's own private party. I'd finally slipped away to try and get a few hours sleep before the morning day-after press conferences.

Hansen, the rollicking Dallas WFAA-Channel 8 sports anchor, had other ideas.

"What the hell are you doing?" he demanded when I picked up the phone.

I mumbled something about trying to go to bed.

"The hell with that," Hansen roared, as only he can roar. "Some of us are having a few beers in Aikman's room. Come on up."

I thought about ignoring him ... for maybe three seconds. Then I thought, Hey stupid, how often do you get to hang out with the guy who just won the Super Bowl? The guy who quarterbacks America's

Team?

Duh!

"Be right there," I told Hansen, who never takes no for an answer anyway.

It was surreal.

After the hoopla and bedlam of the game and the two parties, it was incredibly subdued in Aikman's suite. Even Hansen was finally mellowing out. Beer was iced down on a table with a few bowls of peanuts alongside. Longtime Cowboys' beat writer Mickey Spagnola, who now works for the team's website, was there, but memory fails me on who else showed up. Not many. There weren't more than a half dozen of us all together.

For the next few hours we sipped beer, ate peanuts and chatted about the game with Aikman, who was just killing time until he had to show up downstairs for all the national TV morning shows. Sometime around 6 a.m., he ordered a few pizzas for everyone, then a couple of us followed him around to the network sets in the hotel lobby, watching as he did his obligatory interviews.

I never did get to bed. I remember thinking as I yawned at some point around dawn, "so this is how a Super Bowl winning quarterback celebrates."

Not all Super Bowl-winning quarterbacks, of course. But that was Aikman. He would repeat the process two years later at The Buttes in Phoenix, only with a lot more people in his suite after the team party had shut down. Again the pizza at 6 a.m., and the cycle of the network morning shows afterwards.

Wouldn't have missed it for the world.

To be honest, I was pretty much a Johnny-Come-Lately on the Cowboys' scene. I was still trying to get my career on track at the *Star-Telegram* when the Cowboys first started winning Super Bowls in the early '70s. Then I spent a dozen years covering the Texas Rangers as a beat man before becoming a general sports columnist in 1987. Even then, we had excellent veteran columnists in Galyn Wilkins and Gil LeBreton, first in line to do our Cowboys' stuff. It wasn't until the 1988 season, Tom Landry's last year, that I occasionally began venturing into the kingdom of the legendary Dallas Cowboys.

It was fortuitous timing as it turned out. In February 1989, a new king of the Cowboys would arrive, with a brand new coach and a brand new quarterback, and it wasn't long before America's Team was back. Socks and jocks, Jerry and Jimmy, The Triplets, Super Bowls almost as regular as clockwork. It was a great time to follow the Cowboys.

It would be easy to slip into biblical metaphors when talking about the Dallas Cowboys. America's Team? Not sure that's big enough. How about, World's Team? The Universe's Team? Is there a more prominent, more recognizable sports brand on the planet?

Don't even try to argue that the Dallas Cowboys haven't surpassed the New York Yankees for the No. 1 spot in this country, and that's despite the fact that it's been 20 years since Jones' Cowboys last sniffed a Super Bowl, much less won one. Somehow, the Cowboys have reached that enviable position of continuing to grow more popular despite not winning. Imagine what it will be like if they ever get back to the big game again.

If you're looking for the definitive history of the Dallas Cowboys, this isn't it. Try the library or local book store. There have been volumes written about this team and this franchise. No, this is more of a Cowboys' primer, hitting the high points and talking about many – but not all – of the team's characters that have graced our sports pages over almost 60 years now.

Many of the names and stories you are about to read have reached the level of mythology for Cowboys' fans. The Ring of Honor at Jones' magnificent AT&T Stadium isn't just a roll call of past Cowboys' heroes, it's Mount Olympus itself. Those who wore and who wear The Star have taken on the aura of gods, from Schramm, to Landry, to Meredith, to Lilly, to Staubach, to Dorsett, to Troy, to Emmitt, to Michael, on and on through the annals of NFL history.

It was fun to watch this franchise grow and flourish as a fan in the '60s and '70s and it was an honor to have a chance to cover them in the wondrous '90s. Without a doubt, there is no sports franchise in history quite like the Dallas Cowboys.

But then, you already know that or you wouldn't have this book in your hands.

Jim Reeves
Arlington, Texas

The Architects

CLINT MURCHISON JR.

As football fight songs go, *Hail to the Redskins* is eminently forgettable. Only diehard 'Skins fans would stand up before the game, reverently raise their right hands, and chant/sing:

Braves on the warpath, fight for old D.C.!
Run or pass or score, we want a lot more!
Beat 'em, swamp 'em, touchdown!
Let the points soar!

Takes a lot of pre-game tailgating and cold beer to make those lyrics palatable. Yet, Clint Murchison Jr. was once able to parlay the rights to that song into an NFL franchise in Dallas, Texas. It's how the most recognizable brand in NFL history – the Dallas Cowboys – was born.

Only in America.

With a beginning like that, no wonder the Cowboys have continually captured the imagination of football fans around the world with not only their on-field accomplishments, but with their off-field antics and adventures as well. Long before the term was coined for television, football fans across America realized that the Cowboys were an ongoing reality show, a real-life soap opera that no Hollywood scriptwriter could dream up.

Think about the pantheon of inimitable characters who have either worn or been associated with The Star, from colorful owners like Murchison and Jerry Jones, to the brilliance of Tex Schramm, to the Man in the Hat, Tom Landry, to the Man With the Hair, Jimmy Johnson, to the Texas twang of Don Meredith, to the heroics of Roger Staubach and Troy Aikman, to the resilience and determination of

Emmitt Smith, to the antics of Michael Irvin.

This is the team with the intriguing dichotomy of a stadium with a hole in the roof, so God could watch his team play, but also with the sinfully delicious "White House," where the players could play. Arguably the most popular franchise in the history of sports, this is the team which was also known at one time as the "Cocaine Cowboys," for their propensity to party as hard as they played.

This is the team with eight trips to the Super Bowl, five world championships, and a star player wearing a fur coat in the courtroom, the one who once asked the police the question, "Can I tell you who I am?"

Not really necessary, Michael. Just like it's not really necessary for a formal introduction of America's Team. This is the Dallas Cowboys, the franchise that started with ... well. ...

A song.

• • •

Redskins' owner George Preston Marshall loved the team's fight song. He loved hearing the D.C. crowd sing it before games, during games, after games. It had, after all, been co-written by Marshall's ex-wife, Corinne, and society bandleader Barney Briskin back in the 1950s.

At some point, the original lyrics, which were even more politically incorrect then than they are today – instead of "fight for old D.C.," it was "fight for old Dixie," and "scalp 'em, swamp 'em, we will take 'em big score" – were modified slightly. Corinne, who retained her share of the song rights in the divorce settlement with Marshall, later sold them to Briskin. Unbeknownst to Marshall, Murchison happened to be friendly with the bandleader himself and in the fall of 1959, sent his emissary, Washington lobbyist Bobby Baker, to offer Briskin $2,500 for the rights to the song. Briskin, as the story goes, needed the cash.

Sold!

As the Redskins prepared for a late-season game in 1959, Marshall got a call from Murchison.

"Does the Redskins band intend to play the Redskins fight song?" Murchison innocently inquired, according to Peter Golenbock in his book, *Cowboys Have Always Been My Heroes*.

"They sure will," Marshall answered.

"The hell they will," Murchison shot back. "Nobody plays my fight song without my permission."

That's how Marshall learned that the man who was about to become owner of the Redskins' No. 1 NFL nemesis now owned the Washington team's fight song. All Murchison wanted from Marshall to return the rights to *Hail to the Redskins* was for him to back away from opposing Dallas' entry into the league in 1960. Marshall had vehemently opposed NFL expansion, especially for a team in the south, a territory inundated by his Redskins' radio network.

But he couldn't bear the thought of the Redskins playing without the uplifting, inspiring, *Hail to the Redskins* blaring throughout the stadium. How could the Redskins possibly win without it? Ultimately, he acquiesced to Murchison's backroom deal.

Marshall got his song back.

Murchison — and Dallas — got the Cowboys.

• • •

As the late, great Frank Luksa observed in his book, *Cowboys Essential*, Murchison's understated leadership, always conducted in the background, was never fully appreciated by the public. His wealth, which was substantial, didn't depend on his venture into pro football. He had so many far-flung investments, he once called for a reservation at a hotel he'd forgotten he owned. He hired Schramm as the team's GM, Landry as its coach and Gil Brandt as its first super scout and, of all things, left them alone to do their jobs.

"He never interfered with their decisions or objected to any expense," Luksa wrote, "from flying a team to California for training camp or introducing computer-driven evaluations to the scouting process."

Nor did Murchison, unlike many other owners we could name, ever imagine himself as the team's coach, wearing either a fedora or a hoodie. Not once did he ever send in a play for Landry to run.

"I do not offer suggestions to Tom Landry," Murchison told Luksa. "Furthermore, Landry never makes any suggestions as to how I conduct my sixth-grade football team, which incidentally is undefeated. We have a professional standoff."

In fact, most Dallas fans might have argued that Murchison

could have done as well with the Cowboys in their first four seasons as Landry did, with the team posting a 13-38-2 record. Critics didn't just want Landry's hat, they wanted his head and smart money said Murchison would wield the ax before the 1965 season. Instead, Murchison did just the opposite, signing Landry to a shocking 10-year contract, the kind of security that just wasn't handed out in those days, especially to a coach 25 games under .500 for his career.

"We had lost several games … after we had given Tom the contract," Murchison told Luksa. "And after we had lost one real bad – really been pummeled to death – I had lunch with a friend, and he said there's a silver lining in all this. He said, 'At least Tom's only got nine years left.'"

Rarely quoted or in the public eye, Murchison couldn't help himself after the Cowboys reached the top of the NFL mountain with a 24-3 domination of Miami in Super Bowl VI in New Orleans. Asked for his reaction, Murchison grinned and said wryly, "This is the successful conclusion of our 12-year plan."

Another under-appreciated facet of Murchison's ownership: his sense of humor, which was as dry as a west Texas tumbleweed and equally abundant.

The same would never be said of his successor.

H.R. "BUM" BRIGHT

H.R. "Bum" Bright hated Tom Landry.
Now ask yourself who, for crying out loud, could hate Tom Landry? OK, maybe a few players, but that's all. Has to be an Aggie joke, right? Landry, as any football fan knows, is probably the closest thing to a saint this state has ever seen.

Yet, almost from the moment Bright bought the Cowboys from a financially and physically failing Clint Murchison Jr. in 1984, he had no use for the revered and universally admired Landry, a man Bright resented for his "unapproachable arrogance."

Did Bright's almost visceral dislike of Landry stem from their collegiate backgrounds, Landry coming from the University of Texas and Bright from Texas A&M, where he served as chairman of the school's board of regents from 1981-85? Who knows? What was certain was that there was no love lost between the two men.

They had actually met for the first time way back in 1957, after Bear Bryant left Texas A&M and Bright was among those helping conduct the search for a successor for the Aggies. Landry, according to Bright, contacted him about the job and was granted an interview. Bright later said he was "singularly unimpressed." The feeling, it seems safe to assume, was mutual. Bright was constantly annoyed that Landry generally ignored him at team Christmas parties and other public functions.

Longtime A&M coach R.C. Slocum once described Bright as "a man's man" and his friend's purchase of the Cowboys as something he wanted to do for the city of Dallas and the state of Texas. "When the Cowboys thing came up, he was so worried they were going elsewhere," Slocum said. "Buying the Cowboys was a business deal, but a big part of it was also keeping the Cowboys in Texas."

Bright was a rags-to-riches self-made man. He walked out of A&M in 1942 at the age of 27 with a degree in petroleum engineering and $12 in his bank account. He began buying, selling and trading oil leases. It took him just four years to make his first million.

He was determined, persistent and sometimes ruthless. There are stories about his business deals that have become legend, like the time he allegedly talked a wife into kicking her husband out of the bedroom until he agreed to sell Bright a lease, or when he supposedly tied a pen to a hospital patient's hand to help him sign a contract.

"I play to win," Bright told Golenbock. "I don't care if it's checkers or gin rummy or the oil and gas business. You play the game to win."

Ironically, 20 years later another book, written by David Magee, would be titled *Playing to Win*. It's primary subject: Jerry Jones.

In November of 1982, when Murchison's failing health and crumbling financial empire forced him into the realization that he would have to sell his beloved Cowboys, he asked general manager Tex Schramm to find a buyer. Schramm was nothing if not shrewd. Even though former Murchison business partner Vance Miller and Dallas car dealer W.O. Bankston wanted to buy the team — they'd once plunked down $550,000 to buy up the remaining tickets to a playoff game against the Rams so it could be shown on local TV — Schramm wasn't confident they would continue to let him run the team as he had in the past, or even let him keep his job.

So Schramm brought Bright, another old friend of Murchison's, into the picture. Bright had assured Tex that his intention was to be the same kind of hands-off owner that Clint had been.

Bright, though, was a contradiction in styles from the classy Murchison, who never balked at extra expenses for his precious Cowboys. Though Bright, who earned his nickname because his father thought his brand new son looked like a little hobo all wrapped up in blankets, was at one time one of the 50 richest men in America, he was also frugal to a fault with a great dread of poverty, probably because he had experienced that side of life in his younger years.

"I've been broke once," Bright told the *Dallas Morning News* for a story in October 1986. "I don't want it to happen again."

Bright, as legend has it, charged a Cowboys' employee $1 for individual cigarettes when the man ran out of smokes during the long negotiations to sell the team to Jerry Jones in 1989. He also stalked out of a cafeteria rather than pay 85 cents for a cup of coffee. This is the same man who donated an unrestricted $25 million to Texas A&M in 1997 and another $5 million later to help renovate Kyle Field.

Bright was also a workaholic who demanded as much or more from himself than his employees. He was aghast when he had to have his gall bladder removed and the doctor told him he might need 10 days of hospitalization. Bum quickly located a new doctor, had the surgery without being put to sleep, chatted throughout the operation and checked himself out of the hospital the same night. Two days later he was back at work.

Bright was not a huge Cowboys' fan by any means. His commitment, football-wise, was to A&M and always would be, so when Schramm first approached him, he said he wasn't interested. Schramm persisted and some of Bright's other friends and business partners urged him to step up and buy the high-profile NFL team.

Finally, he put together a group of 11 investors, including Schramm at 3 percent, and made Murchison an offer of $84.5 million. Bright's investment was for only 17 percent of the deal. Schramm convinced then-NFL commissioner Pete Rozelle (who had once been Schramm's PR director when Tex was the Rams' GM) to OK the purchase despite the NFL's professed policy of preferring one investor owning the majority of the stock.

Bright's troubled ownership would last just four seasons, included a 27-37 won-loss record, one division title, one playoff appearance (a 20-0 loss to the Rams in '85), a savings and loan scandal, and the collapse of the oil and gas market (both helping to gut Bright's personal fortune). If there was a silver lining for Bright, it also was the beginning of the end for Tom Landry as disillusionment with the iconic head coach spread from the owner's office, to the media and even to the fans.

The catalyst for dramatic change at Valley Ranch was coming.

His name was Jerald Wayne Jones.

JERRY JONES

There was no getting around it. Christmas 1994 was going to be a miserable affair. At least that's the way it looked for reporters and columnists covering the Dallas Cowboys. The Cowboys were playing the New York Giants at the Meadowlands in New Jersey on Christmas Eve afternoon that year. The airlines were not impressed.

They had canceled flights right and left, apparently for lack of interest that close to the holiday. The only reporters getting home after the Cowboys' game that day would be those who could get their work done in time to catch the team charter after the game. That would not include the reporter/columnists from the *Star-Telegram* and *Dallas Morning News*. We would spend our Christmas Eve stuck in a hotel, away from families, and our Christmas Day would be eaten up just trying to get back home.

Bah humbug.

Not shedding a tear yet? I understand. There are millions all over the world, including thousands of men and women in uniform, who don't get home for Christmas, don't get paid to watch a football game, don't get to travel on somebody else's dime. That fact didn't offer much consolation for the handful of us wimpy newspaper folk that were going to be affected.

Oh, we'd have all survived if we'd missed a Christmas Eve-Christmas at home but it wasn't anyone's idea of the perfect holiday. Some, as it turned out, did have to endure a lonely Christmas Eve in the Big Apple and spent their Christmas Day flying home. But for others, including yours truly, an unexpected hero rode to the rescue on his trusty steed Lear.

His name was Jerry Jones.

Not a name you normally associate with "hero," right? But Jerry Jones is complicated and perception isn't always reality. This is a side of Jerry that few people know or appreciate.

Jones got wind that a number of writers who followed the team were going to be stuck in New York, unable to get home for Christmas. He knew he could do something about that, and after all, it was Christmas. Jones sent word to the press box that he would leave his private jet at a small airport not far from the Meadowlands. He and his family would fly back to Texas on the team charter.

Four of us took him up on his offer (the *Star-Telegram* would later send him a check to reimburse him for at least part of the cost of the flight). When we finished our work at the stadium, we walked outside to find a limo waiting to take us to the plane at a private airport in Teterboro, New Jersey. The jet was stocked with food and drink for the ride home. Most importantly, we were home with our families for Christmas, thanks to an unexpected not-so-secret Santa.

Most casual Cowboys fans, however, don't know that Jerry. The Jerry they know is the one who disgracefully fired arguably the most admired man in DFW sports history, the late and great Tom Landry. They only know the high-roller they see on TV, who too often comes across as arrogant and completely oblivious to his own culpability in his team's continuing failures on the field.

They know Jerry by the barbs – most of them deserving—flung at him by his loudest critics, among them WFAA sports anchor Dale Hansen, and (now retired) sports columnist Randy Galloway, who fired his salvos from both sides of the Metroplex, working for the *Dallas Morning News* and the *Fort Worth Star-Telegram* over a span of 40-plus years while also anchoring the area's most successful sports talk show for much of that time. Jerry provided more ammunition than most of us could ever use.

Jerry is an easy target; he almost never fights back, partly because he's one of those smart guys who figures any publicity is good publicity, and partly because he has little defense to throw up. We are now north of the 20-year mark since the team's last Super Bowl. The glory days are fast fading from memory.

But irrelevant? Heavens no, the Cowboys are many things, but never irrelevant, no matter how suspect the product on the field. There's a reason, even in their lowest moments, why the Cowboys still dominate Dallas-Fort Worth's sportscasts and sports pages.

There is no doubt that Jones has supplanted the late George Steinbrenner, longtime owner of the New York Yankees, as the most despised owner in American sports. Equally certain is that he has rightfully descended to that position. Jerry simply has a knack for publicly rubbing folks the wrong way.

Of course, most of those people have never actually met him. To meet Jerry Jones, to spend any time around him, is to be bowled over by his warmth, his gregarious personality, his essential "fun-ness," to make up a word. He can work a crowd with the best of them.

ESPN The Magazine's Don Van Notta Jr. noted in an in-depth profile of Jones back in August of 2014, how much Jerry, in style, resembles another of Arkansas' favorite sons.

"Instantly I'm reminded of another unstoppable life force, Bill Clinton," Van Notta Jr. wrote of meeting Jones for the first time. "Jerry and Bill: two Arkansas good ol' boys who've made good and know just how to work ya."

It's no state secret that Jerry enjoys his Johnny Walker Blue and the nightlife. Before he and Hansen, who worked for Jones as Brad Sham's sidekick on the Cowboys' radio broadcasts for years, had their falling out and became bitter antagonists, they were regular drinking buddies.

Hansen's voice, as he recounts one of those nights of revelry, can't disguise his fondness and admiration for Jones even today.

"Without question, my favorite all-time Jerry story was in his second year of owning the team," Hansen said. "The Cowboys were in Austin, Texas, (for training camp). Jerry actually calls me back in Dallas and wants me to come back down for his annual media party.

"I come back and we start out at Hooter's. When we left there, we hit another bar. Then another one. Now we hit Sixth Street at about 2:30 in the morning, the bar's closed, but Jerry walks in and says, 'I need drinks for all my guys.' The guy behind the bar says, 'I'm sorry, Mr. Jones, the bar's closed and we can't serve alcohol after 2 a.m.'

"Jerry says, 'Start serving drinks or I buy this bar and you're the first son of a bitch I get rid of.' Five minutes later Jones walks up and says, 'Dale, go take a piss.' So I stagger into the bathroom and there's a guy sitting on the crapper and he says, 'What do you like, margarita, rum and Coke, what?' Jones and I drank until 5:30 in the morning.

"The part that I've never told is that I literally fall off a barstool at 5:30 in the morning, but to my credit, I call a cab. Jerry's still drinking. I get back to the hotel and sleep until 4 in the afternoon and wake up so hung over I can't see. Jones went from that bar at 5:30 in the morning to *Good Morning America* at 7 o'clock. He was at the morning practice, the noon press conference and the afternoon practice. I stagger in about 4:30 to do the 5 o'clock show and there's Jerry, chipper as ever, saying, 'Dale, Dale, I got to tell you what happened after you left.'

"I said, 'Jerry, I don't know, I don't ever want to know.'"

That's Jerry Jones, the best drinking buddy a man could ever have. He'll go until the sun comes up and he always picks up the tab. But like some of his other admirable qualities, that doesn't necessarily qualify him as a great general manager. Jerry's greatest dream, Galloway once wrote, is to be recognized as "a football guy." Until and unless he wins a Super Bowl without Jimmy Johnson, that's unlikely to ever happen.

He is, however, headed to the NFL Hall of Fame in Canton, Ohio, as one of the most important owners in league history. With no salary cap in the NFL, Jerry would have bought several more Super Bowls by now or gone bust trying, and his business acumen has helped make the league billions of dollars. NFL reporters were lavish in their praise of Jones' leadership in relocating the St. Louis Rams back to Los Angeles at the beginning of 2016, and more than one declared that it cemented his place in Canton.

Of course, everyone knows Jones didn't get his Cowboys' ownership off on the right foot. It was, in fact, a nightmarish start, with Jones standing face to face with a tearful Tom Landry in a golf course real estate office near Austin at dusk in late February 1989.

But before we go there and relive that dreadful, fateful night, perhaps we should head for where this all started, at a drive-in fruit stand just outside North Little Rock, Arkansas. That, and the full-fledged grocery store it would become, is where Jerald Wayne Jones would learn the ABCs of "bidness" from his father, Pat Jones.

Born in Los Angeles on Oct. 13, 1942, Jerry was just 2 when his parents, Pat and Arminta Jones, moved back to Arkansas. Pat Jones opened up that fruit stand alongside the England Highway in North Little Rock. Over the years it would grow into a thriving business and those happy foundation years remain etched in Jerry's memory.

Years later, when the Jones clan had relocated to Texas and Pat Jones lay dying in a Dallas hospital in late December, Jerry honored his father by bringing baskets of oranges to his hospital room. He wanted the smell of the citrus fruit to permeate the air there, to remind Pat of those wonderful, growing-up years for the Jones family. Every Christmas Pat would bring baskets of oranges home and their aroma would fill the Jones household.

"For us, that smell meant Christmas," Jones told me. "I wanted to bring Christmas into his hospital room, to bring back those memories."

Jerry would learn much about running a business from his father, who would often hire country-western bands to perform for his customers. Pat himself would regularly wander around the store in cowboy attire, boots and jeans and 10-gallon hat with twin holsters tied down low, twirling a pair of cap-popping six-guns, to the amusement of the clientele. He'd persuade a radio station to do live shows from the store. Arminta would station young Jerry, nattily dressed in a suit and bow tie, next to the entrance, where he would offer to help the ladies as they strolled in to do their shopping.

Pat was on his way to expanding his horizons to include a lucrative insurance company. Like his dad, Jerry was a natural born businessman. He loved football and would play it well enough through high school (as first a quarterback and then fullback) to earn Frank Broyles' notice at the University of Arkansas. But Jerry's dreams were far bigger than his 6-1, 190-pound body, which would limit his football future.

Recruited as a running back, Jones redshirted his freshman year, was switched to guard, and sat on the bench for most of the next three seasons, until the stubby guard ahead of him was moved to the defensive line in Jerry's senior year. That player's name was Jimmy Johnson.

Is it coincidence that Arkansas started winning when Jerry finally had a chance to start? Perhaps, or maybe it was just the famous Jones family luck. Whatever, spurred on by a stunning 14-13 upset of defending national champion Texas, the Razorbacks stormed through the 1964 season undefeated and slipped by Nebraska 10-7 in the Cotton Bowl as Texas was surprising No. 1-ranked Alabama in the Orange Bowl. Arkansas had won the national championship.

By then, Jones was already courting his future wife, Eugenia "Gene" Chambers and had joined his dad Pat in the insurance business. By 1965, he was investing in McDonald's, Kentucky Fried Chicken and a handful of other companies. He was on his way to fame and fortune.

The fortune began to multiply when he got into the oil and gas business. Jones immediately had success, investing in a theory that oil moved in a meandering stream and could be found deep in the Arkoma (Oklahoma) Basin. The Jones family hit on their first 15 wells and when 700 of 2,000 came in flush, Jerry had banked $50 million. The Jones luck again.

A sweetheart deal between Jones' Arkoma Inc. and good friend Sheffield Nelson, who owned ArkLa, a public utility that supplied natural gas to customers in Arkansas, would make Jones another $300 million. The state of Arkansas smelled something fishy but an investigation found no wrongdoing. Meanwhile, Jerry's real dream – to own a professional football team – was inching ever closer.

Business was one thing but football still had its hold on young Jerry. At 23, Jerry had approached his dad in 1966 with the idea of heading up a syndicate to buy the San Diego Chargers for $5.5 million. Pat told him it was a bad idea. Jones took his advice and backed away from the deal. A couple of months later the NFL and AFL merged and shortly after that the Chargers sold for $11.5 million. Pat loved to needle son Jerry about the time he cost him $6 million.

Almost a quarter of a century later, with the Arkoma money burning a hole in his custom suit jacket pocket, Jones was even more set on buying his way into the NFL. That the opportunity would include ownership of the most glamorous franchise in football was something even Jerry couldn't imagine.

Even that came about due to a confluence of events that could not have been predicted. Jones and oldest son Stephen were in San Diego for an oil and gas convention in September of 1988. The Jones boys decided to take a day off and head south to Cabo San Lucas for some sun and fun. They had a fishing boat chartered for the next day, but spent the evening before at the Giggling Marlin cantina, where turistas were regularly strung up by their heels – like caught marlin – and tube-fed as many margaritas as they could drink. No doubt, it did lead to a lot of giggling.

Jerry woke up the next morning with a Hansen-sized hangover and begged off the fishing trip, telling Stephen to go on by himself. Jerry spent the day lounging around the hotel room, nursing his headache. At some point, he opened his briefcase to find the previous day's San Diego newspaper. As was his habit, Jerry regularly devoured the paper, inch by inch, word by word. Buried on an inside sports page, only a couple of paragraphs long, an item caught his eye. It said that Cowboys' owner Bum Bright had hired the investment firm Salomon Brothers to help him find a buyer for the team.

Jones threw the newspaper down and ran for the lobby, where he told a manager he needed to make an international call to Salomon Brothers. He was directed into a room with a telephone and told the international operator would ring when the call had been put through. Jones paced the room, his head pounding. Finally, the phone rang and Jerry snatched it up.

"You don't know me," he yelled into the phone, "but my name is Jerry Jones, and if I live, I'm going to buy the Dallas Cowboys!"

Five months later, he stood face to face with Tom Landry in that room at Hideaway Lakes outside Austin and the legendary Cowboys' coach had tears glistening in his eyes.

"You've taken my team away from me," Landry reportedly told Jones.

It was a scene Jerry could have and probably should have avoided. He could have sent Tex Schramm to confirm the bad news to Landry, but Tex shrewdly told Jones that he should do it face to face himself. No bad guy role for Schramm at this point, and Jerry, to his credit, wasn't going to start his Cowboys' ownership by backing away from his responsibilities. Bright had volunteered to fire Landry as his last act as owner, but Jones felt it was his job to do.

Landry already knew what was coming after a photo of Jones and new head coach Jimmy Johnson having dinner together at Mia's, a Dallas Tex-Mex restaurant that just happened to be one of Landry's favorite spots, had appeared on the front page of the *Dallas Morning News* a day earlier. After 29 years, the Landry magic had worn off and the fedora was showing rust. The Cowboys hadn't had a winning season for three straight years and were a miserable 3-13 in '88. Columnists were publically wondering if the rest of the NFL hadn't finally caught up to Landry and his Flex defense. Fans were openly muttering about a change of head coaches.

Most forgot about that, however, in their outrage and indignation at this Arkansas hick who had strolled into town, had the gall to dine at St. Tom's favorite Tex-Mex joint with his new coach in tow, and then canned Landry without so much as a how-do-you-do.

"The Saturday Night Massacre," as it has been dubbed, on February 25, 1989, will live forever in Cowboys' infamy. Jones was flush with excitement when he arrived for the 8 p.m. press conference that had been hastily called at Valley Ranch. "This is like Christmas," he gushed to the assembled cameras and grim reporters, who may or may not have thought it was time for Landry to go. Whatever their opinions on Landry's coaching, they at least wanted to see him treated with the respect he'd earned, not just brushed aside by this Sooey Pig interloper. And it wasn't just Landry. As Schramm stood grimly by, his back against the wall, Jones declared he would be involved in every aspect of his new team's business, right down to the "socks and jocks." The era of Schramm-Landry-Gil Brandt was coming to an abrupt and torturous end.

For his part, Jones had no inkling of the public relations firestorm he'd ignited. Not even bothering to nod in the direction of Landry's great run of 20 consecutive winning seasons, Jones called Johnson "the best coach in America," a coach "worth five first round draft picks and five Heisman Trophy winners." Peter Golenbock wrote in *Cowboys Have Always Been My Heroes*, "reporters rolled their eyes as Jones began praising the new king without first holding the requisite tribute for the old one. When his remarks appeared in the morning newspapers, every Dallas Cowboy fan who loved and cherished Tom Landry instantly hated Jerry Jones."

Twenty-seven years later, Jones calls it the night he turned himself into "Darth Vader."

Some fans still nurse that grudge, but the success the Jones-Johnson partnership had in quickly turning the Cowboys around certainly mitigated some of the animosity, if not all. Winning three Super Bowls in four years (1992, '93 and '95) has a tendency to do that.

The question still remains, however. Can Jerry Jones win a Super Bowl without Jimmy Johnson? Can he even get the Cowboys back to one? Twenty years and counting, and the answer so far has been a resounding "No!"

Jerry remains resolute and determined. He has turned the Cowboys into a family enterprise and ceded at least some of his authority to oldest son Stephen. Jerry Jr. and daughter Charlotte are also intimately involved in running the Dallas Cowboys empire. It is a Jones family affair and despite their lack of on-field success, the Cowboys continue to grow and prosper. The team that Jones bought for $140 million in 1989 is now worth $4 billion according to Forbes Magazine (September 2015). *Forbes* ranked the Cowboys as the NFL's most valuable team for the ninth straight year with a league record $620 million in revenues, some $125 million more than the next closest team.

This isn't just Jones luck or happenstance. This is because Jerry Jones is a very smart man. Eventually the Cowboys' lack of on-field success may catch up to them – it generally does with every other team in sports – but it hasn't happened yet.

In November 2009, I wrote my last column for the *Fort Worth Star-Telegram*, ending a 40-year career at the same newspaper. Star-Telegram publisher Gary Wortel and executive editor Jim Witt graciously threw a retirement party for me at the Fort Worth Club and asked who I'd like to invite.

Family, of course, and colleagues I'd worked with over the years. A handful of sports personalities I'd become good friends with over time, people like retired Dunbar High School coaching legend Robert Hughes, TCU baseball coach Jim Schlossnagle, former Rangers' president and U.S. ambassador Tom Schieffer, longtime Rangers' all-around great guy Joe Macko and Rangers' catcher and front office executive Jim Sundberg. Tom Grieve, a friend I'd covered as a player, GM and TV broadcaster, was invited along with Rangers' radio voice Eric Nadel. Galloway and other newspaper friends were there, of course.

Nolan Ryan couldn't make it from Georgetown and the Horned Frogs' Gary Patterson was in the middle of a football season and sent his regrets.

But guess who sashayed in, official autographed Cowboys' helmet in hand as a retirement gift, and immediately stole the show....yep, the one and only Jerry Jones.

Jerry stayed for almost two hours, visiting with everyone there, posing for photos with my sons and granddaughters and being a generally good guy, which, in fact, comes naturally to him.

The helmet sits on a bookshelf in my office, with a message Jerry scribbled on it with a Sharpie: "What would you have done without me? – Jerry Jones."

It's a message he could easily send to every reporter/columnist in north Texas. Not sure I have an answer to his question, but I do know this: Whatever it might have been wouldn't have been nearly as much fun.

TEX SCHRAMM

It's ironic, though understandable, that Cowboys' fans were so upset when Jerry Jones bought the team in February of 1989 and immediately fired The Only Head Coach the Cowboys Had Ever Had. Landry, with his square jaw (which always seemed to be clinched) and his squinty stare, had been the face of the franchise for the first 29 years of its existence. It's also true that while many Cowboys fans were themselves beginning to believe that Landry had lost a step by the late '80s, much of the indignation was aroused by Jones' seemingly calloused method of dismissing Landry and what he had meant to America's Team. First, on the eve before Landry's firing, Jones had the audacity to take St. Tom's about-to-be-appointed successor, Jimmy Johnson, to dinner at Mia's in Dallas, one of Landry's favorite Tex-Mex dining spots. Then Jerry capped the coup by flying to Austin to pull Landry off the golf course to deliver the fatal news, which by then was almost merciful.

What fans should have been decrying instead was that Jones' arrival didn't just herald the end of the road for the sainted Landry, but it also meant sayonara to the true architect of the franchise, the man who had supplied the intellect, the guts and the vision to create the myth and legend of America's Team in the first place — one Texas E. Schramm. If the fans wanted something to howl about, they should have been mourning the changing of the guard that would mean the end of an era for those who built the Cowboys from the ground up and who, along with the NFL's growing popularity on television, made it arguably the most glamourous and high-profile franchise in the history of sports.

The wizard behind the curtain was Schramm, a profane, blustering, brilliant football and marketing genius.

I remember the first time I covered a Cowboys' game for the newspaper. I can't tell you who they were playing, or exactly what year it was (sometime in the early '80s). Though I was the paper's beat man covering the Texas Rangers, I was being pressed into off-season duty to handle one of the many sidebars we produced for each home game the Cowboys played.

The game was still in its early moments and the Cowboys had just been flagged for a penalty of some sort when someone exploded in the second row of the Texas Stadium press box. The string of invectives that ensued, directed at the miscreant official who had dared to throw a flag on the Cowboys, would have made a muleskinner blush. I looked back to the second row to see who was breaking the reporter's sacred code — no cheering (or homerism) in the press box — and there sat Schramm between a couple of other Cowboys' officials, his face ruddy with anger, and maybe a scotch or two as well. I looked around at my comrades of the pen and pad, veterans of many such games, and no one else had even raised an eyebrow. This, it turned out, was Tex's typical gameday face. This was a man who was 100 percent invested in his team, 24 hours a day, 365 days a year, and you could quadruple that on Sundays.

Certainly Schramm had his own suite at Texas Stadium (which he had helped design, of course) like most general managers do, but he simply preferred to sit in the press box. The writers liked that, too, because it meant that Tex was easily accessible, before, during and after games, when he would settle in at a large round table at the back of the press box with a glass of J&B scotch and hold court.

"I think, as much as anything, it was because he liked being around sports writers," recalled Carlton Stowers, who covered the Cowboys for the *Dallas Morning News* and later edited *Cowboys Weekly* during the Schramm years. "It made it great for all of us. You could get a column or story without ever leaving your seat.

"It didn't cause anyone to go easy on him, but he understood the role of the media and that it played a key role in what he wanted to accomplish with the Cowboys. I enjoyed being around him. If something had to be dealt with at 10 p.m., you picked up the phone and called him at home. He understood that that was part of the job."

Perhaps Schramm had a soft spot for sports writers because he'd started out as one himself, earning a bachelor's degree in journalism from the University of Texas and then taking a job as sports editor of the *Austin American-Statesman*. Newspapering, however, wasn't enough for Tex Schramm. A friend of his father's helped him land a PR job with the Los Angeles Rams. He worked his way into the GM's office and then jumped to CBS television in 1957, ceding his Rams' job to another PR man by the name of Pete Rozelle, who would one day become NFL commissioner. In 1960, Schramm convinced the network to televise the Winter Olympics from Squaw Valley, the first time it had ever been done, and persuaded iconic newsman Walter Cronkite to do the announcing. It was a huge success and the Winter Olympics have been a TV staple ever since.

Schramm's mission in whatever he did was singular: Never be ordinary; never be irrelevant. The hole in the roof at Texas Stadium, the Cowboys' cheerleaders, the hash marks on the field, the Cowboys' annual Thanksgiving Day game, the Ring of Honor, computer scouting, all can be traced back to Schramm.

"He was such an innovator," Stowers said. "Everything from the hash marks, to the Cowboys' cheerleaders, you name it, Tex thought of it.

"The thing that impressed me a great deal, as much as he loved the Cowboys and devoted 23½ hours of every 24-hour day to the Cowboys, he always put the NFL first. He felt like if the Cowboys were to succeed, the league had to succeed. That was his philosophy and it served him well."

It's a philosophy Jerry Jones still believes in to this day.

Most of the reporters and writers who covered the Cowboys in those days felt the heat of Schramm's legendary temper at one time or another, including Stowers. He still chuckles at a story that the late Steve Perkins liked to tell about Schramm's displeasure with one of his stories that appeared in the *Times-Herald* on a game day Sunday morning.

"Tex had a volatile temper that would last about 20 seconds," Stowers said. "I don't think there was ever a sportswriter who covered the Cowboys who didn't feel his wrath at one time or another. Perkins wrote something that got Tex's shorts in a wad.

"Crack of dawn, Sunday morning, Perkins' phone rang and it was Tex, going on and on about some article, very profane-laced. Tex started with the first paragraph and worked his way through the entire story. Perkins sat through the tirade and then asked Tex, 'Other than that, how did you like the article?' Tex laughed and said, 'I'll see you at the game.' He never held a grudge but he was quick-draw about how he felt about things."

Even mild-mannered Cowboys' radio voice Brad Sham inadvertently ran afoul of Tex back in 1978, Sham's second year as one of the team's radio voices. Sham, as he tells the story in his book *Stadium Stories*, had gotten an unusual phone call from kicker Efren Herrera, who was holding out during training camp. Herrera liked Sham and said he was coming to Thousand Oaks the following day, but not to report to the team. He wanted to hold a news conference and asked Sham to let his reporter buddies know.

As Sham wrote, "The Cowboys didn't take kindly to holdout players. I told Herrera that I thought he was making a mistake and he ought to just come to camp, but he was adamant. Would I spread the word or not? I said I would. Another mistake I only made once."

To his credit, the first thing Sham did was notify a couple of Cowboys' officials about Herrera's call. Then he let the Cowboys' press corps in camp know about it. By the next day, Schramm was livid, Sham knew it, and sought an audience to try and clear up the apparent misunderstanding.

Sham would describe Schramm's eruption as something akin to a "nuclear explosion." The Cowboys' president/GM accused his radio man of acting as Herrera's agent and as such, was "on the verge of being sent packing." Seems that the club officials Sham had notified had failed to relay the news to Tex.

Sham survived the confrontation and learned what veteran Cowboys' reporters already knew: Schramm could blow up like an erupting volcano one moment and be cool and calm the next. And he almost never carried a grudge.

Herrera, however, might not feel the same way. He was released and Rafael Septien wound up being the Cowboys' kicker in 1978.

Schramm was obviously astute at hiring talented people and like any good manager, he gave them latitude to do their jobs, whether it was Landry, top scout Gil Brandt, or his PR people. The one thing Schramm did himself was negotiate contracts, and as Stowers notes, it often "wasn't a pleasant experience" for the player involved.

A legendary Cowboys story tells about the time Roger Staubach decided to negotiate his own contract and showed up for a meeting with Schramm back when the Cowboys still had their offices in a business tower on Central Expressway, not far from SMU. Staubach waited and waited in a lobby outside Tex's office until he finally lost all patience, crawled out a window and scurried along a ledge until he was outside Schramm's office window, 11 floors up. A startled Tex looked up from a phone call to see his grinning star quarterback standing on a narrow ledge and plastered against his 11th-floor window. He was not amused.

"I guess I got his attention," said Staubach, who was quickly ushered into the office for his meeting.

GIL BRANDT

If Schramm was the genius pushing the buttons inside the Cowboys' offices, Gil Brandt was Tex's man-on-the-street, giving the Cowboys a face and a presence on college campuses from sea to shining sea. Brandt, a baby photographer in an earlier incarnation, had worked for Schramm as a part-time talent scout in L.A. and when Tex moved to take over the Cowboys, one of the first things he did was to hire Brandt fulltime.

"I knew he was good because when I was with the Rams, we had used him when we needed some kind of project done," Schramm told Peter Golenbock for his book *Cowboys Have Always Been My Heroes*. "If I needed someone to go see someone, or for someone to find out something, he was the guy we used on that kind of stuff. And I knew he always got it."

Brandt had the same kind of relentless zeal, the same kind of intensity, which drove Schramm. There was no book of rules they had to follow. They made it up as they went along, and in the process, basically developed scouting college players into the science it has become today.

With Brandt in the field, the Cowboys had an edge they would exploit over and over again in the 1960s and '70s. It was Schramm and Brandt who would define computerized scouting for players, figuring out which numbers could best lead to an accurate and quantifiable evaluation. They realized that good football players weren't only to be found at the big collegiate football factories, like Michigan, Alabama and Ohio State. They discovered running back Don Perkins at the University of New Mexico, Jethro Pugh at tiny Elizabeth City (North Carolina) State, Drew Pearson at Tulsa and Cliff Harris at Ouachita Baptist (Arkansas). Brandt knew almost as many basketball coaches as he did football coaches and they told him about the best athletes they had who wouldn't play in the NBA, players like Cornell Green and Pete Gent. They looked at other sports, too, and brought in track sprinters Bob Hayes and Mike Gaechter. They went out of the country for soccer players like Toni Fritsch.

The Cowboys were the first to administer psychological and intelligence tests to help gain a better understanding of their players' personality traits. They were a good 10 years ahead of the rest of the NFL in their scouting strategies and tactics.

"I think Gil was the first scout to ever time guys at 40 yards, because he knew that was football speed," Stowers said. "The first to use computers — Tex's deal. They hired a guy to set up a computer program for their scouting while other teams were still going through their Street and Smith magazines.

"The remarkable thing about Gil Brandt was the fact that he knew everybody involved in college or pro football. He was a great salesman for the Cowboys, much like Schramm was. He was the guy who'd call up the Oregon State coach and ask him about the player, how his wife was, how his kids were. He was a computer himself."

Brandt also knew the value of public relations. He would send Cowboys' T-shirts and souvenirs to prospective players and to their coaches.

"Gil Brandt fit perfectly into what the Cowboys were trying to do, particularly in the early years," Stowers said. "Every team was looking for an advantage. The Cowboys found one. Gil was just damn good at his job. He had a tremendous reputation throughout the NFL. A lot of coaches called him for advice and that's the kind of person Tex wanted."

Eventually, the NFL would catch up. The Cowboys would help to set up the scouting combine that leveled the playing field and it wasn't long before every team was using a computer scouting program.

Not every player loved Schramm and Brandt, however. Some would feel used or taken for granted. Others felt they'd been misled, including the rebellious Gent, who would write the acerbic and revealing novel *North Dallas 40*, a fictional account of a Dallas professional football team based on his experiences with the Cowboys.

"In my next book," Gent told Mark Ribowsky in his book *The Last Cowboy*, "I'm going to create the most evil person I can think of and call him Schrandt."

Love them or hate them, there's no denying what Schramm and Brandt meant to the Cowboys. They laid the foundation for one of the greatest franchises in American sports history.

The Coaches

TOM LANDRY

There's a story about Tom Landry that has etched itself into legend, as so many stories about him have, and whether it's mostly myth or absolutely 100 percent truth has faded into the fog of time. Frankly, I'm not sure it matters any more. What we know is true is that Landry, a co-pilot at 20 years old, flew 30 Air Force missions from Suffolk over Europe during World War II. His B-17 bomber once crash-landed in a French forest, losing both wings and with the nose of the plane coming to rest softly against a giant tree.

In this particular story, though, the engines in Landry's bomber sputtered to a stop during a fuel transfer and young Tom gave his crew the order to bail out. Just before the first crewman jumped from the plane, a desperate Landry reached out, jiggled the fuel switch one more time, and the engines miraculously sparked and began to cough themselves back to life. Rather than having to bail out over German-occupied Belgium, with sure capture and a prison camp – if not death – in their future, Landry and his men flew safely back to England.

This story resonates with me on a couple of levels. One, my uncle, Weldon Jeffress, died in 1944 when his bomber exploded over Belgium on his 15th mission. Though I never met him, I owe my middle name to him. Second, the image of Landry jiggling a switch and pulling a miracle out of his famous hat is something he seemed to do so often during his 29 years as Cowboys' head coach. Some came to call it simply Landry Luck.

The Cowboys were a quarter century into their history, and Landry in his final years as coach, before I had a chance to finally meet the great man. For me, a longtime Cowboys' fan who had to painfully learn the cynicism and neutral demeanor required of a sports writer during a dozen years on the Rangers' beat, it was still a meaningful moment. It was a routine interview with one or two other writers at the Cowboys' old practice facility sometime in the mid-'80s, just before they moved out to Valley Ranch. I found Landry cooperative, helpful, even cordial. Rumors of a total lack of personality, I decided, were unfounded. If he was a robot, as some insisted, I could see no signs of obvious seams or plastic skin.

Tex Schramm, himself no dummy, knew he was hiring a certifiable football genius when he handpicked Tom Landry as the Dallas Cowboys' first – and for 29 years, only – head football coach back in 1960. He was getting a born-and-bred Texan, a man who had grown up in the Rio Grande Valley in Mission, just north of the Mexican border. Landry was a standout high school quarterback who would go on to star at the University of Texas as a fullback and defensive back and then later for the New York Giants.

It was while he was with the Giants that Landry built a double-edged reputation, first as a vicious tackler and competitor and second as a brainy defender with an almost uncanny ability to know where a play was going before the ball was even snapped. Landry learned how to do this by studying film – an unheard of strategy in those days – and looking for trends and keys from the offense that would help him sniff out the play before it began to develop. His coaching brain was already engaged at a young age because he knew it made him a far better football player than his limited physical abilities – he wasn't particularly fast or quick – should have allowed.

Landry's keen analytical intellect made him fully prepared when new head coach Jim Lee Howell asked his defensive star to be player-coach in 1954. Coincidentally, Howell brought with him a new offensive assistant as well, a young coach from West Point: Vince Lombardi. The two would become close friends and bitter rivals, even on the same team. Landry introduced the Giants and the NFL to his new 4-3 defense, the one that would eventually evolve into "The Flex." Landry's new defense depended on a tough and mobile middle linebacker and he found his man by converting guard Sam Huff to defense.

Lombardi, meanwhile, believed in teaching his offense a handful of basic plays that it would execute so well, they couldn't be stopped.

Both were perfectionists and Howell could only rarely allow his two first-team units to oppose each other in practice.

"It got pretty heated," Dick Nolan, who played defensive back for the Giants and would follow Landry to Dallas an assistant coach, told Peter Golenbock in *Cowboys Have Always Been My Heroes*. "Boy, talk about hitting. Some people got their brains beat out."

Landry and Lombardi would continue trying to beat each other's brains out throughout their coaching careers, both reaching legendary status in Dallas and Green Bay. Lombardi had departed the Giants to become the Packers' head coach following the 1958 season, after the Giants had lost to Johnny Unitas' Baltimore Colts in overtime in the championship game. Many believe it was the most pivotal game in NFL history, in that it was televised nationally and the overtime drama captured the heart of sports fans across the country. For Landry, it was simply pure heartbreak, and the beginning of a pattern of close losses in huge games that would continue to haunt him, first in the Cowboys-Packers iconic Ice Bowl championship game matchup at Lambeau Field, and then in Super Bowl losses to Baltimore and Pittsburgh (twice).

Landry faced a decision after the '59 season in New York. He had obtained his degree in industrial engineering and spent six months of the year working in the real world. But his heart was always with football. As an assistant in New York, he was making only $12,000 a year. He needed more. There were rumors that Howell would step down and Landry would assume the head coaching reins, but they never panned out. There was a brief flirtation with Bud Adams and the Houston Oilers of the AFL, but the always-conservative Landry, while entertaining the idea of returning to his home state, just wasn't comfortable taking a gamble on the new league. That's when Landry got a call from Tex Schramm. Talk about your perfect timing. Landry, seizing the opportunity to build his own team from the ground up, couldn't say "yes" fast enough.

Landry's 29-year reign in Dallas can easily be broken down into the decades it encompassed: the '60s, when he took basically the dregs of the NFL and turned them into "Next Year's Champions;" the '70s, when Landry and the Cowboys went to five Super Bowls; and the '80s, the last half of which began the team's slow, agonizing slide to perdition and ultimately that devastating encounter with Jerry Jones at Hidden Hills on Lake Travis, just outside of Austin.

His 270-178-6 record represents the third-most wins by a coach in NFL history, ensuring his spot in the Pro Football Hall of Fame in Canton, Ohio, that came in 1990. He won two Super Bowl titles, took his team to five NFC championships games, won 13 NFC East titles and posted an amazing 20 consecutive winning seasons.

Despite his success, Landry could never quite catch the perfection that drove him so relentlessly. His aloof nature – an approach he felt was required in order to do his job – made him appear cold and calculating, or as running back Duane Thomas would so famously put it, a "plastic man." Those players looking for a father-figure in their head coach came away disappointed. Yet, many others glimpsed the man behind the frozen mask, and loved him all the more.

After he retired, fullback Walt Garrison was once asked if he'd ever seen Landry smile. "Nah," Garrison drawled, "but I only played for him for nine years."

Another story that has made the rubber chicken circuit tells about the time the Cowboys were in a tense home game at Texas Stadium. During a timeout, quarterback Roger Staubach trotted to the sideline to strategize with the head coach. He found Landry in a reverie, gazing up through the hole in the roof. When the coach finally turned his attention back to his quarterback, Staubach's keen sense of humor kicked in and he said to Landry, "I always wondered where you got those plays."

True to his nature, Landry never even smiled. He simply told Staubach the play he wanted run. Staubach nodded, ran back to the huddle, and led the Cowboys to another victory.

JIMMY JOHNSON

If Jerry Jones immediately became the most hated man in Texas for so rudely dismissing "the only coach the Cowboys have ever had" on that bleak late February night in 1989 – known far and wide as "The Saturday Night Massacre" – imagine the outrage if the brash and brazen college coach he brought in to replace the legend had fallen flat on his face.

Already a pariah, Jones might have been run out of town on the proverbial rail, complete with tar and feathers. Some, no doubt, would contend that such decoration would have improved Jerry's looks.

Most coaches, especially those stepping straight out of the college ranks, might have been intimidated trying to fill the coaching cleats of the great Landry. Most, undoubtedly, would have been humbled at the very prospect of treading the same sideline where the Man in the Hat once walked. Humble, however, is not an adjective anyone would ever use to describe Jimmy Johnson.

If ever a man coached with his hair on fire, it was Johnson, and with that perfectly-lacquered coiffure, it would have only taken a spark to start the conflagration. A defensive coaching genius in his own right, Johnson was not inclined to defer to Landry, or anyone else for that matter, including Jones, as history would eventually teach us. The immoveable hair was a red herring, folks. Inside that head, the wheels were always in motion.

Remember, Jimmy was a psychology major at the University of Arkansas, where he played defensive line on the Razorbacks' national championship team with a spunky, over-achieving offensive guard named Jerry Jones, and he put that education to work as a coach. And not just with his players.

I remember being granted a one-on-one audience with Johnson during training camp in Austin one summer and was amused when Jimmy began our session by asking me about the Texas Rangers and how they were doing that season. Surprised, yes, but fooled? Not really. I knew Jimmy couldn't care less about the Rangers and, in fact, hated small talk like that. I immediately knew he'd been prepped for our interview (I suspect PR man Rich Dalrymple was doing his job), and had learned that I'd spent a dozen years as the Rangers' beat man before becoming a general sports columnist just a few years earlier. He was pandering to me. I suppose I should have been flattered. It didn't offend me, but it immediately made me wary. This, I recalled, was the same guy who'd had Dalrymple make calls to the highest profile media guys in Dallas (Dale Hansen, Randy Galloway, maybe Blackie Sherrod) when he first arrived in town, just to say "howdy," and to give Jimmy a call if they needed anything. Like I said, smart man.

This is the guy who told Mike Fisher, in his 1993 book *Stars and*

Strife, that he hated having to talk at "functions" while serving as head coach at Oklahoma State and the University of Miami. "What I really want to be is just a football coach," Johnson said. "I hate small talk. I hate jokes. I like funny stories. I like cuttin' up with the guys in our circle. I laugh hardest when (the stories) have something to do with football."

At training camp, and sometimes back in Dallas, Johnson saw the benefit of occasionally spending some time shooting the bull with the reporters and columnists who covered the team, convening at a Tex-Mex joint for nachos and his favorite cool-down beverage, Heineken over ice. Mostly, though, Johnson was all business, and his business was football.

Business started a little rough when he arrived in Texas, arm in arm with Jerry Jones on February 24, 1989. Jimmy knew it probably wasn't a good idea for the two of them to slip out of the hotel for dinner at Mia's, one of Tom Landry's favorite hangouts, but Jerry wanted some nachos and beer. Bad idea.

Mia's was crowded and the duo was spotted by *Dallas Morning News* college football writer Ivan Maisel, who quickly phoned his desk for a photographer. The next day's front page photo, showing the smiling Jimmy and Jerry practically toasting each other over Landry's soon-to-be-dead body, shocked the Dallas-Fort Worth sports world to its core and confirmed the worst: St. Thomas had fallen. It was not an auspicious start for the new Cowboys' regime.

While Jimmy was smart enough to get "the hell out of Dodge" and back to Miami the next morning, Jerry was grimly prepping his jet to fly to Austin to settle things with Landry. Johnson would strategically miss the evening's press conference back at Valley Ranch when Jones, innocently ecstatic at closing the biggest deal of his life, told the assembled media, "It's just like Christmas!"

The resulting gasp echoed west to El Paso, north to the Panhandle, east to Texarkana and south to Houston and Del Rio. The Promised Land was being invaded and the despicable culprits were those real estate rootin', cow pasture killin' Hawgs from Arkansas. Fortunately for Jones, the only things pointed at him were cameras and wagging fingers.

Whatever the fans and even the indignant media thought of

Jones, it would eventually become obvious to everyone that he'd at least been smart enough to hire the right man for the job ahead. First though, came the big chill, as Johnson realized exactly what had to be done to bring Dallas, 3-13 in 1988, back to a competitive level. What the triumvirate of Schramm-Brandt-Landry had accomplished in building a team from scratch back in 1960, Jones, Johnson and his staff were going to have to virtually duplicate, starting in '89.

One of the first things Johnson told his staff (80 percent of which had come with him from Miami) after the first mini-camp in April was that he would not be meeting personally with the players as often as he normally would have.

"I can't lie to them," Johnson wrote in his autobiography *Turning the Thing Around: Pulling America's Team out of the Dumps and Myself out of the Doghouse*. "I can't go in one day and tell them about being a close-knit group and having unity, having feeling for one another, when I'm going to cut three or four of them the next day."

The talent level, Johnson realized, was abysmal, far worse than he had ever imagined. America's Team had become rotten to the core.

"So rather than even talk to the players, it was as if I blocked myself out and treated the situation a little more coldheartedly than I would otherwise," Johnson wrote. "I suppose that chill filtered through the team and out into the media by osmosis, and so the image problems kept getting worse. I couldn't let that matter. This was an absolutely necessary part of the massive radical surgery needed to begin getting this thing turned."

Johnson knew he would have to be brutally cold-hearted at times. But he also knew that dealing with some of the iconic Cowboys veterans, men like Randy White, Too Tall Jones and Danny White, men in the twilight of monster careers, would have to be handled with finesse and respect, both from a public relations standpoint but also because they'd earned it with what they had accomplished.

As bad as things looked, Jones and Johnson had one ace in the hole ...

The No. 1 draft pick, and a franchise quarterback coming out of UCLA named Troy Aikman.

The NFL, however, is rarely kind to rookie quarterbacks, especially rookie quarterbacks playing behind a ridiculously porous offensive line on a rebuilding team. Jones and Johnson easily beat San Diego 20-3 in their first exhibition game and the Cowboys would skip through the pre-season schedule with a 3-1 record. Then the regular season started and a crushing roof called reality came crashing down. What ensued was a pitiful 1-15 season. The Cowboys lost their first eight, beat Washington 13-3 at Texas Stadium, then lost their last seven. That Aikman even survived the weekly maulings was a miracle.

The revolving door at Valley Ranch continued to spin as the 1990 season began, but fresh blood was arriving almost daily. Of most importance was the arrival of a stubby running back out of Florida named Emmitt Smith. Wide receiver Michael Irvin, who had starred for Johnson at Miami, had been drafted in '88 and fullback Daryl Johnston out of Syracuse was a second-round pick in '89. The Cowboys didn't know it at the time, but The Triplets and the man who would set the table for Smith were now in place.

The steps were incremental but Johnson, and even the fans, could see the progress: 7-9 in 1990 and an amazing 11-5 and a wild card win in the playoffs in '91, just two years after bottoming out with that horrendous 1-15 showing. Jones was doing what he'd promised to do, spending whatever money it took to revitalize the Cowboys and Johnson and his staff were finding players both in the draft and on the free agent market.

The big bonanza, the catalyst for the Cowboys' turnaround, was Johnson's ballsy decision early in the '89 season to trade the team's greatest asset, running back Herschel Walker, who had a combined 2,019 rushing and passing yards in '88 ... while the Cowboys were fading to a worst-in-the-NFL 3-13 ledger.

Johnson had no intention of building his offense around Walker in '89 anyway, so why not use the blue chip player to get what the Cowboys really needed: extra high draft choices. On the surface, the Minnesota Vikings' trade of five mostly marginal players and a No. 1 pick for Walker seemed heavily weighted in Minnesota's favor. That's what Johnson wanted everyone to think.

The reality was that each of those Minnesota players coming to Dallas had a conditional draft pick attached to them. If the Cowboys wound up cutting them within a year, they would get a draft pick instead. Vikings' GM Mike Lynn felt safe because he knew how depleted the Cowboys' roster was. What he didn't know was how clever and how desperate Johnson was. The deal would net the Cowboys a bounty of valuable extra first and second-round draft picks, used to select players named Emmitt Smith, Russell Maryland and Kevin Smith, among others, all who would play key roles in helping the Cowboys win three Super Bowls in four years.

When Johnson publicly announced the trade and called it "The Great Train Robbery" in Dallas' favor, the DFW media all but laughed him off the podium and scorched him in print. Johnson, as he often did, had the last laugh and probably still giggles about it even now, as he fishes off his boat "Three Rings," near his home in the Florida Keys.

Johnson was the head coach for two Dallas Super Bowl wins, conquering perennial bridesmaid Buffalo each time. Troy Aikman led the Cowboys to a 52-17 destruction of the Bills in the Rose Bowl in Pasadena at the end of the '92 season and Emmitt Smith was the catalyst in a 30-13 victory in Atlanta the following year.

And then, perhaps inevitably considering the egos involved, it all fell apart between Jimmy and Jerry. The subsequent stunning divorce was all about credit. Jimmy, essentially, wanted it all and truth be told, maybe he deserved it. But he regularly antagonized the man who signed his paycheck by publicly dissing Jones' ability to judge football players.

Johnson knew that by becoming the first coach to ever win both national collegiate championships and a Super Bowl (two others, Barry Switzer and Pete Carroll, have done it since) that his options were wide open. Once he was out from under his Cowboys' contract, finding another job would not be difficult and he already had his eye on one of the Florida teams so he could live close to his beloved Atlantic ocean.

The final break between two proud men came at the NFL's winter meetings in Orlando in March 1994. During the league's gala at Disney's Pleasure Island theme park, Johnson sat at a table with former Cowboys' assistant coaches Dave Wannstedt and Norv Turner and former team executive Bob Ackles. Johnson was in the middle of telling the story about how Jones had asked him to look in his direction when the Cowboys' war room was on camera during the last NFL draft, so it would appear that they were discussing the next pick, which in fact, Jimmy was making, when Jones walked up.

The table went quiet. Jones, giddy over the Cowboys' back-to-back Super Bowl successes, proposed a toast to these coaches who had helped make the Cowboys a success. The response was half-hearted and then it went silent again. No one suggested a reciprocal toast to the owner. Jones knew he was again being dissed by his head coach, and in turn by the men he'd just complimented and to whom he'd paid millions of dollars in salaries. His pride pricked, Jones stormed away in a huff.

He returned to the Hyatt Regency bar to drink with friends and at a table adjacent to four reporters. It was there that Jerry repeatedly made his infamous statement, "I should have fired him and brought in Barry Switzer. There are 500 coaches who could have won the Super Bowl with our team."

When that quote hit the newspapers the next morning, my sports editor was on the phone to me down in Port Charlotte, Fla., where I was watching the Rangers wrap up spring training. I was on the road to Orlando within the hour. Early that evening, I was face to face with Jones in his suite at the Hyatt Regency.

What I hoped to hear was that somehow this rift could be patched up and that Jones' flippant remark about Switzer was Jerry's way of putting the needle back to Jimmy for the previous night's insults. Jones knew Jimmy had no use for Switzer, who had been at Arkansas at the same time they were.

"C'mon, Jerry," I said to the Cowboys' owner that night. "You wouldn't really hire Switzer, would you?"

"Why not?" Jones replied, cutting me off before I could even make my argument.

From that point on, it was just a matter of working out the details. Back in Dallas, Jones demanded that Johnson make a five-year commitment to stay as the Cowboys' head coach. That's when the realization that had been bubbling in Johnson's subconscious finally stood up and screamed, "No, that's not what I want!" The two settled on a $2 million buyout of the remaining five years on Johnson's 10-year contract and Jimmy left Dallas for a temporary gig as a Fox Sports analyst while he waited for Don Shula to retire in Miami.

The perfect partnership that had rebuilt the Cowboys in just four short years and had won two Super Bowls was dissolved, just like that. And Jerry? Beware of what you wish for ... Jerry did indeed bring in his old friend, Barry Switzer, the bootlegger's boy, to be the third head coach in Cowboys' history.

BARRY SWITZER

Barry Switzer was a Hawg from the same pigpen that had produced Jones and Johnson, an assistant coach and dorm supervisor when Arkansas won the national championship in 1964. When Switzer was named head coach at the University of Oklahoma in 1973, he beat out a couple of close friends: Jimmy Johnson and Larry Lacewell.

Lacewell, who grew up with Switzer, just calls it "The Switzer Luck." How else to explain a college football coach, sent home in disgrace because of the outlaws who had scandalized his program at OU, a man with not even one scintilla of NFL experience, being handed the keys to a legendary pro franchise that had just won two straight Super Bowls?

"It's like hitting the lottery," is how Switzer described it.

Maybe Jones was right, maybe any one of 500 coaches could win with that Cowboys' team, led by Troy Aikman, Emmitt Smith and Michael Irvin, but give Switzer credit, he tried really hard to be No. 501, the guy who couldn't win with what was easily the best team in the league.

The coaching staff was in place. The players were there and they knew what it took to win in the league. All Switzer really had to do was stay out of the way and from a coaching aspect, he mostly did that. But Switzer, a great motivator of college players, hadn't changed. He was proud of the fact that at 56, he could still out-party players 30 years younger and he had no problem telling them that when he showed up at Valley Ranch the next morning after a long night on the town. The players would absorb their head coach's lifestyle and reflect it right back, weakening and infecting the team. If the coach could party and play all night, why can't we?

It was about this time that wide receiver Alvin Harper rented a house that backed up to the Cowboys' practice field. It would become known as the infamous "White House," a hangout for Cowboys' players and, according to neighbors, an infinite revolving door of beautiful young women and even drugs.

Switzer's loose attention to detail and discipline would eventually take its toll and alienate Aikman and other key players. The Cowboys would lose to the San Francisco 49ers 38-28 in the NFL championship game at Candlestick Park in 1994, then win their third Super Bowl in four years by beating Pittsburgh 27-17 in Tempe, Arizona, in 1995, culminating a tumultuous season in which players admitted that the feeling afterward was more of relief that it was over than delight with the victory.

On the dais after the game, Switzer and Jones seemed to be wrestling over the Lombardi Trophy as Switzer screamed into the TV cameras, "We did it, baby! We did it!"

The Cowboys, though, were falling apart even as the celebration began. The next season, the Cowboys were beaten badly, 26-17, at Carolina in the divisional playoff game when Michael Irvin dislocated his right shoulder on the second play of the game. In '97, all the wheels came off and they floundered to a 6-10 record, losing their final five games.

"This didn't happen overnight," Aikman said in Frank Luksa's book, *Cowboys Essential*. "We've been declining the last couple of years to where we are now. But I think we're better than 6-10. We didn't play as well as our talent would indicate we would."

It was an indictment of the four-year Switzer era and it was right on the money.

"I told Jerry he ought to get rid of the whole damn bunch of us," Switzer declared at the time.

Jones at least agreed that it was time for the head coach to go. Jerry was about to celebrate the start of his 10th year as owner of the Cowboys by hiring his third head coach.

CHAN GAILEY

The search didn't start well. Jones zeroed in on former UCLA coach Terry Donohue, only to suffer the embarrassment of having Donohue turn down the job as the next head coach of America's Team. It's doubtful Jones had ever dreamed something like that might happen. Donohue might have been one of those 500 coaches who could take the Cowboys to another Super Bowl title, but he didn't even want the chance.

As first-alternate, Chan Gailey seemed to be an inspired choice. He was the opposite of the loud and often obnoxious Switzer, soft-spoken, easy-going, and by all accounts an offensive virtuoso. Gailey was the Steelers' offensive coordinator and had served two years as head coach at Birmingham of the World Football League.

But another aspect of Jimmy Johnson's departure and Switzer's four-year reign was a loosening of the chain of command at Valley Ranch. Aikman, who didn't even speak to Switzer during the season's last six weeks and the team's run to the Super Bowl in 1995, now had the owner's ear.

That didn't seem to be a problem in '98, when Gailey restored order and the Cowboys flip-flopped their 6-10 record of a year earlier to 10-6. They suffered a disappointing 20-7 defeat to Arizona in the NFC wild card game, however, slipped to 8-8 the following season and again lost a wild card game, this time to Minnesota 27-10. With Aikman publicly unhappy with Gailey's offensive schemes, the trigger-happy Jones swung the ax yet again.

Jones would admit in years to come that firing Gailey so quickly was probably a major mistake. The team's subsequent 15-33 ledger with the next head coach over the next three seasons might have prompted that rare confession.

DAVE CAMPO

Dave Campo never had a chance. Campo was the affable and highly competent defensive backfield coach Johnson had brought with him from Miami. He had been promoted to defensive coordinator in '95 under Switzer and helped the Cowboys win a Super Bowl.

Jones did Campo no favors by handing him the reins to the team after Gailey was sent packing. Where Johnson had coveted and cherished high draft picks as the best way to build a team, Jones had squandered two first-round picks to bring in flashy wide receiver Joey Galloway in 2000. The Cowboys had already gone dry in the draft with consecutive high picks of Shante Carver, Sherman Williams, Kavika Pittman and David LaFleur. If that wasn't enough bad news, Galloway would tear up his knee in his first game and never play another down all season.

To put the cherry on top, Aikman retired following the 2000 season. So much for the great Aikman-to-Galloway pairing. It never materialized.

Campo was cursed with the worst predicament in the NFL: No quarterback. With Aikman gone, Jones floundered, looking under every rock for a competent, NFL-caliber signal caller. He struck out time after time. Veteran Tony Banks was cut in training camp, Quincy Carter, taken with a second-round pick when no other NFL team had him rated that high, failed time after time. So did Anthony Wright, Randall Cunningham, Clint Stoerner, Ryan Leaf and Chad Hutchinson.

Campo tried so hard to find the bright side of things during this dismal stretch, I finally dubbed the poor man "Coach Polyanna" in the *Star-Telegram*. He deserved better, both from Jones and from me. It just wasn't his fault.

BILL PARCELLS

On the surface, it was an unimaginable pairing, like a dollop of ice cream on a greasy bowl of chili. It was the immovable object meeting the irresistible force. No way in hell Jerry Jones and Bill Parcells could co-exist as owner and head coach of the Dallas Cowboys. Jones was the intensely involved owner who vowed to handle even the "socks and jocks," when he took over the team. Parcells was of the Frank Sinatra ilk: he did things his way. Period.

"If you're gonna cook the meal," Parcells was fond of saying, "then you need to be the guy buying the groceries." The meaning was clear: If he was going to coach a team, he was also going to be responsible for acquiring the players through the draft, trades and free agent signings, a territory that Jones had staked as his own since Johnson's departure.

Las Vegas all but posted odds on how long this oddball relationship could last. The over-under was maybe six weeks, including training camp. At some point, the pundits were sure, Parcells would simply reach out and grab Jones by his scrawny, turkey wattle of a neck, and shake him like a dog with a squirrel.

The pundits, however, were wrong. Jones did the unthinkable, relinquishing authority and responsibility to the 30-year coach with three Super Bowls on his résumé. Parcells would last four years, three of them winning seasons, left of his own volition and still insists working with Jones was never a problem.

"I think there's a definite misperception," Parcells said in an interview for Dallas Cowboys *Star Magazine* back in 2013. "I just think everyone thinks a certain way. I didn't see it to be that way.

"I think Jerry is a good businessman and a good listener. What you have to do is make sense to him. If he thinks you're making sense, he'll alter his opinion. I enjoyed him. I like him a lot."

Jones brought Parcells in to change the culture of the team as much as he did to change its won-loss record. Both efforts succeeded. Parcells brought instant credibility and his own brand of iron-handed discipline. There was never a question about who was in charge when "The Big Tuna" was in town.

Parcells worked a veritable miracle in 2003, carving out a 10-6 record with inconsistent Quincy Carter at quarterback, leading an offense that was shut out twice and, including a 29-10 loss to Carolina in the wild card game, scored but a single touchdown in seven other games. Only defensive coordinator Mike Zimmer's No. 1-ranked defense and Parcells' iron will kept the 'Boys afloat.

Nothing could do that in 2004 when Carter was abruptly released in training camp for drug test violations and the Cowboys were forced to go with 42-year-old Vinny Testaverde at quarterback. His 76.4 quarterback rating directly correlated to the team's 6-10 record.

Parcells brought in Drew Bledsoe, another of his former QBs, in 2005 and somehow coaxed a 9-6 record out of his team, but not a playoff spot.

His final season, 2006, brought his highest highs and his lowest lows. He uncovered and signed an undrafted free agent quarterback out of Eastern Illinois named Tony Romo to develop as a backup to Bledsoe. In the season's sixth game, Romo took over for Bledsoe in the second half of an eventual 36-22 loss to New York and never looked back.

In Romo's first start the following week, he led the Cowboys to a 35-14 upset at Carolina. The Cowboys' quarterback, the most important piece for any NFL team, was in place for at least the next decade.

The Cowboys won five of six in the middle of the season with Romo at the helm and even though they would stumble to the finish line losing three of their last four, they still earned a chance to play at Seattle in the wild card game. Late in the fourth quarter, trailing 21-20, the Cowboys drove the length of the field, where they set up for what should have been a game-winning field goal inside the Seahawks' 10-yard line with just over a minute to play.

Somehow, in a pivotal play that haunts him to this day, Romo failed to hold the snap, fumbled the ball away, and the Seahawks took over on downs and escaped, 21-20. It was the last game Parcells ever coached. Tired and discouraged, he elected to retire after the season.

WADE PHILLIPS

Jerry Jones' choice to lead the Cowboys in the wake of Parcells' departure had royalty written all over it. He handpicked "Son of Bum," 60-year-old Wade Phillips, as Parcells' successor, out of a field of 10 candidates, with former Cowboys' Super Bowl offensive coordinator Norv Turner the easy favorite. When Phillips began his Cowboys' tenure with a 13-3 record and a romp to the NFC East title in his first season in 2007, it looked like a genius hire.

Not so fast.

Phillips, who won his first Super Bowl as defensive coordinator of the Denver Broncos following the 2015 season, is, without a doubt, one of the great defensive minds in NFL history.

As a head coach, though, his judgment and feel for his team was, at best, questionable, and at worst, non-existent.

Blessed with a bye in the first round of the playoffs after that spectacular 2007 season, Phillips thought it might be a good idea to give his players a break and allowed them take a long weekend off, during which players scattered to the four winds. After playing on the beach in Cabo San Lucas with girlfriend Jessica Simpson and assorted teammates, Tony Romo may have come back fresh, but he was far from sharp against the New York Giants, who upset the Cowboys at home,

21-17. This, despite the fact that the Cowboys had easily beaten the Giants twice during the regular season.

As good as Phillips often seemed to be during the regular season – he was 82-64 overall as a head coach in the NFL – he just couldn't seem to get it together in the playoffs. The loss to the Giants dropped him to 0-5 in postseason games and gave credence to the media's contention that he couldn't win the big one. He would never quite escape the shadow of the Cabo fiasco during his three-plus seasons as Cowboys' head coach.

Needing a win to qualify for a wild card game in the final game of the season in 2008, Phillips' Cowboys gagged in a 44-6 loss to the Philadelphia Eagles, finishing 9-7 and out of the playoffs. In 2009, Phillips took over defensive coordinator duties himself and the Cowboys streaked to an 11-5 record. This time, Dallas whipped Philly in the wild card round, snapping the Cowboys' six-year drought without a playoff win and handing Phillips his first and only postseason victory as a head coach.

The Cowboys started a disastrous 1-7 the next season and in Phillips' final game, on national TV on a Sunday night in Green Bay, his team was destroyed 45-7 by the Packers, forcing Jerry Jones to do something he'd never done before – replace a head coach in-season.

Phillips was plagued throughout his Cowboys' tenure by claims that he was a nice guy who was far too soft on his players, earning him the media nickname, "Coach Cupcake."

JASON GARRETT

The eighth head coach in Cowboys' history is also the first former Cowboys' player to ever hold the job. Jason Garrett, the Princeton-educated carrot-top with the football family pedigree, spent seven years as a backup quarterback in Dallas, under-studying Troy Aikman on three Super Bowl teams. In nine emergency starts, Garrett posted a 6-3 record, ironic because the Cowboys stumbled to a miserable 4-12 mark in 2015 for lack of a quality backup QB.

Son of longtime Cowboys' personnel scout Jim Garrett, Jason was hired as the team's offensive coordinator in 2007 and anointed the head coach-in-waiting even before Jerry Jones picked Wade Phillips to hold the fort until Garrett was ready.

That time came eight games into the 2010 season when the Cowboys found themselves smothering at 1-7. Intelligent, positive, but bland with the media, Garrett was quickly dubbed "Coach Process" in honor of one of his favorite words used to describe his coaching philosophy.

Garrett's 15 minutes of fame as a backup quarterback came on Thanksgiving Day 1994, after both Aikman and Rodney Peete were injured and unavailable. Making just his second career start, Garrett led the Cowboys to a remarkable 42-31 victory over Green Bay at Texas Stadium. Garrett guided the Cowboys' offense to a club record 36 second half points and was named NFL Offensive Player of the Game.

He brought the 2010 season home with a 5-3 record after Phillips' firing and hope flamed anew. Alas, it was short-lived. The Cowboys found themselves mired in mediocrity for the next three seasons, posting back-to-back-to-back 8-8 records.

That changed in 2014. With DeMarco Murray leading the NFL in rushing and Tony Romo keeping his gunslinger instincts under control, the Cowboys romped to a 12-4 ledger. They outlasted the Detroit Lions 24-20 in the wild card round of the playoffs but fell at Green Bay, 26-21, in the divisional round when Dez Bryant's spectacular, sprawling touchdown catch was overturned by instant replay. The play sparked controversy and debate over what should or should not constitute a catch that continues even today.

Garrett signed a new five-year contract for $30 million after the season and the Cowboys hoped to pick up where they'd left off in 2014. Instead, with Murray gone to Philadelphia via free agency, Bryant knocked out by a broken foot in the season opener and Romo felled by a broken collarbone twice, the Cowboys belly-flopped to a 4-12 record, the third worst finish in franchise history. Only the team's 3-13 log in Tom Landry's last year in 1988 and the 1-15 mark in Jimmy Johnson's first were worse.

Any thought that the Cowboys might be for searching for their ninth head coach, and eighth in Jones' nearly three-decade tenure as team owner, were quashed almost as soon as the season ended.

"Let me be real clear," Jones said. "There's no thought of replacing

Jason. At all. I only say that to get ahead of anything that might be said about me addressing coaching."

That's a good sign. One of the hallmarks of the Cowboys' first three decades was the stability they built with one head coach, one philosophy, essentially one voice that matters in the locker room. Given good players and a smidgen of luck, Garrett can win in the NFL.

The Quarterbacks

DON MEREDITH

When Pete Gent turned his thinly-disguised memoir of life as a Dallas Cowboy into the novel *North Dallas Forty*, Hollywood reacted by choosing country singer Mac Davis for the key role of quarterback Don Meredith in the movie. It was Davis' first feature role and most folks would be hard pressed to name another film he appeared in; there were only a handful. But Davis' laid-back, twangy-version of country-cool "Dandy Don" was spot on, earning Davis a nod on Screen World magazine's list of "Promising New Actors" for 1979. Even better, Davis' signature song, *It's Hard to Be Humble*, captured Meredith's essence in a nutshell.

"Jeff and Hazel's baby boy," was the first of Dallas' "golden boys," a strong-armed – and strong-willed – quarterback who had set the Southwest Conference on fire while at SMU in the late '50s. Because Dallas was getting a late start on the draft in 1960, the NFL allowed owner Clint Murchison Jr. to sign Meredith and New Mexico running back Don Perkins to personal services contracts even before the league had voted to give Dallas the franchise. Meredith, a two-time All-American, had been such a popular figure on campus, fans had started calling it "Southern Meredith University." He was a perfect fit for Dallas' fledgling NFL franchise, a name and face fans would recognize.

Which then begs the question: Why did the Cowboys spend so much time and effort trying to get Meredith killed? Meredith took over as the team's starting quarterback after veteran Eddie LeBaron retired following the 1963 season. Meredith may be the only quarterback in NFL history who had a statistic invented specifically for him by *Dallas Times-Herald* sports writer Steve Perkins: yardage lost attempting to live.

That was life, if only barely, for Meredith as he tried to survive a Swiss-cheese offensive line during the Cowboys' growing years into the mid-'60s. Meredith's ability to keep coming back after taking horrific poundings became legendary.

He blew out a knee cartilage during an exhibition game one season but never missed a game, playing the entire year hobbling around on the bad knee. Landry called it "perhaps the most courageous and gutsy season any professional quarterback ever played," in Peter Golenbock's book, *Landry's Boys*.

Besides his exceptional passing ability, Meredith had one other absolute necessity going for him in those days: a terrific sense of humor.

Meredith simply refused to take himself seriously, which in and of itself wasn't a bad attribute. Unfortunately, that philosophy often also extended to the game of football, which infuriated head coach Tom Landry. During practice Landry would send in a play for the offense to run. Meredith, humming a country song in the huddle, would almost immediately forget the play or maybe just ignore the coach.

"Ah, hell," he'd drawl to his teammates, "just run the last play all over again."

This was like déjà vu for Landry, bringing back bad memories of his college years at the University of Texas. The one former teammate Landry could never understand was Longhorns' quarterback Bobby Layne. Landry saw Layne's immense talent, but instead of admiring his accomplishments, both at Texas and later in the NFL, he wondered how much better Layne might have been if he'd taken the game seriously instead of partying till the wee hours every night. Now Landry was seeing Layne all over again in his own fun-loving quarterback.

It was almost more than he could bear. Landry expected his players to take the game as seriously as he did. Those who didn't, and who were expendable, were disposed of as quickly as possible. Meredith wasn't expendable, at least not yet, so Landry resorted to the only avenue left to him: he regularly lectured Meredith and other Cowboys "sinners" on the dangers of having fun while playing football.

Landry and the Cowboys made matters worse for themselves in 1964 when they brought in a kindred soul for Meredith, veteran wide receiver Buddy Dial. Dial, who had excelled at Rice, had played with and been enamored by Layne in Pittsburgh. Now here was Meredith, cut from the same swashbuckling cloth.

"Don and I were roommates, and I was a terrible influence on him," Dial admitted to Golenbock. "I played the guitar and (Meredith) loved to sing and drink, and we just stayed in trouble all the time. We almost stayed in jail for three years, because of Landry, 'cause he never knew what we were going to do."

Meredith's carefree attitude obviously worried Landry enough for the Cowboys to draft Tulsa's Jerry Rhome, who still had his senior season to play, as a future pick in 1964 and then add cannon-armed Craig Morton out of Cal-Berkeley a year later (imagine that, Cowboys' fans, actually stocking up on talented quarterbacks!). If Meredith was insecure before, he was even less comfortable now, especially since both rookie quarterbacks were getting paid more than Meredith was making in a new three-year contract.

To top that, the Cowboys would also take a future pick in Heisman Trophy winner Roger Staubach, who wouldn't be free of his naval duty and able to play until 1970. How secure could a starting quarterback feel with three legitimate contenders for the position waiting in the wings?

The Cowboys obviously weren't shying away from a quarterback controversy in 1965 and, five years into life in the NFL, they were finally feeling as if they might be getting their sea legs under them.

Not so fast.

This was the season in which Landry again at times resorted to a quarterback shuttle, first playing Meredith, then Morton, then Rhome. Seven games into the season, the Cowboys ham-handed their way to a 22-13 Halloween Day loss at Pittsburgh, their fifth straight. Landry, in tears in the locker room afterward, pointed the finger at himself for not having his team adequately prepared, at which point Meredith stood up and took the blame on his own shoulders.

Going into the next week, the media fully expected an announcement that Morton would start the upcoming game against San Francisco. Late in the week, Landry called a grim Meredith in for a face-to-face meeting. Meredith expected the worst, a demotion and a seat on the bench, but instead an emotional Landry told Meredith he was sticking with him, and both men broke down and cried. The Cowboys would win five of their last seven to finish 7-7.

One of the two losses, however, was especially painful. It came at the Cotton Bowl against Cleveland in late November when Meredith threw two key interceptions, including one from the Browns' one-yard line. One-yard line!

It prompted what is arguably the most famous and unforgettable lead paragraph about the Cowboys and Meredith in DFW sports page history. Paraphrasing the great Grantland Rice, Gary Cartwright wrote in the *Dallas Morning News*: "Outlined against a grey November sky, the Four Horsemen rode again Sunday. You know them: Pestilence, death, famine and Meredith."

The furor over Meredith's failures would overcome the public's good-natured affection for him. Meredith would hold off Morton for three more seasons, during which the Cowboys posted a 31-10-1 regular season record. The first two, 1966 and 1967, ended with losses to Green Bay in the championship game, including the infamous Ice Bowl following the '67 season. Meredith led the 'Boys on a dominating 12-2 regular season march in '68, only to lose to Cleveland 31-20 in the first round of the playoffs, with a struggling Meredith (three interceptions) being pulled in the second half for Morton.

With Landry talking about giving Morton an equal chance to win the starting job at training camp in '69, Meredith requested a July 4 meeting with Landry to tell him he was thinking of retiring. Meredith went through the myriad list of reasons why he might quit, including the fact that two weeks earlier his wife Cheryl had given birth to their daughter Heather, who had serious birth defects.

Friends would say later what Meredith really wanted was for Landry to give him some validation, to try to talk him out of quitting. He was hoping, deep inside, for a fatherly pat on the back, even a hug, and perhaps for Landry to tell him to sleep on it for a few days before doing anything rash. Instead, the iron-jawed, expressionless Landry looked across his desk and said, "If that's the way you feel, then retiring is probably the right decision."

At only 31 years old, Meredith walked away from the game, but certainly not out of the public eye. He would go on to indelible fame on as Howard Cosell's foil on *Monday Night Football*, a successful acting career and a valued private life in Santa Fe, New Mexico.

The story that perhaps best sums up Meredith and his career comes from Walt Garrison, who was aghast when he once watched Dandy Don spend $400 buying drinks for the house in a favorite saloon.

As Mark Ribowsky tells it in *The Last Cowboy: A Life of Tom Landry*, Garrison told Meredith, "God darn, Meredith, how can you afford to blow all that dough?"

"Whadda ya mean?" Meredith retorted. "I just made $400."

"How do you figure that," Garrison wondered.

"Hell," Meredith drawled, "I had $800 worth of fun."

Now, though, as he walked out of Landry's office that sad day, it was time to turn out the lights. The party was definitely over.

ROGER STAUBACH

Some things are simply meant to be. I'm convinced that Roger Staubach, a character straight out of Marvel Comics, was born to be the quarterback of America's Team. There just couldn't be any other way. Yet, it's almost preposterous that it ever actually happened when one considers all the dominos that had to fall into place for "Captain America" to wind up in Dallas, leading the Cowboys to NFL prominence in the 1970s.

First, Tex Schramm and Gil Brandt had to be prescient enough and bold enough to be willing to take Staubach in the 10th round of the 1964 draft, even though they knew they'd have to wait five years for him to complete his senior season at Navy and then his four-year naval commitment. Second, they had to fend off Lamar Hunt, who also drafted Staubach for the AFL's Kansas City Chiefs and almost stole him away by offering a $10,000 signing bonus and $500 a month while Staubach was serving his country. The Cowboys quickly agreed to match the deal and when Hunt offered to go higher, Staubach said he didn't want to get into a negotiating battle.

Who does that?

It was the Dudley Do-Right in him, one of the great character traits that made Staubach so attractive to teams in the first place, that they were willing to wait half a decade for him to finally show up.

Even before that, things had to fall in place for Staubach to emerge as a potential NFL quarterback and Heisman Trophy winner for Navy in 1963. Like a lot of superb all-around athletes, Staubach played football, basketball and baseball at Purcell High School, an all-boys Catholic school in Cincinnati. He was a tight end and defensive back as a freshman, switched to quarterback as a sophomore, but broke his hand as a junior and played strictly on defense. His senior year in high school was essentially his first full season at quarterback.

Besides that, Purcell ran strictly a T-formation offense and Staubach rarely threw the football more than half a dozen times a game. He did, however, have ample opportunity to display his skills as a runner for college scouts, who would also soon learn that he had developed an outstanding arm playing third base during the spring and summer.

Purdue saw the potential in Staubach and offered him a scholarship. Navy was also interested. Notre Dame, Staubach's first love as a loyal Catholic kid, arrived late to the party and offered him a scholarship after the North-South high school All-Star game in June. By then, Staubach had made his commitment to Navy, and as everyone would learn, when the man made a commitment, he stuck by it.

After a year at New Mexico Military, Staubach found himself fifth on the quarterback depth chart at Navy, stuck behind two seniors, a junior and another sophomore. How to climb over five players ahead of him on the depth chart? Then one of the seniors went down with an injury. The sophomore was hurt so badly he lost a kidney. Suddenly, Staubach was the third-teamer, taking a few snaps late in games. After an 0-2 start, with both quarterbacks ahead of him struggling, Staubach was waved into the game by head coach Wayne Hardin. He led the Midshipmen to a quick score and ultimately a 41-7 victory and started the next game. His career was off and running.

"I was a scrambling quarterback and our team needed that," Staubach told Peter Golenbock in *Landry's Boys*. "We didn't have the protection, so I ended up doing a lot of scrambling and making things happen, and that was it. If I was in trouble, I ran. (The coaches) knew I wanted to win, and they put up with it."

Knowing he had a four-year stint in the Navy ahead of him after college, Staubach hadn't put a lot of thought into the possibility of playing football professionally. In fact, he figured it was more of an impossibility. If he did play in the NFL, it would be as a 28-year-old rookie. Not many of those around.

There was also the fact that the Cowboys weren't exactly twiddling their thumbs while waiting for Staubach to finally arrive. They'd hedged their bets by also drafting Tulsa's Jerry Rhome in 1964 and followed that by selecting Craig Morton in '65. Those two were next in line behind starter Don Meredith, who was only 26 when the Cowboys drafted Staubach.

In fact, Staubach figured his best chance of playing in the NFL might be with another team, if the Cowboys would trade him once he joined them in 1969. Turns out, that wasn't necessary. Worn out both physically and emotionally, Meredith retired at only 31 years old. Rhome was traded to Cleveland.

Staubach found himself backing up the talented Morton, but approaching 30 himself, the former Naval officer wanted his own command, especially as he watched from the sidelines as the Cowboys and a sore-shouldered Morton lost to Baltimore 16-13 in Super Bowl V.

"I was frustrated as far as not getting a chance," Staubach said in an interview for this book. "I told Coach Landry on the plane back to Dallas that I wanted to be traded, that if I couldn't play when Craig was hurt I didn't deserve to be on the team."

Tom Landry liked Morton, but he was a smart enough football man to understand that he had something special in Staubach.

"He told me, 'You will have your chance to quarterback this team in '71,'" Staubach said.

Both quarterbacks played well as the Cowboys won all six of their preseason games with Staubach and Morton alternating starts. With the season opener looming at Buffalo, Landry still couldn't make a decision. Staubach, he said, would start against the Bills and Morton would quarterback at Philadelphia the next week.

But even Landry's plans were subject to unpleasant surprises. Staubach had suffered a broken blood vessel in his leg in the final exhibition game against Kansas City and doctors recommended he rest it for a week. So Morton started against the Bills instead. Calvin

Hill ran crazy, scoring four touchdowns, and Morton was 10-for-14 for 220 yards and two TDs in a 49-37 Cowboys' victory.

Staubach started the next week at Philly, as Landry had promised, and on the third play of the game, was intercepted by Bill Bradley. On the same play, Eagles' defensive lineman Mel Tom slammed a forearm into the side of Staubach's helmet, "a dirty shot," Staubach said. Knocked woozy, Staubach found himself on the sidelines again, watching Morton hammer the Eagles 42-7.

Citing momentum, Landry started Morton the third game against Washington and the Cowboys lost 20-16. Staubach started the fourth game and the Cowboys led the Giants 13-6 at halftime, when Landry replaced him with Morton. Staubach believed taking a quarterback out in the middle of the game was "the ultimate insult" and again told his coach to just trade him. Again, Landry smartly declined.

By the time the seventh game of the season against Chicago rolled around, the Cowboys were 4-2 and no one knew who the quarterback was. The team was beset by the dreaded quarterback controversy. Unbelievably, it would still get worse before it got better.

"Craig had a lot of friends on the team and I had friends so the team was divided," Staubach remembered. "Coach Landry was unbelievably organized, but in football, things happen out there emotionally and players have to believe in other players. He knew there was a problem.

"Then it got worse against Chicago because he had us alternating plays. Craig and I thought he was kidding when he announced it that week. Then Craig came in at the end of the game (a 23-19 loss) and finished up and so I thought I was toast again. We had a really good team but we were 4-3 because we just hadn't had the continuity."

Staubach was almost beside himself. He wanted to start. He wanted the team to win. And he wasn't sure that his NFL future lay in Dallas.

"There was a Monday charity thing we had to go to that week and I figured Landry was going to announce that Craig was the starting quarterback because even he knew it wasn't working having two guys," Staubach said. "Then (assistant coach) Ray Renfro came up to me and said some of the coaches had gone to talk to Landry. He said, 'You're going to be the starting quarterback.' I was more excited than at any time in my whole athletic career. It was as if this huge weight was lifted off me. It meant I didn't have to be perfect all the time." Of course, there are those who will still claim today that Staubach has always been pretty darn perfect.

"We went on to win the next 10 games in a row (right through Super Bowl VI), but I'm convinced Craig would have been successful, too," Staubach said. "He was a good quarterback and a good guy."

After under-studying Morton for two years, the Cowboys were now Staubach's team. He led the NFL in passing in 1973. Morton would be traded to the Giants halfway through the '74 season.

Staubach was on his way to becoming "Captain Comeback," leading the Cowboys to an amazing 23 come-from-behind, fourth-quarter victories. Fourteen of those came with less than two minutes to play or in overtime.

It was after one of those dramatic comebacks that Staubach would coin a line for the ages, one that is repeated dozens of times now each football season. In the 1975 playoffs in Minnesota, the Cowboys found themselves trailing 14-10, facing a fourth-and-16 at their own 25-yard line with less than a minute to play. Staubach called a corner-post route for Drew Pearson, who hadn't caught a pass all day. He caught this one for 22 yards and a first down.

Preston Pearson dropped a short pass, which was probably for the best, since it saved some time on the clock. There were 26 seconds left.

Staubach and Drew Pearson figured they could get cornerback Nate Wright to bite on a deep turn pattern. Staubach pump faked to hold safety Paul Krause for a split second, then found Pearson deep down the right side. Pearson came back a step to haul in the under-thrown pass, which he trapped between his elbow and hip. He scored when Wright slipped down trying to make the play and the Cowboys won, 17-14. They were headed to their second Super Bowl championship.

In the locker room, reporters clamored around Staubach, asking him what he was thinking when he unleashed the game-winning touchdown pass to Pearson. Staubach pulled his answer straight from his grade school days at Cincinnati's St. John the Evangelist Catholic School.

"I got knocked down on the play ... I closed my eyes and said a Hail Mary," Staubach said.

And thus, the lexicon of the game was changed forever and the "Hail Mary pass" was born.

As straight-laced as Staubach was, a fiercer competitor never wore the star. He was also blessed with a sense of humor and there's the legendary story of the time he used it to almost scare poor Tex Schramm to death.

Early in his career, Staubach had grown weary of waiting in Schramm's outer office for a contract meeting. Looking around the Cowboys' offices on the 11th floor of Expressway Towers, Staubach realized he could get out on the ledge and sneak around to Schramm's corner office. There was lattice-work on the east and west sides of the building that would help protect him from falling. Once he got to the northwest corner and Schramm's office, however, he would be on his own.

"I got around there and peeked around the corner," Staubach said. "Tex was sitting there with his feet up on the credenza, kind of staring out the window. He was on a conference call with (then commissioner) Pete Rozelle and some other people. They told me later he gasped so loud when I jumped out, they thought he'd had a heart attack."

Schramm told Rozelle his future quarterback had just flashed before his eyes – on a window ledge, 11 floors up.

"Looking back, it was probably a stupid thing to do," Staubach said. "I took too many risks in those days. But I darn sure didn't have to wait (to see Schramm) any longer."

Staubach's accomplishments speak for themselves. He was a six-time Pro Bowler, a four-time NFL passing champion, MVP of Super Bowl VI, won two Super Bowls, five NFC titles and seven division championships. He is enshrined in the Pro Football Hall of Fame in Canton and in the Cowboys' Ring of Honor.

But he meant so much more to the Cowboys than just the amazing numbers he accumulated. He embodied what the Cowboys wanted to be to their fans. He married his childhood sweetheart, Marianne, and made it clear that he would always be faithful to her. He spurned the nightlife and wild parties. He really was a real life Dudley Do-Right.

Walt Garrison tells about the time when he and his wife had their first child, a son, and Staubach, who had four girls at the time, asked him how he did it.

"Well, I really can't explain it, Roger," Garrison reportedly drawled, "But I'll tell you what, if you bring Marianne by the house, I'll try and getcha one."

Staubach wasn't amused about that, or the time that Garrison convinced him to try a pinch of snuff. He threw up twice during a quarterbacks meeting. But he understood it was all in fun. He wasn't quite so forgiving with Clint Longley in 1976.

Longley, a big-armed quarterback out of Abilene Christian, came in as Staubach's backup in 1975, but he hated the discipline Tom Landry demanded of his players, a regimen endorsed by Staubach as quarterback and leader of the team. When Longley fell to No. 3 on the depth chart after Danny White's arrival at camp in Thousand Oaks, California, in 1976, Longley's attitude went totally south. He challenged Staubach to a fight on the practice field and was embarrassed when Staubach easily flipped him upside down.

The next day, Longley waited in the locker room until Staubach was pulling his pads over his head, arms up, essentially defenseless, and cold-cocked him, knocking him into a set of nearby scales and cutting his head. Staubach recovered in time to grapple with Longley. When the two were separated, Longley quickly slipped away to his dorm room while Staubach's injury was treated by the team trainer.

Once Staubach convinced the trainer he was OK, he sprinted out of the locker room, looking for Longley to finish what Clint's cheap shot had started. Longley had already wisely decided it was time to get out of Dodge and was headed to the airport.

Much like Nolan Ryan's showdown with Robin Ventura at Arlington Stadium years later, the Longley incident only solidified Staubach's stature with the fans. Staubach, perhaps more than any other player in Cowboys' history, somehow made the star on the helmet shine a bit brighter.

DANNY WHITE

Imagine, for a moment, being the guy who replaced John Wayne in the re-make of the epic western, Stagecoach (it was Alex Cord, in case you've forgotten). Or just as challenging, supplanting Anthony Hopkins as Dr. Hannibal Lector in *Silence of the Lambs*.

Now you have an inkling of how Danny White must have felt back in 1980, when he found himself stepping into the rather large cleats of the absolutely irreplaceable Roger Staubach.

Welcome to the NFL, kid. Have a great time.

Danny White was about to learn the validity of one of the NFL's great and mysterious truisms: the backup quarterback is the most beloved player on the team; the starter … sometimes, not so much.

At 38, Staubach was coming off a season in which he'd suffered three concussions, finding himself dazed on the sideline and unable to return to the game. In the 1979 playoffs against the Rams, linebacker Jack Reynolds slammed Staubach to the ground so hard that Roger would admit later that he wasn't all there mentally by the time the game ended.

After consulting with doctors following the season, Staubach assessed his options and decided it was time to hang it up rather than risk permanent brain damage. He knew he was leaving the Cowboys in good hands with White at quarterback.

"We had been in three Super Bowls in four years, and Danny White was definitely ready to play," Staubach told Peter Golenbock in *Landry's Boys*.

There was no question of that. White had patiently bided his time, backing up Staubach for four seasons once he'd joined the team in 1976 from the defunct World Football League's Memphis Southmen. The Cowboys had used a third-round pick on White, thinking of him mostly as a punter, following the '74 season but Memphis promised him a chance to play quarterback and offered more money, so he tried the WFL first.

"I played two years in the World Football League and had a lot of success there," White said for an article for the Cowboys' *Star Magazine*. "When I came to the Cowboys I knew right away there was going to be a learning curve. And at the time I didn't know how long it was going to be, but I knew Roger was in his late 20s before he even started playing so I knew he wasn't going to play forever, that my chance would come and it did."

Staubach could see the talent that White had and knew he was a good fit in Dallas. He advised his understudy to remain patient, telling him his day would eventually come.

"He would say, 'I'm not going to play much longer; you need to stay here, people love you here.' He was so positive about my career and my future in Dallas," White said. "That meant a lot to me."

There are those who say that White was the best Cowboys' quarterback to never win a Super Bowl, and while that's probably an accurate assessment, it's not technically correct. White does have a Super Bowl ring, backing up Staubach in Super Bowl XII after the end of the 1978 season.

What he doesn't have is a Super Bowl ring as the Cowboys' starting quarterback. He is more often remembered as the quarterback who couldn't "win the big one," taking the Cowboys to three straight NFC title games (1980-82) on the road and losing each one, despite being favored.

Most painful was the 1981 loss in San Francisco when Dwight Clark leaped high to rescue Joe Montana's high floater in the back of the end zone for what would become known in NFL lore as "The Catch." That touchdown put the 49ers up 28-27 with 51 seconds to play. White subsequently hit Drew Pearson with a long pass and for a moment it looked as if Pearson would break away to score, but 49ers' DB Eric Wright caught just enough of the back of Pearson's jersey to trip him up and prevent a 75-yard touchdown play. Two plays later, with the Cowboys almost within field-goal range, White was sacked and fumbled, the 49ers recovered and the game was over.

White was the best Cowboys' quarterback never to win a Super Bowl and the numbers are in the Cowboys' record book to prove it. When he left the game, he owned several team passing records, including most career touchdowns (155), single-season TDs (29) and single-season yards (3,980). Over eight seasons, he won two-thirds of his starts, including five playoff games, and his ability to punt through the '84 season allowed the Cowboys to keep an extra player on the roster.

But did White ever escape Staubach's enormous shadow? Maybe not.

"I think what makes White somewhat under-appreciated – and I do think he was under-appreciated – was the fact that he wasn't Staubach," Cowboys' radio voice Brad Sham said in that article for

Star Magazine. "He followed Staubach, didn't get to the Super Bowl.

"When you assess what he did on the field, he's clearly under-appreciated to me. I would say, 'Three straight championship games – you go do that.' "

In fact, only one Cowboys' quarterback in history – Troy Aikman – did better, taking the Cowboys to four straight championship games from 1992-1995.

"Danny White did one hell of job, really," Staubach told Golenbock. "They just lost some tough games. But it was still a very good team for three or four years."

For his part, White has made peace with himself and with the past. He knows how good he was and how close he came to greatness, to joining Staubach and Troy Aikman as Super Bowl-winning quarterbacks for the Dallas Cowboys.

After his playing career with the Cowboys, White became a highly successful coach and player personnel director in the Arena Football League, guiding the Arizona Rattlers to championships in 1994 and 1997. Starting in 2011, he became a color analyst on Cowboys' games for Compass Radio Network.

TROY AIKMAN

If there was every any doubt that Jerry Jones was born under a lucky star – and not just the star on the Cowboys' helmet – it was totally removed less than two months after Jones bought the team when the NFL draft rolled around in late April.

What better gift to a brand new owner and brand new head coach than the No. 1 overall draft pick, especially when a franchise quarterback was sitting there, ready to rock and roll. Troy Aikman, come on down.

For Jimmy Johnson, it was about time. Johnson had tried desperately to recruit Aikman for Oklahoma State after Aikman starred in football and baseball at little Henryetta, Oklahoma. The coach ultimately lost him, ironically, to Barry Switzer at the University of Oklahoma when Switzer promised the Sooners would throw the ball all over the field with Aikman at quarterback. That promise, however, was based on the presumption that OU was going to move to an I-formation offense with new tailback Marcus Dupree lining up behind Aikman.

That plan fell through when Switzer and Dupree didn't see eye to eye and the star running back hightailed it back to Mississippi. Aikman found himself ground-bound in Switzer's bread-and-butter Wishbone offense. After Aikman had his leg broken in a 1985 game against Johnson's Miami Hurricanes – the coincidences just keep mounting up – Aikman transferred to UCLA, where he became an immediate star.

"He's a tremendous competitor, intelligent, with a strong arm," Johnson wrote in his 1993 autobiography *Turning the Thing Around: Pulling America's Team out of the Dumps and Myself Out of the Doghouse.* "I knew he could be one of the cornerstones in building an outstanding football team."

No doubt about that, but there were a handful of other future All-Pros at the top of that draft, giving rise to some speculation as to whether the Cowboys gave consideration to anyone else besides Aikman. The second pick was gigantic offensive lineman Tony Mandarich, projected by some to become the best NFL lineman of all time. After he was cut by Green Bay in 1992, *Sports Illustrated*'s cover headline proclaimed Mandarich "The NFL's Incredible Bust."

A pretty good running back out of Oklahoma State named Barry Sanders was the third pick of the draft, linebacker Derrick Thomas was fourth and flashy cornerback Deion Sanders was fifth. Four out of the top five picks in 1989 are now in the Pro Football Hall of Fame in Canton, Ohio.

For the Cowboys, it was Aikman or bust. He was everything God meant an NFL quarterback to be: tall, piercing blue eyes, blond hair, a million-dollar smile that caused young women to swoon and a stud-sized personality that captured the hearts of fans and teammates alike.

During two long days of contract negotiations with agent Leigh Steinberg and Jerry Jones in the back room of a Dallas restaurant after the draft, word that Aikman was in town eventually leaked out and a crowd of young women waited outside the restaurant for a glimpse of the Cowboys' latest heart-throb. A waiter mentioned this to Aikman and told him that he'd advised the women that it was just someone who looked like Aikman, not really the new Cowboys' quarterback-to-be.

Aikman, according to a story in Jones' 2008 book *Playing to Win*, told the waiter it was OK, to let the crowd know he would be out after lunch. When he emerged to spend an hour or more signing autographs, Jones knew for certain he'd made the right choice when he went with Aikman as his No. 1 pick.

The record books, of course, attest to the same thing. Aikman was exactly the cornerstone that Jones and Johnson needed to construct their team around. If anything, Troy was even better than advertised. He proved to be as tough as Meredith and Staubach, probably even more talented than either of them at throwing the football, and with the intelligence to understand what it would take to win under the electron microscope that comes with being the quarterback of America's Team.

Yet, the statistical record books don't really define Aikman's greatness. He is only 32nd in passing yards in NFL history, already surpassed by Tony Romo and behind such NFL "legends" as Dave Krieg, Kerry Collins and Steve DeBerg.

The one number that Aikman owns that no other Cowboys' quarterback can match: THREE Super Bowl rings. Only Tom Brady, Terry Bradshaw and Joe Montana, with four each, have more.

"The thing about the Triplets that doesn't get enough credit. ... Troy was motivated only by winning games," popular Cowboys' fullback Daryl "Moose" Johnson said of the Cowboys' star triumvirate of Aikman, running back Emmitt Smith and wide receiver Michael Irvin. "He wasn't driven by anything but that, and certainly not the numbers. Michael was the heart and soul of our team and Emmitt was on his way to becoming the league's all-time leading rusher, but Troy was what made everything click.

"Those guys were not dominated by egos. All three of them only wanted to win. They knew their legacy would be defined by winning championships."

Aikman's 90 victories in the 1990s made him the winningest starting quarterback of any decade in NFL history to that point (since surpassed in the next decade). He won six NFC East titles, three NFC championship games and the three Super Bowl titles. He was a six-time Pro Bowler, MVP of Super Bowl XXVII and was 1997's NFL Man of the Year. Aikman's five-year stretch (1992-1996) in which he posted a 56-19 regular season record and an 11-4 post-season ledger may never be surpassed in Dallas.

"He cares more about being great than anyone I've ever known," Norv Turner, the Cowboys' offensive coordinator in 1992-1993, said after presenting Aikman for induction into the Pro Football Hall of Fame in Canton, Ohio, on August 5, 2006. "He not only drove himself, he drove everyone around him."

Turner, who spent 15 years as a head coach with three NFL teams, said if he had one game to coach, he would want Aikman as his quarterback.

"Because I want to win," Turner explained. "If you look at Troy's greatest plays, they came in the most critical situations, they came against the best teams and they came in the playoffs. In an era of super egos, he never let his get in the way of winning. Super Bowls were more important than statistics."

The irony is that after his election to the Hall of Fame, Aikman sent out invitations to family and friends to attend the ceremony and illustrated the invitation with a photo that he felt symbolized his career. It didn't show him smiling – didn't even show his face, in fact – and it didn't show him winning.

The photo is from the back and shows Aikman's grimy, mud-caked jersey, his arms laced with tape, his pants drenched with sweat. He is walking off the field at San Francisco's old Candlestick Park on Jan. 15, 1995, after the Cowboys lost to the 49ers, 38-28 in the NFC championship game. Their chance at an unprecedented third straight Super Bowl victory vanished into the mist and muck that day as well.

This, it's fair to ask, is how Aikman wanted to remember his career?

Absolutely. Maybe you had to be there, but it may have been Aikman's finest moment. He never stood taller in his life.

"That photo embodies my career, or at least I hope it embodies it," Aikman said. "That game was probably the one game in my career I was proudest of."

He could have picked Super Bowl XXVII, when his pinpoint passing (73 percent completion) and four TD passes helped decimate

Buffalo 52-17 and earned him MVP honors. Or the game he feels was his best ever, that 38-27 win over Green Bay in the 1996 NFC title game.

But no, the game that meant the most to him was a loss.

The Cowboys were down 21-0 just 7 ½ minutes into the game but fought back like cornered tigers.

"We knew we had talent," Aikman said. "Our character was demonstrated that afternoon at Candlestick Park. I think we learned something about ourselves, too. We'd won two straight Super Bowls, but you don't really know who you are until you've faced adversity."

Finally understanding just how tough and resilient they could be that afternoon would help the Cowboys win their most difficult Super Bowl a year later.

Troy Aikman's amazing will to win wouldn't have it any other way.

TONY ROMO

I love the enigma that is Tony Romo. I love that he is, at once, both so good and so bad. As a fan, I even love the agonizing mystery he brings to the TV screen each Sunday during the season. Is he going to be good today? Is he going to be great? Or is he going to throw three of those back-breaking, pick-six interceptions that snatch defeat from the jaws of victory one more time?

If he was a movie, Romo would be unlikely to ever be nominated for an Academy Award. He is not going to be gushed over by the critics. From an aesthetics standpoint, he'll probably come up short. But you know that when you sit down in your seat, the lights go off, and the action starts, there may well be more than one popcorn-throwing moment ahead. He brings that kind of excitement.

Does he even deserve to be mentioned in the same breath with Cowboys' quarterbacks Don Meredith, Roger Staubach, Danny White and Troy Aikman? What would he think if he picked up this book, turned to the quarterbacks section, and found he had been left out, simply ignored, listed with the also-played, like dozens of others. Maybe he should be.

But I couldn't do that. Talent-wise, Romo deserves his place here and not just here, but in the discussion with the best of the best that have worn the Cowboys' star. Yet, I can also understand those who would howl that that's nonsense, pointing to his measly two career playoff victories after 13 seasons in Dallas, the last eight as the team's fulltime starter.

The funny thing is, Romo himself would probably come down on the side of the latter. He knows, as much as Staubach or Aikman ever did, what constitutes greatness. And he knows he'll never be there until he takes the Cowboys to a Super Bowl and wins it. He told us as much back in October of 2014, when S. L. Price wrote a revealing in-depth *Sports Illustrated* profile on arguably the most polarizing quarterback in Cowboys' history.

"I will tell you straight up: Without winning a championship, it's going to be very hard to have fulfilled what I set out for," Romo told *SI*. "You just can't be considered one of the best without it. Only some people can — the Dan Marinos and Jim Kellys of the world. Everybody else, it comes down to that. Is it unfair? It doesn't matter. It is what it is. So you'd better go do it. You have no choice. There are no excuses. Did you get the job done or didn't you?"

For all that Romo has accomplished, the team passing records he has obliterated, the four Pro Bowl selections, the 25 fourth-quarter comebacks, virtually everything positive about his career also has a rebuttal. Sure, he's had two magnificent 500-yard passing games in his career, but he's also had two five-interception games, including in one of those 500-yarders, a 51-48 shootout loss to Peyton Manning and Denver in 2013. The 13 wins he led the Cowboys to in 2007 tied the franchise record, but that was also the Cabo year, and it ended miserably when a tanned Romo and the Cowboys were absolutely abysmal in their upset playoff loss to the Giants.

At one moment he's the bashful undrafted free agent with the dimpled smile, the plucky kid from little Burlington, Wisconsin, and the next he's exactly what Bill Parcells told him not to be, the Jessica Simpson-dating, beauty pageant-judging, Cabo-partying celebrity quarterback who too often seems to love golf more than football.

Somehow, as good as he is, as good as he can be, he's just one monumental fumbled field-goal attempt snap, one irresponsible fumble, one blatantly stupid interception, from being the bane of every Cowboy fan. If there's any Cowboys' quarterback he most resembles, it's the star-crossed Meredith, who also too often simply tried to do too much with too little.

The contradictions are littered throughout Romo's career. We are told by those who know him best that the guy often tabbed as simply not caring enough is an incredible perfectionist, a relentless grinder, a film room and practice field rat, who outworks everyone around him in his pursuit of excellence.

"I've been doing this 30-plus years," Roy Wittke, Romo's coordinator at Eastern Illinois and a former assistant coach at Arkansas and Arizona State told *SI*. "He was, by far, consistently the hardest-working kid in practice I've ever been around."

Nothing's changed since Romo arrived in the NFL.

"I've never seen somebody try to perfect their craft he way he has," tight end Jason Witten told Price.

Former Cowboys' quarterback Danny White, who had to follow in the footsteps of the great Roger Staubach and, not surprisingly, came up a little short of that greatness, analyzes Cowboys games for the Compass Radio Network and has come to appreciate Romo's talent.

"I can relate to what Tony's going through, and if I could get inside his head and tell him one thing, it's he's one of the great quarterbacks in the history of the Dallas Cowboys," White said in an article in the *Cowboys Star* magazine. "People keep saying, 'You've got to win the big one.' Well, he doesn't have to win the big one.

"There are 10 other guys out there on the field and 46 on the field as a team. And everybody plays a big part in that, and if you really think about it, everybody else on the offense has to do their job before the quarterback gets to do his. The quarterback gets more credit and blame than he ever deserves."

Romo headed into the 2016 season at 37 and coming off a collarbone that was broken and surgically repaired twice in 2015. He is realistic enough to understand that the challenge is only growing more difficult, but optimistic enough to believe it can still be met.

"It should be hard," he told *SI* back in 2014. "If it was easy, it wouldn't be as great when you actually accomplished it. I like to think that we might be good enough to actually do that. And that makes me excited going forward the next four or five years."

There is no question that Romo has become a smarter, better-prepared, thinking-man's quarterback after more than a decade in the NFL. He can still avoid pressure and extend plays as well as almost any quarterback in the league. He is not the reckless gunslinger he once was. His team records and the respect he's earned around the NFL are not flukes.

But he is still searching for that postseason payoff that has eluded him for all these years. The key question is whether he can find it before the Cowboys simply can't put Humpty Dumpty back together again and the Romo era fades into history.

Three plays into the third preseason game of the 2016 season, Humpty Dumpty was shattered once again. Jerry Jones immediately sent trainers scurrying to the nearest hardware store for more Super Glue.

Considering that intended backup quarterback Kellen Moore had already been sidelined for the season with a broken fibula in training camp, Cowboys fans could be forgiven for wondering if the 2016 season had just swirled down the toilet.

The only quarterback left standing was rookie fourth-round pick Dak Prescott, who wasn't even the project quarterback the Cowboys had hoped to land in the draft. Who knew he would show up wearing Superman's cape?

First, Romo's injury. Scrambling out of the pocket, a slow-moving Romo was caught from behind by Seattle defensive end Cliff Avril and landed awkwardly with Avril on top.

Five games into the season, the Cowboys were 4-1 behind Prescott and Jones was dealing with a full-blown quarterback controversy. Prescott had yet to throw his first NFL interception and, with rookie running back Ezekiel Elliott leading the league in rushing, the Cowboys offense was running as smoothly and effortlessly as a fine-tuned Ferrari.

Jones continued to insist that Romo would return to his role as the Cowboys starting quarterback as soon as he was healthy while the debate raged about whether the team should make any change at all when things were going so good.

One thing seemed certain: The Cowboys had unexpectedly found their "quarterback of the future."

The Running Backs

DON PERKINS

The NFL of the 1950s and '60s was a running backs league. Alan Ameche, Jim Taylor, Jim Brown, Joe Perry, Frank Gifford, Elroy Hirsch, John David Crow, Paul Hornung, Gale Sayers were the names emblazoned in the sports page headlines.

Sure, there was room for the Otto Grahams, the Bobby Laynes, the Johnny U's, but it was the big bruisers, pounding through the mud and the muck, who captured the hearts of the blue collar fans who made up the majority of those who were coming to love this new American professional game.

That Don Perkins, the Cowboys' first running back, carved out his niche in that line of great runners despite playing his entire career behind a patchwork offensive line on a ragged expansion team speaks to the type of player and person he was. It's why his is among those 21 names in the Cowboys' Ring of Honor.

It's also why Tex Schramm, given the chance by the NFL to sign two star college players to personal services contracts after the 1959 NFL season (the franchise didn't even exist at the time of the draft), chose Perkins to go along with native Texan and SMU star Don Meredith as the cornerstones of the new team. Knowing the new franchise would already be far behind the rest of the league after a weak expansion draft, it was the NFL's way of giving Schramm and new owner Clint Murchison Jr. a break.

Schramm knew what he was doing. In a league known for its hard-nosed fullbacks and halfbacks, Perkins would validate the GM's confidence by giving the new franchise credibility and professionalism. He was the college all-star from the University of New Mexico that no one knew: quiet, polite, introverted, tough. He was coming to a team in the south on the fringes of the Jim Crow era, to a city that at the time didn't even have a decent hotel to accommodate black players. Team and city leaders had to convince the Ramada Inn next to Love Field to not only accept the Cowboys' black players until they could find housing, but those from visiting teams as well. Perkins, grateful for the opportunity to play football for a living, would never complain or cause a problem.

Perkins would miss the entire 1960 season after reinjuring his foot – he'd broken it as a junior in college – at the college all-star game, but when he returned for the 1961 season he made an immediate impact, giving the Cowboys a bona fide running threat, rushing for 815 yards (4.1 yards per carry) and earning NFL Rookie of the Year honors. He was the first Cowboys running back to record a 100-yard rushing game (106 on 17 carries vs. Minnesota).

He came close to giving Dallas its first 1,000-yard rusher the following year, finishing with 945 yards and being named to the All-Pro Team. Six times in his eight Cowboys seasons he was a Pro Bowl selection and finished among the top 10 in NFL rushers each year. When he retired, his 6,217 yards ranked him fifth on the NFL's all-time rushing list.

Bob Lilly was the Cowboys' first Ring of Honor inductee in 1975. Perkins and Meredith would follow a year later.

CALVIN HILL/DUANE THOMAS

After Perkins' retirement following the '68 season, the Cowboys would depend on young fullback Walt Garrison, a tough Oklahoman who was a real-life cowboy, and versatile Dan Reeves, but their next real star at running back would come from perhaps the most unexpected place of all – the Ivy League.

Calvin Hill was intelligent, introspective, well-educated and outspoken – something that sometimes made Tex Schramm and Tom Landry uncomfortable – but he was also 6 feet, 4 inches and 235-pounds of muscle, speed and force. He was just what the Cowboys needed as the decade of the '70s began.

"Calvin made a big impression, because he was the closest thing to Jim Brown I've seen," cornerback Cornell Green remembered in *Landry's Boys*. "Calvin could fall forward for five yards. He could get yards without even passing the line of scrimmage. I just thought he was a great back."

Hill's career with the Cowboys would be short but definitely sweet. In his first pro action, an exhibition game against the 49ers at San Francisco's Kezar Stadium, Hill rushed for 106 yards. In his second regular season professional game, running what would become a Cowboys' bread-and-butter sweep, Hill rambled for 138 yards on 23 carries. For the first nine games of the 1969 season, he racked up 807 yards and was the best back in the league. But he also broke a toe in that ninth game, a 150-yard splurge against the Redskins, and the lingering injury would eventually shorten his career. He would gain only another 137 yards total over the season's final four games.

Hill would battle injuries and not be nearly as productive for the next two years but the Cowboys had also discovered another option in an enigmatic young power back named Duane Thomas, out of West Texas State. Worried about Hill's ability to stay healthy, the Cowboys had surprisingly made Thomas their No. 1 pick (23rd overall) in the 1970 draft. After all, Hill had just won Rookie of the Year honors and finished second in the league in rushing. Thomas would usurp some of Hill's carries over the next two years. They would, at times, even both start in the same backfield in 1970-71, but it was Thomas who led the NFL in rushing touchdowns (11) in '71.

In the 1970 playoffs, it was also Thomas who carried the Cowboys to the Super Bowl, lugging the ball 30 times for 135 yards in a slug-it-out 5-0 victory over the Detroit Lions in the first round and then toting it 27 times for 143 yards in a 17-10 win in the championship game against the San Francisco 49ers. But he could gain only 35 yards in the heartbreaking 16-13 loss to the Baltimore Colts in Super Bowl V while Hill watched from the sidelines.

Thomas' relationship with the Cowboys blew completely apart in the off-season when Tex Schramm refused to renegotiate his contract and Thomas made his now infamous claim that Landry was a "plastic man." In July, 1971, the Cowboys thought they'd ridded themselves of their problem child, trading Thomas to the New England Patriots for running back Carl Garrett. Three days later, the Pats sent Thomas back, saying they couldn't handle him, and commissioner Pete Rozelle voided the trade.

Thomas spent the first three days of the '71 season on the inactive list, then returned to action for the Monday night game against the New York Giants. When Hill was injured four plays into the second half, Thomas came into the game and gained 60 yards on nine carries.

Upset with the media over the way his training camp holdout had been portrayed, Thomas refused to talk to reporters for the rest of the season. He may have been silent, but he could still run, averaging better than 4½ yards a carry for the rest of the season, leading the league in TDs and helping the Cowboys back into the playoffs. He rushed for 95 yards and a touchdown in Dallas' dominating 24-3 triumph over the Miami Dolphins in Super Bowl VI, after which he finally broke his long public silence. It was his last game in a Cowboys uniform and after two lackluster years in Cleveland, he was out of the league.

Hill stepped back in as Dallas' primary back in 1972 and became the Cowboys' first-ever 1,000-yard rusher (1,036). He trumped that in '73 with 1,142 yards on a whopping 273 carries. His last season as a Cowboy came in 1974, when he gained 844 yards on 185 carries.

It would be two more years before a new, even brighter star would emerge in the Cowboys' backfield.

TONY DORSETT

If there was ever any doubt that the Cowboys' star was a lucky star, that doubt faded completely away on draft day in March of 1977, when Tex Schramm smugly announced that the Cowboys had traded four draft picks – their first-rounder and three seconds – to the Seattle Seahawks for the rights to the second overall pick.

The trade was also contingent on Tampa Bay, which owned the first overall pick, taking USC running back Ricky Bell. In other words, if Tampa took University of Pittsburgh's four-time All-American and Heisman Trophy winner Tony Dorsett, the deal was off. Dorsett was the Cowboys' one and only target. The Bucaneers happily obliged by taking Bell and Dorsett fell smack dab into Schramm's lap, just as he and Gil Brandt had planned.

Other NFL coaches and executives were furious.

"Dallas and Seattle must be sleeping together," fumed Vikings' coach Bud Grant. "I don't understand it at all."

Baltimore Colts' general manager Ernie Accorsi nailed it even more succinctly and with amazing precognition.

"The Cowboys got themselves a Hall of Famer for four draft choices," he sighed.

It was as if divine intervention was working in the Cowboys' favor: the most glamorous and popular pro football franchise in the country had just swapped a handful of beans for the flashiest and best player in the country. The trade would pay enormous dividends for the next 11 seasons.

Dorsett, Dallas' first million-dollar player, had shattered college records by running for more than 6,000 yards at Pitt. He would more than double that as a Cowboy.

There was skepticism among the veterans and media when Dorsett arrived at his first Cowboy training camp. Remember, the Cowboys were accustomed to big running backs, like Calvin Hill and Duane Thomas, and here was Dorsett, all 5-foot-9, 185-pounds of him after a chicken fried steak and cream gravy dinner. It only took a few practices, however, for the rest of the team to realize that something special had arrived.

"Once he hit the practice field, you could see the talent, the quickness, the speed, and this was one thing he never got enough credit for: his acceleration," Drew Pearson said in Peter Golenbock's book *Cowboys Have Always Been My Heroes*. "He could start from zero and be at 60 miles an hour in no time flat. That's what made Tony Dorsett what he was all through his career; his ability to accelerate so quickly."

Dorsett was joining a Cowboys' team that had gone 11-3 in 1976 before losing the divisional playoff game to the Los Angeles Rams, 14-12. With Dorsett joining Roger Staubach in the backfield, and with Drew Pearson and Tony Hill as wideouts, the Cowboys had the ability to dominate offensively.

"Tony Dorsett had a big difference when he came in '77," Staubach told Golenbach. "Getting Dorsett was a real shot in the arm. He had speed and he was tough, could run inside. With him, we had a very balanced game."

Dorsett, of course, had to learn the Landry ropes. Preston Pearson continued to start at running back while Dorsett waited. He carried seven times in the second game of the season and scored two touchdowns. He had 72 yards on 10 carries in the third game and, though he didn't start Game 4, he dashed for 141 yards on 14 carries and scored two touchdowns playing behind Pearson.

He would start just four of 14 games, all in the last five weeks, and still rang up 1,008 yards, averaged 4.8 yards and scored a dozen touchdowns. The Cowboys finished 12-2 and Dorsett would play an integral role in their march to Super Bowl XII and a 27-10 victory over Denver in New Orleans. Dorsett was named NFL Rookie of the Year.

It was the beginning of an auspicious 12-year career that would end with – as Accorsi had predicted – Dorsett in the Pro Football Hall of Fame, and in the Cowboys' Ring of Honor. Along the way Dorsett was a four-time Pro Bowler, an All-Pro and set an NFL record that will never be broken.

On Jan. 2, 1983, the last day of the regular season, playing before a *Monday Night Football* national TV audience against the Minnesota Vikings, Dorsett took a handoff from quarterback Danny White in the Cowboys' own end zone. It was a simple dive play up the middle with the Cowboys merely hoping to get some breathing room away from their own goal line. But Dorsett got superb blocks from Tom Rafferty and Herb Scott and "I jumped through that hole," he would say. Then he did what he had always been taught: "Run to daylight."

He ran like Tony Dorsett always ran. Fast. Hard. With total abandon, veering right and accelerating to warp speed in just a few steps. Drew Pearson threw a key block down field. Ninety-nine-and-a-half yards later Dorsett owned the record for the longest touchdown run in NFL history (officially 99 yards).

When he retired after the 1988 season (11 years in Dallas, one in Denver), Dorsett had rushed for 12,739 yards, second only to Chicago's Walter Payton. He now ranks fifth all time behind Emmitt Smith, Payton, Barry Sanders and Eric Dickerson.

"A lot of people said I wouldn't last in this league," Dorsett said at his retirement. "I was the skinny little kid from Aliquippa, Pennsylvania, who wasn't supposed to make it."

Oh, he made it all right.

"Tony Dorsett," Staubach said, "is one of the greatest backs in NFL history."

There is a final tragic addendum to Dorsett's story. The many hard hits he suffered in his career have taken their toll and his frequent memory losses have caused doctors at UCLA to suspect he is a victim of chronic traumatic encephalothopy (CTE), a disease affecting many former NFL players.

EMMITT SMITH

It is ironic that the greatest running back in Dallas Cowboys' history – in NFL history – wound up wearing the star because of another big-name running back. Without Herschel Walker, there wouldn't have been an Emmitt Smith, not in Dallas at least.

And just like with Tony Dorsett, hindsight tells us that it took another blockbuster trade that turned out to be nothing less than highway robbery in the Cowboys' favor. Call it living under that lucky star again.

Jimmy Johnson calls it something else and devotes a whole chapter to it in his 1993 autobiography, *Turning the Thing Around: Pulling America's Team Out of the Dumps and Myself Out of the Doghouse*. He named the chapter, "The Great Train Robbery."

It all came together when Johnson and his assistant coaches were walking back to Valley Ranch after their daily lunchtime jog. The Cowboys were a not unexpected 0-3 in 1989 and the coaches were brainstorming about how they could get better faster.

As Johnson recounts it, defensive coordinator Dave Wannstedt asked the key question.

"What asset do we have that would allow us to do something to get a jump start?" Wannstedt wondered.

Clarity of thought often came to Johnson on these jogs and he didn't hesitate in answering Wannstedt.

"We could trade Herschel Walker," Johnson said.

As shocked as his assistants were, it actually made sense. After all, the Cowboys didn't have many tradeable assets anyway and had just drafted a franchise quarterback in Troy Aikman. Walker, the 1982 Heisman Trophy, Maxwell Award and Walter Camp Award winner, had the name and the mystique and was still only 27 years old at the time. Johnson knew if he floated Walker's name on the NFL marketplace, he would get some definite nibbles.

Besides that, Walker didn't fit Johnson's idea of a great NFL running back. Sure, he was big enough and strong enough to run over someone in the open field and he could outrun most anybody if he could get to daylight. But he wasn't, in Johnson's words, a "nifty" runner. He couldn't make the quick cuts and moves that were necessary to be consistently successful in the NFL.

By this time, Johnson had realized the only way for the Cowboys to get better was to somehow accumulate multiple high draft picks. Johnson knew he was not going to build his team around Walker and that he was more valuable as a trade chip than he was in the Cowboys' backfield. He also knew that trading Walker, if he could get Jerry Jones to agree to do it, would set off a firestorm of negative reaction in the Dallas media and fan base. He was willing to take the heat.

A few days later, Cleveland GM Ernie Accorsi called and mentioned Walker. Then the Cowboys checked in with most every other team, mentioning Walker in passing. The team that bit hardest was Minnesota and GM Mike Lynn.

For Walker, the Vikings loaded up the bus and shipped five players they didn't think they needed any more to Dallas. The only player who even stuck around for a year was defensive back Isaac Holt. But Johnson had an ace up his sleeve: each of the five players had a specific round and year for a conditional pick attached to his name. If any of them were not on the Cowboys' roster as of February 1, 1990, Dallas would receive the corresponding draft pick, or picks.

If exercised, those conditional picks added up to a veritable bonanza: first and second-round choices in both 1990 and 1991 and first, second and third-round choices in 1992. The Cowboys capitalized on almost all of them and used one of those extra picks to trade up to acquire Emmitt Smith with the 17th pick in the first round of the 1990 draft. They were also used to land first-rounders Russell Maryland (defensive tackle, 1991) and Kevin Smith (cornerback, 1992).

The Cowboys had done it again.

The Wide Receivers

BOB HAYES

For every stud quarterback the Dallas Cowboys put behind center during their first 65 years of existence, you can bet there was at least one star wide receiver with the ability to fly down the field and flag down the "Hail Marys" those quarterbacks would fling.

None flew faster than "The Bullet."

None almost single-handedly changed the game like Bob Hayes, who forced defensive coordinators to come up with something other than man-to-man coverage to be able to cope with "The Bullet's" inhuman speed. Hayes was directly and fully responsible for the development of the zone defense and bump-and-run coverage in professional football. Defensive coordinators had to do something. It wasn't enough, but it was all defenses could think to do in response to the blur that was Bob Hayes on a football field.

Frank Clarke was the Cowboys' first standout wide receiver, virtually Don Meredith's only deep threat on a bad football team in the early 1960s. But Hayes' arrival in 1965 coincided with the Cowboys becoming NFL relevant for the first time. During his nine-year run as a starter, the Cowboys went 90-34-2, the best and longest run of sustained success in their history. It was not a coincidence.

Hayes was another product of Tex Schramm and Gil Brandt's ability to think outside the box. Their conviction that particularly good athletes could adapt from basketball or track to play football led to the signings of cornerback Cornell Green, receiver Pete Gent and safety Mike Gaechter, among others. And it led to the Cowboys spending a seventh-round future pick in the 1964 draft on Hayes, who had played football as a fullback at Florida A&M but had stunned the world by becoming "The World's Fastest Human" at the 1964 Tokyo Olympic Games, winning the 100-meter dash in 10.05 seconds. He won the event by an unheard of four full meters. He was alone and practically coasting the last 10 meters.

If that wasn't enough, Hayes also anchored the U.S. team's 4 by 100 relay team. When the baton hit his hand, Hayes was behind five other teams. In the space of one circuit of the track, Hayes made up 9 meters and again won going away, beating the second-place team by 2 meters. He ran his leg in an unbelievable 8.6 seconds.

They didn't time players in the 40-yard dash in those days – that's something else the Cowboys' scouting department would eventually introduce – but Hayes had been timed at 5.6 in the 60-yard dash and at one time held world records in the 60, 100-yard dash, 220-yard dash and Olympic 100-meters simultaneously.

"World's Fastest Human," indeed. No wonder the Cowboys were willing to wait a year for Hayes' to complete his Olympic commitment before they could get him in uniform.

But could he play football? Oh, yes, he could play. This was no slender, fragile track star who shied away from contact. Hayes, who had played fullback/wingback of all things at Florida A&M, had the classic deep chest and over-developed thighs of an NFL running back. But it was his speed that made him special and the Cowboys knew he would be at his best in space. Put him outside and dare NFL cornerbacks to cover him one-on-one.

Clarke tried to explain to ESPN's Ralph Wiley what it was like watching Hayes play, and basically take his job as the Cowboys' No. 1 wideout.

"It was like he was melting, he was so fast," Clarke said.

There was no way any NFL cornerback, running backwards, could hope to cover Hayes. It was a total mismatch and teams soon recognized that they had to change their way of thinking on defense in order to cope with the special talent Hayes brought to the table. Cowboys' wideout Pete Gent said he used to love playing on the opposite side from Hayes because he knew he would always face nothing more than single coverage. Everybody else was on the other side, trying to keep up with Hayes.

Meredith and Roger Staubach, who had played with Hayes in the College All-Star Game, also quickly grasped the new weapon at their disposal and leaped to take advantage of it. Hayes caught 25 touchdown passes in his first two seasons with the Cowboys, including a 95-yarder from Meredith that still stands as a team record.

Hayes' 71 touchdown receptions also remained a team record at the end of the 2015 season, as does his career 20.0 yards per catch. In 1970, he averaged 26.1 yards on his 34 receptions, 10 of which went for touchdowns. The next season, he would average 24 yards a catch. He was virtually unstoppable. Hayes led the team in receiving three times, was a three-time Pro Bowl selection and a four-time All-Pro.

Jerry Jones – not Tex Schramm, surprisingly – inducted Hayes into the Cowboys' Ring of Honor on September 23, 2001. On Aug. 8, 2009, just short of seven years after his death from complications of prostate cancer, Hayes was inducted into the Pro Football Hall of Fame in Canton, Ohio, with his son, Bob Hayes Jr., and Roger Staubach as co-presenters.

During his Hall of Fame speech, Staubach said it took him awhile to adjust to Hayes' speed.

"I would think I was over-throwing him every time," Staubach said. "Instead, I was always under-throwing him. I had to learn to get rid of the ball quicker."

It was Staubach who stepped up to help Hayes after he spent time in prison following a controversial drug sting operation after Hayes had retired from football. Once out of prison, Hayes fell back into alcohol and drug abuse. Staubach paid for him to go back into rehab and gave him a job when he had finished.

The only thing that could stop Bob Hayes was death. And as Wiley said so vividly in his Hayes obituary, the real surprise was that even death could finally catch him.

DREW PEARSON

The man who would eventually supplant Hayes as the Cowboys' No. 1 receiver wasn't particularly fast. He wasn't especially big. In fact, coming out of college, Drew Pearson was known more as a quarterback than a wide receiver, a position he moved to his last season at the University of Tulsa.

But what Drew Pearson had that was as good as any possessed

by any Cowboys' receiver, past or present, was a pair of hands that caught everything. High. Low. Wide. Behind him. Too long. Too short. Didn't matter. Pearson would find a way to catch it. Legend has it that when Roger Staubach tossed his sweaty underwear toward the laundry hamper in the Cowboys' locker room, Pearson was there to make the grab.

Pearson ranks third on the Cowboys' list for career receptions with 489. It was Pearson's ability to make the clutch, game-winning play that set him apart. The Pro Football Hall of Fame honored Pearson's game-breaking ability by naming him to the All-Decade Team of the 1970s.

Pearson was a loosely wound combination of intelligence, quickness, those amazing hands and a terrific work ethic. He's the perfect example of someone who willed and worked himself to be more than the sum of his parts. Not bad for an undrafted free agent who showed up for his first training camp in 1973 as the eighth wide receiver on the depth chart.

Besides his own considerable attributes, Pearson had a significant "believer" in his corner: One Roger Staubach, who was about to step in as the Cowboys' fulltime starter at quarterback. When Staubach started showing up at the Cowboys' practice field in June of 1973, looking for someone to throw to, the only one there most of the time was the kid free agent from Tulsa.

"Drew was out there all the time," Staubach said. "I could really see that Drew was good. We kind of clicked and I had a lot of confidence in him.

"Drew made it because he worked so hard. He wasn't the fastest guy in the world, but if you look at film, when he got behind a defender, the guy didn't catch him. You just felt good about throwing it to him. You knew he was going to be where he was supposed to be and he was going to battle for the ball. Drew had those instincts and those intangibles that they didn't recognize in the draft."

By 1974 Pearson had become Staubach's favorite target, leading the Cowboys in receiving for the next four seasons. In 1978, Tony Hill arrived, giving the Cowboys two feared wideouts who would combine for 968 career catches and 99 touchdowns.

Drew not only made the spectacular catches, he made the routine ones. He wasn't afraid to go over the middle.

Although Pearson made dozens of incredible catches, many for game-winning touchdowns, the one that lives in NFL history has its own name: "The Hail Mary." Along with "The Catch," "The Immaculate Reception," and a handful of others, it goes down as one of the most famous and remarkable pass plays ever.

Its uniqueness comes from the situation as well as Roger Staubach's postgame locker room anointing that made it ... well, holy. It came in the first round of the 1975 playoffs, when the Cowboys found themselves trailing the Vikings in Minnesota, 14-10. Pearson had just caught a desperation 22-yard pass on fourth-and-16 for a first down at the 50. Preston Pearson dropped a pass, so it was second-and-10 with 26 seconds left in the game and the Cowboys had no timeouts.

In the huddle, Staubach told Drew to make a move on cornerback Nate Wright and go deep. Staubach would pump fake to hold safety Paul Krause so that he couldn't get over to help Wright. Ironically, Wright had Pearson played perfectly. If the pass had been on target, the Vikings' DB would have been able to make a play on it and the game would have been over.

Instead, the ball was slightly underthrown. Pearson saw it and reached back to make the catch. Vikings fans will swear today that he pushed off Wright, who slipped and fell on the icy field. Even then, the ball slipped through those glue-like hands and Pearson had to trap it against his hip with his elbow. As Krause arrived and began jawing with the closest official, Pearson turned and ran the final five yards into the end zone. The Cowboys had pulled off a miraculous comeback.

"Miracle," must have been what Staubach was thinking when reporters asked him about the play in the locker room afterward.

"I said, 'I got knocked down on the play ... I closed my eyes and said a Hail Mary,'" Staubach remembered on the play's anniversary a few years ago. "What was I going to say, that I intentionally underthrew it?"

The nuns at St. John the Evangelist grade school in Cincinnati, where Staubach attended, must have been so proud – in fact, they wrote Staubach later to tell him exactly that.

Not being Catholic, Pearson didn't even know that Staubach

meant he'd thrown up a prayer.

"The play never dies," Pearson said. "It was a great play but there are a lot of great plays. It's the name that keeps it alive."

Unbeknownst to them at the time, Staubach and Pearson had combined to add to the lexicon of football. Now, wherever the game is played, from peewees to the pros, every desperation pass is known as a "Hail Mary."

Pearson retired as the fourth-leading receiver in NFL history, once caught a pass in 58 consecutive games, was a three-time Pro Bowler and helped the Cowboys win six straight NFC East Division titles. He was inducted into the Cowboys' Ring of Honor in 2011.

"Let's be honest, he belonged in there a long time ago," longtime Cowboys' radio voice Brad Sham said at the time.

Jerry Jones' decision to finally admit Pearson – the two had some legal battles over Pearson's apparel company at one time – was influenced by Roger Staubach.

Once again, the Staubach-to-Pearson connection had produced another come-from-behind victory for the Cowboys.

MICHAEL IRVIN

If Troy Aikman was the engineer and Emmitt Smith was the little engine that could on the Cowboys Super Bowl teams of the 1990s, then the man who stoked the locomotive and made it all go, the man who was the heartbeat of America's Team, was Michael Irvin.

Aikman was implacable, immovable and relentless. Smith's batteries never seemed to run down. Teams did not want to be behind the Cowboys in the fourth quarter, because if they were, they knew what was coming ...

Emmitt left, Emmitt right, Emmitt up the middle. It was the Cowboys' way of grinding it out, hammering the last vestiges of hope out of an opponent.

But Irvin ... Irvin gave those Cowboys teams the breath of life. He gave them the spark they needed to become something special. His teammates believed in him. When, in the throes of despair it seemed that all was lost, it was Irvin who insisted that the Cowboys would somehow find a way to win. And they usually did.

"I never coached a guy who had as much passion for the game as Michael Irvin," said Jimmy Johnson, who also coached Irvin at the University of Miami. "He was also the guy who I knew at crunch time I could depend on to come through with a key play."

Irvin's spirit permeated everything the Cowboys did, starting with practice. That's the irony. Irvin's off-the-field problems dominated the headlines late in his career so many fans have the idea that he must have also let those problems affect what he did on the field. That was never the case.

"You can't get to Canton, Ohio, without exceptional talent," Cowboys' owner Jerry Jones said at Irvin's induction into the Pro Football Hall of Fame in 2007. "But athletic ability alone was only a part of Michael's gifts. His hard work is legendary. In two-a-days, the grind of all it, when (the players) would be on the field in the morning and in the afternoon, someone would look around and say, 'Where's Michael?' He'd be down on the field with pads on in the hot sun, getting some more (work) in."

"He was the heart and the soul of those championship teams."

Former Cowboys' offensive coordinator and NFL head coach Norv Turner remembered Irvin the same way.

"At the end of our practice each week we would do a two-minute drill," Turner said. "You would think it was Super Bowl week the way Michael competed."

The 15th of 17 children, Irvin grew up understanding that he would have to fight to get anywhere in life. It was that drive that made him a college star at Miami and brought him to the Cowboys as their No. 1 pick, 11th overall, in the 1988 draft. Troy Aikman would join him in Dallas a year later and Emmitt Smith the year after that. Irvin was the last Tex Schramm/Gil Brandt pick before Jerry Jones bought the team and Schramm pronounced that Irvin would be the player who would accelerate the Cowboys' "return to the living."

As usual, Tex was right.

Irvin caught 32 passes, five for touchdowns, and averaged 20.4 yards a catch as a rookie but it wasn't until after Aikman and Smith arrived that he established himself as the Cowboys' far-and-away best receiver, hauling in 93 catches for 1,523 yards and eight TDs in 1991. Like the Cowboys themselves, "The Playmaker" had come alive.

Over the next eight seasons Irvin averaged just under 83 catches per season, including an incredible 111 for 1,603 yards in 1995 as the Cowboys marched to their third Super Bowl championship in four years.

"Troy Aikman often said the greatest thing about Michael Irvin is you could throw him the ball when he was covered or you could throw him the ball when he was open, and the results were usually the same ... it was a completion and most of the time it was for a first down," Jones said. "Now when you've got a quarterback that has that kind of confidence in (his) receiver, you can have some offense. That's how you earn the name Playmaker, and that's how you keep it."

Despite having his career cut short by a spinal cord injury in 1999, Irvin's 750 career catches and 11,904 yards are both Cowboys' records. When he retired, he either owned or was tied for 20 team receiving records. His 47 100-yards receiving games placed him third in the NFL and he was selected to five Pro Bowls. He is a member of the Cowboys' Ring of Honor and was inducted into the Pro Football Hall of Fame in Canton in 2007.

"His passion, his competitiveness, were really possibly his greatest gifts and he shared them with his teammates on a daily basis," Jones said. "He practiced every day with the determination of a rookie that was hanging by a thread to make the team.

"I don't know that we'll see again a professional football player with a combination of his strength and skills as an athlete on the field and his unbelievable people skills. (He had) the kind of charisma and tremendous will with the strength to get the respect of the team."

Irvin's off-field problems began in 1996, following the Cowboys' third Super Bowl win of the '90s. He is the first to tell fans and admirers that he made many mistakes and has used his life lessons to become a powerful motivational speaker as well as an analyst for the NFL Network. He and is the kind of person who inspires loyalty, which is why Aikman showed up in the courtroom when Irvin was on trial on drug charges in '96.

He appeared, Aikman said, to be there for him as a friend.

"I know what kind of individual he is," Aikman said of Irvin's election to the Hall of Fame. "I know what he means to me. I know what kind of friend he was.

"I'm biased, (but) if there was ever a receiver that had a Hall of Fame career, in my opinion, it's Michael Irvin."

DEZ BRYANT

What Jerry Jones didn't know when he talked about Michael Irvin being one-of-a-kind at Irvin's Hall of Fame induction was that a close facsimile was on the way to become the third outstanding wide receiver to wear Cowboys' jersey No. 88. Like Irvin before him, Dez Bryant is big, strong, physical and intense.

Just the way the Cowboys like them.

If anything, Bryant may actually out-intense Irvin himself, who played the game as if it might be the last thing he does on this earth. Who knows, that may well be exactly how both Irvin and Bryant want it.

Both receivers are all about winning. Both have hands as soft as a freshly-powdered baby's behind. Both were willing to spill every drop of blood in their bodies to simply catch a football, where ever it was thrown. If it was high, they would somehow climb an invisible ladder to get to it. If it was low, they'd dig a tunnel. If it was wide, they'd turn into Rubber Man, stretching themselves like contortionists.

One huge difference: Irvin is in the Hall of Fame. And, oh yeah … he owns three Super Bowl championship rings. Bryant? He needs more time. Without question, in his first five seasons he had established himself as one of the top 5 wide receivers in the NFL. Then came 2015, a season essentially lost to an off-season contract dispute, a broken bone in his foot in the season's first game, a twice-broken collarbone for quarterback Tony Romo and an abysmal 4-12 finish.

"He was never healthy, but his problems began in the spring and summer (of 2015) when he missed the whole off-season, because of the contract holdout," Cowboys' radio play-by-play man Brad Sham noted. "In my opinion, that combined with his lack of patience and impulsiveness and led to his being injured in training camp, and then getting hurt in the first game. That all goes back to his absence from the off-season program."

There are other differences between Irvin and Bryant, too. Irvin's childhood, while difficult as one of 18 siblings, had definite structure.

His mother was a strong influence in his life. He quickly realized, standing on a roof helping his dad work one day, that this was not the kind of life he wanted. He found more structure on the football field in high school and a father-figure in college in Jimmy Johnson.

Bryant, the son of a 15-year-old drug addict and crack dealer, came up in a different world. His grandmother was a crackhead. Growing up, he never knew for sure where he was going to sleep at night, or whether there would be something to eat for dinner. He remembers going door to door, begging for food stamps. His foster mother kept a lock on the refrigerator.

All of this was detailed in an in-depth interview Bryant did for *Rolling Stone* magazine in late August of 2015, during which he raged about his frustration with Cowboys' owner Jerry Jones over his contract situation, which would shortly be resolved to Dez's satisfaction.

Rage, or something like it, is how Bryant deals with much of life. He is trying to learn how to channel his seemingly out of control emotions into a positive direction.

"He came in here and he was maybe 12 years old (emotionally)," Sham said. "He's only about 14 now. Before he got here, he had never been made accountable for his adult actions. He still goes crazy. That's the lack of maturity."

The Cowboys, who moved up to make Bryant the 24th overall pick in the 2010 draft, understood that this was what they were getting when they went after Bryant, who had been suspended for lying to the NCAA while at Oklahoma State. His strengths and weaknesses were detailed, virtually to the letter, in this scouting report from the NFL Combine:

Strengths: *Bryant has a really impressive combination of size and speed. Possesses the quickness and agility necessary to consistently gain separation as a route runner. Very good ball skills, catches the ball softly away from his body and is outstanding at high-pointing the jump-ball and really fights for the football. Runs angry after the catch and is a load to bring down in the open field.*

Weaknesses: *There are some questions surrounding Bryant's maturity level. Does not always show a high level of effort away from the ball. Was able to get open with pure athleticism in college but needs to run more precise routes at the next level.*

Did the scouts nail it, or what?

The good news – and it has shown up on the field – is that Bryant is willing to learn and work hard to make himself better. No, he doesn't have Michael Irvin's work ethic, which was off the charts, but few ever have.

"There were a lot of players last year (2015) who didn't like the way Dez behaved and the way he was treated by upper management, kind of coddled," Sham pointed out. "But that came from his frustration of his body, for the first time ever, not being able to do what he wanted it to do."

During the three-year span from 2012 to 2014, Bryant was an absolute beast. He averaged 91 catches a season and scored a remarkable 41 touchdowns, leading the NFL with 16 in 2014. He went to the Pro Bowl in 2013 and 2014 and was first-team All Pro in '14. With his holdout and injury-plagued 2015 behind him, the Cowboys have no reason to believe that the 27-year-old Bryant won't return to the dominance he showed previously.

"Besides their physical traits, they shared incredible determination," Sham said of Irvin and Bryant. "Every receiver wants the ball. There are a lot of guys who want their catches. Dez and Michael simply want to win.

"Dez is a catalyst and leader for his position group. He can be a very positive influence because of his passion, but it has to be channeled right. He's clearly a dominant player at his position in the league."

The Tight Ends

BEFORE BILLY JOE

If someone rattled off the names Doran, Bielski and Folkins to most Cowboys fans, they might think it was Jerry Jones' law firm, not the foundation of a Cowboys' Pro Bowl legacy at tight end. But, in an era in which the tight end was generally expected to be rarely seen and never heard from – unless it was to expound on an exceptional block he'd just made that allowed Don Perkins or Amos Marsh to score – that's exactly what those three men built.

Before DuPree, before Cosbie, before Novacek, before Witten, there were Doran, Bielski and Folkins, not to mention Norman, Ditka and Smith. The Cowboys' tradition at tight end is much richer than the casual fan might ever realize at a cursory first glance.

When the Cowboys were born in 1960, the tight end was basically an after-thought in NFL teams' offensive scheme, a lunch-pail toting, card-carrying extra offensive lineman who just happened to also be eligible to catch passes once in a while. Of course, the passing game itself was still in its infancy in those days. It was still the Nothing Fancy League, just three yards and a cloud of dust, or on a really entertaining day, three yards and a face full of mud.

Ironically, Jim Doran holds the honor of not only scoring the first touchdown in Dallas Cowboys history – on a 75-yard pass from Eddie LeBaron on September 24, 1960 – but also has the distinction of being the franchise's first-ever Pro Bowl player. Try those trivia questions out for size on your neighbor who swears he's the greatest Cowboys' fan who ever lived.

Doran had spent nine seasons in Detroit, starting his career as a defensive end/wide receiver in 1951 and even being named MVP in the Lions' championship season in 1952. His encore was to catch the game-winning 33-yard touchdown pass as the Lions won the title again in '53. In 1957, having moved to tight end, he led the Lions in receiving, despite the NFL's prevalent thinking that a tight end was little more than a glorified extra tackle. But when the expansion draft rolled around in 1960, Doran was 33 and the Lions included him on a list of available players from which the new Dallas Rangers (they hadn't changed their name to Cowboys yet) could choose (each team had to list nine players, but could lose no more than three).

Doran immediately added a touch of class to the rag-tag expansion Cowboys in 1960, giving LeBaron and rookie backup Don Meredith an experienced receiving target. Again, he surprisingly led the team in receiving with 31 catches for 554 yards and three touchdowns.

The Cowboys had wisely also added a second experienced tight end in the expansion draft, selecting five-year veteran Dick Bielski from Philadelphia. Bielski was a college fullback from Maryland who had been taken by the Eagles fifth overall in the 1955 draft.

In 1961, Bielski supplanted Doran as the Cowboys' No. 1 target at tight end, catching 26 passes for 377 yards and three touchdowns and earning a trip to the Pro Bowl. His greatest distinction: catching the unofficial league record shortest TD pass in NFL history, a two-incher from LeBaron against the Redskins on Oct. 9, 1960.

In 1962, the rival Dallas Texans used a 16th-round draft pick on a little known wide receiver out of Johnson C. Smith University. NFL teams ignored Pettis Norman because the Texans allegedly spread rumors that he'd already signed a contract, which turned out not to be true. Miffed, Norman chose instead to sign a free agent contract with the Cowboys.

By 1963, the Cowboys' tight ends were Norman and Lee Folkins, who had come to Dallas via a trade (an 8th-round draft choice) from Green Bay. Norman, who had also starred in track in college, was fast enough that the Cowboys sometimes used him at wide receiver and started Folkins at tight end. Like Doran and Bielski before him, Folkins was a favorite Meredith/LeBaron target, hauling in 39 passes for 536 yards and six TDs. And like Doran and Bielski, Folkins was tabbed for the Pro Bowl, the third different Cowboys' tight end in three years to earn that honor.

Norman took over the position from 1963-1970 and did far more blocking than catching as the Cowboys' offense leaned toward its wideouts (Bob Hayes arrived in 1965) and its backs. Also, Norman was sharing time with a pseudo-tight end named Pete Gent in those days, who was involved in more of the passing downs. It wasn't until former Bears' great Mike Ditka reminded the Cowboys of the damage a pass-catching tight end could do that a Dallas tight end would catch 30 passes in a season again in 1971. Before we begin the Ode to Billy Joe, we must call for a moment of silence for another Hall of Fame tight end who made little more than a cameo appearance for the Cowboys in 1978, yet his name will live in infamy among Cowboys' fandom as long as there's a star on the helmet.

Jackie Smith had carved out an illustrious career for the St. Louis Cardinals and had retired after the 1977 season, having lost his starting job to J.V. Cain. When Cowboys' backup tight end Jay Saldi broke his arm in the fourth game of the season, ironically in St. Louis, Tom Landry personally called Smith and asked him to come out of retirement to provide depth for the Cowboys.

Smith did so, playing entirely as a blocker in goal line situations. He didn't catch a single pass during the regular season, but in the NFL Divisional playoff game, he made a critical catch for a game-tying touchdown from Danny White after Roger Staubach had been injured. The Cowboys would rally to win the game, 27-20 with Smith contributing three catches.

He would make his only trip to the Super Bowl a few weeks later and fate would catch up to him there. Trailing 21-14 to the Steelers late in the third quarter, the Cowboys sent in a three-tight end set on a third down play from the 11-yard line. The pass play was designed to go first to Billy Joe Dupree in the left corner, then to the fullback in the right flat. Both took defenders with them and Steelers' linebacker Jack Lambert, blitzing up the middle, was laid out by Scott Laidlaw.

Smith was all alone in the middle of the end zone, uncovered.

Under pressure, Staubach had to release the ball a little early, before Smith made his turn. The pass was low, but catchable.

"It was a great call, a great play if Pittsburgh blitzed, and they loved to blitz deep in their territory, so it worked like a charm," Roger Staubach remembered years later. "But Jackie was surprised, and the ball hit him in the chest, and he couldn't catch it. We had to settle for a field goal, so it was 21-17 Pittsburgh instead of a tie."

The Cowboys would lose 35-31 and Smith would retire again, this time for good, even though the Cowboys wanted him back. He had a great career and deserved a better ending.

BILLY JOE DuPREE

At 6-4, 225, Billy Joe Dupree, the first of the Cowboys' outstanding modern day tight ends, looked like he was born for the position. He was both an outstanding blocker and an inviting target for Cowboys' quarterbacks. In fact, DuPree is tied with Drew Pearson for the most touchdowns passes (27) caught from quarterback Roger Staubach.

In a January, 2013 edition of *Athlon Sports* magazine, DuPree (24) was included on a list of the 25 best tight ends in NFL history, a list, by the way, that also included Ditka, Jay Novacek and Jason Witten.

DuPree is widely recognized as the greatest tight end in Michigan State history, even though the Spartans rarely passed the ball while he was there. DuPree's blocking in the Spartan's run-oriented offense was invaluable and he also led the team in receiving one season with 25 catches for 414 yards and three touchdowns.

Once he arrived in Dallas, Billy Joe was still called upon to do much of the grunt work on the offensive line but Tom Landry also began to see DuPree's value as a surprise receiver. The 20th overall pick in the first round of the 1973 draft, DuPree immediately stepped into the Cowboys' lineup as a rookie and led the team in receiving yards (392) and was second in touchdown receptions (5).

DuPree was actually more valuable to the Cowboys than his numbers – 267 receptions, 3,565 yards – would ever indicate. As evidence, he's 14th all-time in the Cowboys' record book as far as number of catches (and the fourth-ranked tight end behind Jason Witten, Jay Novacek and Doug Cosbie) but eighth overall with 41 TD grabs.

"Billy Joe had an outstanding career despite the fact he was a victim of the era's philosophy on tight ends, especially at the beginning of his career," former *Dallas Morning News* Cowboys beat man Carlton Stowers recalled. "Tight ends throughout the league were mostly after-thoughts in the passing game. Their role was to go 10-to-12 yards and across the middle to the sideline.

"The emergence of DuPree's eventual replacement, Doug Cosbie, signaled the first sight of a change in Landry's plan for the position. Whereas Drew Pearson and Tony Hill had been the deep threats, Landry hinted prior to the '84 season that deep routes would be added to the tight end duties."

Stowers said Landry's slow but sure recognition that the tight end could play a major role in the vertical passing game was the beginning of a significant change in team philosophy.

"My recollection is that the two tight-end scheme also really developed in Dallas with Cosbie's arrival, first teaming him with DuPree and then later with Jay Saldi," Stowers said. "Thus, more attention to the position as a viable offensive weapon."

DuPree was definitely recognized for his accomplishments by his peers and by the NFL, going to three consecutive Pro Bowls (1976-78). He led the Cowboys with four catches for 66 yards in their 27-10 pummeling of the Denver Broncos in Super Bowl XII.

DuPree was also known for his durability, never missing a game in his 11-year career. His 41 TDs stood as the franchise record for a tight end until Jason Witten broke it in 2012.

DOUG COSBIE

As Billy Joe DuPree's career began to wind down, what had been a timeshare at tight end between he and Doug Cosbie shifted dramatically towards the latter, at the same time that the Cowboys were fully committing to making the tight end an integral part of their downfield offense.

The position was trending toward even bigger, faster players than Billy Joe, if that was possible, and Cosbie, at 6-6, 236 pounds, fit the profile perfectly. Drafted in the third round out of Santa Clara University in 1979, the Cowboys thought so highly of Cosbie they ignored the highest-rated player remaining on their draft board to instead reach for DuPree's eventual replacement. The player they passed on sitting at the top of their board?

Some guy named Montana.

History tells us he would turn out not to be just another Joe.

Don't be too hard on the 'Boys. The Cowboys, at that time, still had Roger Staubach and Danny White, with Glenn Carano developing in the wings. Who needed an under-sized quarterback from Notre Dame with those guys already in place? Oops. Staubach, concerned about repeated concussions, would retire at the end of the '79 season, prompting Tex Schramm to call the decision not to take Montana the worst in his career as Cowboys' general manager.

It certainly wasn't Cosbie's fault that Montana would wind up as the catalyst to multiple Super Bowls for the San Francisco 49ers or that Joe would become a particular nemesis for the Cowboys. Cosbie was a good player in his own right, just not Joe Montana.

Cosbie would become the first Cowboys' tight end to ever exceed 50 catches in a season, hauling in 60, in fact, in '84, the year after DuPree's retirement. Cosbie's 300 career catches ranks him 11th on the Cowboys' all-time list and third among tight ends behind Jason Witten and Jay Novacek.

During the prime of his NFL career, a three-year span from 1983 to 1985, Cosbie caught 170 passes. Only wide receiver Tony Hill (181) caught more in those three seasons and Cosbie was All-Pro each of those years. He finished with 300 catches for 3,728 yards and 30 touchdowns, all records for a Cowboys' tight end at the time.

Cosbie's final three years with the Cowboys were hampered by injury, in particular a partially torn Achilles tendon that required surgery in '88.

In a post-career interview with the *Fort Worth Star-Telegram*'s Carlos Mendez, Cosbie noted that it was Bill Parcells, head coach of the New York Giants at the time, who not too subtly let him know it might be time to do something else for a living.

"My last year with the Cowboys, when we played at New York, Bill Parcells came up to me after the game," Cosbie recounted. "He asked me if I had any plans about what I was going to do after football.

"I said I didn't have any idea. I got to thinking, it must be time to retire if even the opposing coach is asking you if you're going to retire. He kind of inspired me to hang up my cleats."

Later, after Parcells came to Dallas to coach the Cowboys for Jerry Jones, Cosbie told Mendez he had an opportunity to get in his own little dig.

"I told him it was nice to have him on the good side now, with the good guys," Cosbie said. "Not with the dark side."

By then, Cosbie had moved on to a post-playing career as a high school and college coach and from there spent four years as marketing director for Shangri-La Entertainment, promoting movies in Hollywood.

Thanks to Cosbie, the Cowboys had finally discovered what a great weapon a pass-catching tight end could be, but Cosbie's success was only a precursor of things to come. It would get even better.

JAY NOVACEK

Until Jason Witten arrived, easily the best and most productive tight end in Dallas Cowboys' history was a man who honestly felt more comfortable in a Stetson than he did a football helmet with a star on its side. Jay Novacek was a cowboy – a real cowboy – long before he was a Dallas Cowboy.

Raised in tiny Gothenburg, Nebraska, Novacek was – and still is --as country as a beatup pickup truck. There's a rumor his cologne was called "Alfalfa." He's as at home today atop a world class cutting horse as he once was running free down the middle of the football field, waiting on a Troy Aikman bomb to settle into his strong and nimble fingers.

Novacek is one of those players who arrived in Dallas in 1990, just in time to save Aikman from near certain death, or at least dismemberment. The Cowboys' rookie quarterback had all but been annihilated trying to survive behind Dallas' atrocious offensive line in 1989, the year Jerry Jones and Jimmy Johnson arrived to try to rebuild the Cowboys from the ground up. The question was whether they would be able to accomplish that before Aikman was literally buried in that same ground.

Acquiring Novacek, who had spent five mostly under-appreciated and under-used years with the Phoenix Cardinals, was essentially like throwing a drowning Aikman a flotation device. Novacek was the safety-valve that Aikman desperately needed, a receiver who somehow always managed to find a nook, or a cranny, or a crease where a defender wasn't. As the Cowboys built toward three Super Bowl championships in the mid-'90s, he would become Aikman's favorite third-down receiver, and for good reason.

Bringing Novacek in as a Plan B free agent, a new rule that had just been implemented in the NFL, was a brilliant move by Johnson, who admitted in his book, *Turning the Thing Around*, that the Cowboys had nothing to lose by tossing out the equivalent of a seining net into the free agent pool in hopes of upgrading their woeful talent.

"Since there was no limit on these guys, we were seining through and taking a bunch, realizing that only a few would pan out," Johnson said. "Three who panned out were linebacker Vernon Smith and safety James Washington, who also were destined for the Super Bowl with us, and most importantly, tight end Jay Novacek, who would become a Pro Bowl starter."

Novacek was a rock in his six years with the Cowboys, dependable, steady, and surprisingly productive as a downfield receiver. He'd been a decathlete in high school and college and had surprising speed and quickness for someone 6-4, 235 pounds.

Novacek also brought his small-town values and country toughness with him. He'd already made a commitment to Wyoming University when his home state university, Nebraska, sashayed in late and offered him a scholarship, too, figuring it could easily snatch up another local kid on its name and prestige alone. Novacek allowed as how he'd already given his word to Wyoming and he wasn't going to back out on it.

After Novacek had been with the Cardinals for five years, new head coach Joe Bugel arrived expecting his tight ends to block and play as an H-back. Novacek wasn't seen as a good fit, so the Cardinals declined to match the Cowboys' free agent offer.

The Phoenix braintrust very likely had second thoughts about that decision when Novacek immediately snagged 59 passes for 641 yards and four touchdowns in '90. As far as Aikman was concerned, it was love at first sight. When the quarterback was in dire straits, Novacek was the target who seemed to always find a way to get open.

"I knew nothing of him when he joined us," Aikman told reporters before the Cowboys' Super Bowl victory over Buffalo in 1992. "But after two weeks of throwing the ball to him, I knew he was something special. Because of him, we have a lot of opportunities on third down. He's like a wide receiver playing tight end."

In his six years in Dallas, Novacek caught 339 passes for 3,576 yards and 22 touchdowns. Every pass he caught seemed to be critical. Except, that is, to Novacek, who once explained to reporters that he simply didn't buy into the concept of pressure. And he only did that then because he was compelled to speak to the media during Super Bowl week, and went along with the mandate against his better judgment.

"You can't see pressure," Novacek insisted to the assembled media. "It does not exist. Pressure is an excuse."

But what about your first play in the Super Bowl, someone asked. Won't you get butterflies? That's pressure.

"No," Novacek shrugged, "that's butterflies."

What if you're taking an EKG examination, someone else asserted. "Isn't that pressure?"

"No, that's stress," Novacek said.

OK, another reporter said, what if the game-winning pass in the Super Bowl is coming at you in the end zone; isn't that pressure?

"No," the laconic Novacek said with a grin, "that's a touchdown."

Check and mate.

Starting in 1991, Novacek went to five straight Pro Bowls, something only two other tight ends in NFL history had ever done at the time. He's in three different Halls of Fame: the National Collegiate Hall of Fame, the University of Wyoming Athletics Hall of Fame and the Texas Cowboy Hall of Fame.

It's not difficult to make a case that Novacek should also be included in the Cowboys' Ring of Honor, because he was such an integral part of three Super Bowl teams, but with Jason Witten's extraordinary career coming right on his heels, it seems unlikely that will happen now.

Knowing Novacek, I doubt he's losing any sleep over it anyway.

JASON WITTEN

There's an iconic photo from a family album that *Sports Illustrated* ran with a feature story in December, 2015. It's from 1986 and was taken in the bowels of RFK Stadium in Washington, D.C., right after the Redskins had crushed the Dallas Cowboys 41-14. It shows a distinguished Tom Landry, fedora in place, posing with three young boys, his hands on the shoulders of the two oldest.

Standing just to the left and a little forward of the group is a tow-headed 4-year-old, unsmiling, his eyes wide, as if to say, "Can we just get this over with so I can go play?" Strangely, considering what had just happened on the field outside, Landry is smiling. Maybe he had a premonition that the little blond boy, slightly removed from the coach and his brothers Ryan and Shawn, would someday grow up to be the most prolific pass catcher in Cowboys' history.

S.L. Price's insightful and brilliantly written story on Jason Witten – the little blond in the photo – explains how it came to be taken and of Witten's often painful but always amazing story of survival in a family stricken and split by domestic abuse. Witten has talked frankly about the demons that plagued his 6-foot-8-inch, 300-pound father Eddie and while that tale is riveting, it is Witten's own relentless dedication to become one of the greatest tight ends in NFL history that ultimately gives the story its true bottom line.

On a team with a proud legacy of Pro Bowl tight ends, Witten stands alone as, hands down, the best of them all.

Price himself describes Witten thusly: "Witten is low-altitude, rock-solid, the tight end you take home to mother."

But only if there's not a game to play, you understand, because absolutely nothing will keep Witten off the field if it's humanly possible for him to be there. His toughness, his durability, his unyielding pursuit of perfection, has become legendary and the standard Cowboys' coaches hold up to other players.

This is the player who, in 2007, caught a pass over the middle, had his helmet popped off by a would-be tackler, then rumbled, bare-headed, downfield for another 25 yards. It is the perfect microcosm of just who Jason Witten is.

In Week 5 of his rookie season, Witten made a catch and was

smashed hard in the side of the face, fracturing his jaw. He somehow ran off the field before stumbling to his knees, spitting blood onto the turf. Doctors told him he needed a four- to six-week recovery period and head coach Bill Parcells, the man who insisted the Cowboys draft Witten because he reminded the coach of rugged former New York Giants tight end Mark Bavaro, sneeringly presented him with a jar of baby food (sweet potatoes) the next day. Witten took it as a challenge and missed one game. He hasn't missed another game since.

In 2008, Witten played at various times with a separated shoulder, torn rib cartilage, broken ribs, high ankle sprains on both feet and still caught 81 passes for 952 yards. In the first game of the 2012 season, Witten suffered a lacerated spleen. Doctors recommended 6-8 weeks of rest. Witten played the next week. It would be his best season ever: 110 catches, his fourth 1,000-yard season.

After the 2012 season, he was presented with the Bart Starr Award and the Walter Payton NFL Man of the Year Award. He is a 10-time Pro Bowler and ranks second in all-time receptions (1,020) for a tight end behind only Tony Gonzalez. But all the awards and all the numbers are simply a reflection of who the man is and the one number he may be proudest of is his Cowboys' franchise record 203 consecutive games played.

"I want to be the best," Witten told the *Fort Worth Star-Telegram*'s Clarence Hill. "I want to be a part of a team that's about that. I love that process of doing it and doing it at a high level. When I can't, it's time for me to get out of it."

Witten is a coach's dream, a perfectionist with a work ethic that's off the charts. He won't quit until he gets it right. Tony Romo once said that if all the Cowboys' quarterbacks were hurt in a game, Witten is the one player who has a good enough grasp of the team's offensive concepts to step in and play the position.

"He wants to be a great player," head coach Jason Garret said. "He has been that and it's because of the approach that he takes. He has a great feel for the game. But what he is all about is what makes Jason Witten the player that he is – his dedication to be the best that he can be in every single opportunity that he has.

"The standard he has for himself about doing things the right way every minute of every day is as high as any player that I have ever seen. There's never a wasted moment."

Those cut scenes on TV before games of Witten firing up and motivating his teammates on the sidelines are part and parcel of what he has become to his Cowboys' teammates. They look to him to set the tone, because it's what he does naturally, and to lead them into battle.

Former Cowboys' backup quarterback Stephen McGee summed up the aura that Witten brings to his team this way in an ESPN.com article: "He's the one teammate or the rare athlete that when we're all sitting around the dinner table one day, I'll hope to tell my son about. He's that guy. There's no other teammate I played with that I hold with as high regard as I hold Jason Witten."

Brandon Weeden was even more effusive in the same article.

"He's the ultimate pro, in my opinion, the best total football player in the last 10-15 years," Weeden said. "He's just the complete package. He's basically a quarterback playing tight end. He can run block, he can catch the ball down the field, he can catch the short or intermediate routes.

"He's just so smart. He (had) complete control of what we (were) trying to do. I've been around a lot of good athletes and guys like that, but I've never seen a guy who does his business the way he does."

Witten is proud of what he has accomplished. He is proud of his legacy as a Dallas Cowboy. As a four-year-old, he may not have fully grasped the import of that photo with the legendary Tom Landry, but he gets it now.

Maybe that's why when his wife Michelle gave birth to a baby girl late in 2012 (they have four children now), Witten decided to name her Landry.

And maybe that's yet another reason why Tom's smile was so big in that 30-year-old photo.

The Linemen and Defense

UPON THIS ROCK ...

Someone once wrote in a pretty important book that a wise man builds his house upon the rock, not the fickle shifting sand. No one ever said that Tom Landry and Jimmy Johnson, the two men who built Super Bowl dynasties during their coaching tenures with the Dallas Cowboys, weren't intelligent men. Winning those five Super Bowls in the '70s and in the '90s would take flamboyant players like Roger Staubach, Drew Pearson, Tony Dorsett, Troy Aikman, Emmitt Smith and Michael Irvin. But Landry and Johnson also recognized that the foundation of those dynasties must be fashioned on the backs and arms, the sheer strength, of offensive linemen that the casual fan might never know, of defensive linemen and linebackers who didn't mind getting their uniforms smeared with mud and blood, of defensive backs who not only had speed but the willingness to sacrifice their bones and their bodies to make game-deciding plays.

It would be these too often under-appreciated men who would protect the Staubachs and the Aikmans, the Dorsetts and the Smiths, men who would come together as a unit to form an impenetrable wall on offense and defenses so feared, so respected, they would earn the nickname "Doomsday" and "Doomsday II." No Cowboys' history would be complete without paying homage to the men upon whose backs the Dallas Cowboys were built.

Though there have been many outstanding offensive and defensive linemen, linebackers and defensive backs in Cowboys' history, it is no coincidence that the nine men who played those positions and have since been enshrined in the Ring of Honor essentially come from Landry's Super Bowl teams of the '70s or Johnson's championship teams of the early-to-mid '90s. It is also true that in a sense, men like Bob Lilly and Rayfield Wright, the cornerstone pieces of the defensive and offensive lines of those '70s teams, represent more than just themselves in the Ring of Honor. Offensive and defensive lines are only as good as their weakest link. They operate, not as individuals, but as a complete unit. When that happens, they become more than the sum of their parts. Each man does his individual job, but it is teamwork that makes it successful.

No one was more about team than "Mr. Cowboy," Bob Lilly. Lilly, from little Throckmorton, Texas, was the Cowboys' very first draft pick out of TCU in 1961, taken first overall in the country. Tex Schramm and Gil Brandt could not have done any better.

Lilly would suffer through the Cowboys' growing pains of the '60s while immediately supplying them with credibility, work ethic and the talent that would make him the premier defensive lineman in the NFL. Besides great strength at 6 feet, 5 inches and 260 pounds, Lilly was exceptionally quick, which allowed him to shed blockers and shoot through gaps to be on a quarterback almost before he could turn around.

By the time the Cowboys reached their first Super Bowl in 1970, Lilly was recognized throughout the league as the leader of the Cowboys' vaunted "Doomsday" defense and opposing offensive coordinators knew that they would have to somehow account for the red-haired terror in the middle of the Dallas line. Lilly regularly beat double and sometimes triple-teams on play, after play, after play.

Landry, who would introduce Lilly for his induction into the Pro Football Hall of Fame in Canton, on more than one occasion said, "There won't be another Lilly in my lifetime. We're observing a man who will become a legend. Nobody is better than Lilly."

The rest of the NFL and the sporting world thought just about as highly of Lilly as Landry did. Eight times he was a first-team All NFL selection. *The Sporting News* named him to its All Century NFL team and "the greatest defensive tackle in NFL history." He was a member of the NFL's All-Decade Team of both the '60s and '70s. In 1999, *The Sporting News* ranked Lilly 10th on its list of the 100 best NFL players of all time. Although the Cowboys don't make a practice of retiring jerseys, no one else has ever worn No. 74, a silent nod to Lilly's brilliance.

Despite all the accolades, Lilly understood better than anyone that he was part of a unit that succeeded because of each individual part that made up the whole. "All of us are here today for one reason," he said during his induction speech at the Hall of Fame in 1980. "We played on teams that were winners. To sum it up, I deserve just a small part of this award today. It took teamwork."

Lilly was paying homage to the men who were all equal parts of the original "Doomsday." He was recognizing the efforts and talents of players like Larry Cole, Jethro Pugh, and George Andrie. He was tipping his hat to that outstanding linebacker corps of Lee Roy Jordan, Chuck Howley, Dave Edwards and, later, D.D. Lewis, and to the resilience and toughness of Mel Renfro, Cornell Green, Cliff Harris and Charley Waters and others in the secondary.

Rayfield Wright would do much the same thing for the offensive line when he was inducted at Canton in 2006. He wanted everyone to know that he represented more than himself there, that figuratively standing alongside him on that stage were men like Dave Manders, John Niland, Blaine Nye, John Fitzgerald, Ralph Neely and Tony Liscio.

Wright was one of those Gil Brandt specials, a 6 foot, 7 inch, 255-pound tight end out of tiny Fort Valley State (Georgia). Originally a basketball player – Wright was heading to the NBA before Brandt called – he was practically shanghaied by Fort Valley State football coach Stan Lomax, who recognized talent when he saw it. It was Lomax who introduced Wright at the Hall of Fame induction.

"Someone once said I would rather see a sermon than hear one any day," Lomax said. "For more than 12 years, Rayfield Wright, with displays of commitment and determination, delivered his message clearly and emphatically each Sunday afternoon. Primarily, he had two admonitions. One, thou shalt not touch Roger. The second was, thou must not impede the forward progress of Calvin (Hill) or Tony (Dorsett)."

Wright started his Cowboys' career as a tight end and once asked Don Meredith, "Don, you remember throwing me a touchdown pass against the Eagles?" Wright said Meredith laughed and replied, "Rayfield, I wasn't throwing the ball to you. You was just so tall, you got in the way."

Two years into his career, Landry came to Wright to tell him he wanted to move him to tackle. Wright said, "but coach, I've never played there before". Landry explained that the Cowboys were bringing in a quarterback by the name of Roger Staubach who had an aversion to staying put in the pocket. "He's going to need some extra protection," Landry said.

That's how one of the NFL's greatest offensive tackles was born. Wright took his coach's words to heart.

"Offensive linemen are taught to protect the quarterback, the same way that the Secret Service protects our nation's president," Wright said at his induction. "In this case, Roger Staubach was our president. The director of our Secret Service was our offensive line coach, Jim Myers. He built an offensive line that was unmatched. Today, I cannot accept this honor without bringing Coach Myers and his line into the Hall with me."

The Cowboys were fortunate that just as Lilly reached the end of his career in 1973, they had drafted a young defensive end out of East Texas State that same season. Harvey Martin, like Lilly, would team up with future Hall of Famer Randy White to terrorize NFL quarterbacks for more than a decade. Martin, who died of pancreatic cancer at the young age of 51 in 2001, was a pass-rushing specialist. He would lead the Cowboys in sacks in seven of his nine seasons as a starter, including an amazing 23 sacks in a 14-game season in 1977. The NFL didn't begin recognizing sacks as an official stat until 1982, so the official all-time leader is Michael Strahan with 22.5 sacks in 16 games in 2001. Martin, though, remains the unofficial record holder.

Ironically, Cowboys coaches would initially wonder if Martin would be aggressive enough to be an effective defensive end and urged him to develop more of a killer attitude while on the field. They apparently got the message through, because Martin would soon earn the nickname, "Too Mean." Martin would cap that wonderful 1977 season with a Super Bowl victory over Denver in which he was co-MVP with Randy White.

No one ever had to worry about White's aggressiveness. The challenge for the Cowboys' coaches was trying to figure out whether his incredible strength was better suited at linebacker or on the defensive line. Selected second overall out of the University of Maryland in the 1975 draft, White was initially seen as the perfect replacement for the soon-to-be retiring middle linebacker Lee Roy Jordan. Instead, the Cowboys quickly realized that Bob Breunig, picked in the third round of the same draft, had better instincts at linebacker. In his third year, White settled into the right defensive tackle slot previously occupied so ably by the great Lilly. With Martin lining up just to his right, opposing offensive lines had to pick their poison.

The 1977 season was White's breakout year. He made All-Pro for the first time, went to the Pro Bowl and shared co-MVP honors in the Super Bowl with his linemate, Martin. The following season White, nicknamed "The Manster" (half man, half monster), was named the NFL's defensive player of the year. For nine straight seasons White was named All-Pro and to the Pro Bowl.

White, who reportedly once bench-pressed 450 pounds 10 times in a row, was also the Cowboys' unofficial in-house enforcer when things got chippy. It was White who stepped in to separate Roger Staubach and Clint Longley at Thousand Oaks in 1976 when the two tangled after Longley sucker-punched Staubach. And when talented but mouthy linebacker Thomas "Hollywood" Henderson, playing for Miami, came into the Cowboys' locker room and slapped White, Randy picked him up and deposited him into an empty locker.

"Hollywood took the first shot and Randy retaliated twice," a witness told the *Dallas Morning News*' Dan Barreiro in 1985. "Hollywood got up the first time, like a fool. Randy ended up picking him up with one hand and pinning him."

Actually, both White and Henderson said White never threw a punch, for which, Henderson said later, he was eternally grateful.

"It pissed me off. I grabbed him by the hair and smashed his face down into the floor," White said in Henderson's book *In Control*, co-written with Frank Luksa. "I could have drilled him but I didn't. I let him up. He came back at me and I grabbed him and stuffed him in a locker. I'd been listening to all this crap about (how) he wanted to kick my ass. I knew in the back of my mind that there hasn't been a day gone by that Thomas Henderson was going to do anything to me."

Said Henderson in his book, which was written after he'd kicked his addiction to drugs and alcohol: "I've always respected Randy White. Like myself, I never saw him back down...I made a mistake when I slapped him upside his head in 1981. He manhandled me but he didn't hit me...Now that I think back, I never had a chance in that fight. Here you have one of the strongest men in the history of the NFL and me on crack...If I was in an alley fight and could have just one person to choose to be at my back, it would be Randy White."

Lee Roy Jordan, Chuck Howley and Dave Edwards, the trio who played directly behind Lilly and Co. in Tom Landry's Flex Defense, were as solid a linebacking crew as there was in the NFL in the '70s. Jordan was an under-sized middle linebacker with hit like a sledgehammer and was just as tough. Howley had field-awareness rarely seen in players and remains the only player to win Super Bowl MVP honors for a losing team after intercepting two passes and recovering a fumble in Dallas' 16-13 loss to Baltimore in Super Bowl V. Edwards was Mr. Dependable, seemingly always in the right place at the right time.

Mel Renfro was a highly regarded running back out of Oregon when the Cowboys drafted him but Landry looked at his instincts and speed and saw a great defensive back. He was right. Renfro went to the Pro Bowl in each of his first 10 seasons in the NFL. He still holds the team record with 52 interceptions, spending his first six years at free safety before moving to cornerback. Landry called him, "the best in the league at free safety" during his stellar 1969 season. He also holds the Cowboys' all-time record for kickoff returns with an average of 26.4 yards.

Cliff Harris, an undrafted free agent out of tiny Ouachita Baptist in Arkansas, followed in Renfro's footsteps after the Cowboys signed him in 1970. Harris made six Pro Bowls and was named to the NFL's All-Decade team of the '70s. He teamed with longtime friend Charley Waters to give the Cowboys one of the best safety combos in the league.

Jimmy Johnson's Super Bowl teams of the early-to-mid '90s were also built on the rocks of an offensive line that featured guards Kevin Gogan, John Gesek and Nate Newton, along with tackles Mark Tuinei and Erik Williams and center Mark Stepnoski. Larry Allen, a future Ring of Honor honoree, would come along after that group had already won two Super Bowls and would become the best of all of them.

"It was an interesting group," Aikman recalled. "When I came in in '89, Tuinei was there and so was Newton and they weren't a heralded group as an offensive line. This (current Cowboys') team they have now has essentially four first-rounders. That wasn't our line. In the early years there were those who thought we would never get where we wanted to go with those guys. But they proved everybody wrong and they were proud of that and it will be talked about as one of the great offensive lines in the game."

Aikman, as a quarterback, appreciated what his offensive linemen did for him personally and always seemed to have an offensive lineman's mindset himself. He knew how difficult their job was and the challenges they faced.

"Mark was as athletic a guy as I'd ever been around in the offensive line," Aikman said. "There weren't many players who could run like he could or were as strong. As a quarterback, I never had to worry about my blind side.

"Jimmy and offensive line coach Tony Wise saw something in Step, who'd been a guard, and turned him into a center and it was amazing how great he was. Then we had big Nate at right guard and he got better and better. Erik Williams was a third-round pick and a great talent and he just imposed his will on people and intimidated people more than anything else.

"The other guard position kind of rotated out with Gogan and Gesek and then Larry Allen arrived. Where Larry gained my respect was that NFC championship game we lost in '94 at San Francisco and he was struggling. But he never complained and never thought about coming out of the game. He just fought his ass off. He never got embarrassed again after that."

On the other side of the ball, the Cowboys will be eternally grateful that Charles Haley had this habit of hacking people off, even those on his own team. After he had confrontations with head coach George Seifert and quarterback Steve Young in 1991 and allegedly urinated on a teammate's car in the players' parking lot, the 49ers decided they'd had enough of Haley's antics, despite his elite production on the field. The Cowboys, who desperately needed a high-octane pass rusher, gave the 49ers a second round pick in 1993 and a third-rounder in '94 for the right to put up with Haley's often boorish behavior. If one player can make a very good team a Super Bowl team, Haley was it for the Cowboys. Tony Tolbert manned the other defensive end spot with Tony Casillas and Russell Maryland at tackles. Robert Jones and Ken Norton Jr. gave the Cowboys excellent play at linebacker while Larry Brown, Thomas Everett, Ike Holt and James Washington combined to form an aggressive and effective secondary. Leon Lett, Darren Woodson, Kevin Smith and Brock Marion would all be key additions as the Cowboys won three Super Bowls from 1992-1995.

There are those who believe that the Cowboys' current offensive line of left tackle Tyron Smith, left guard La'el Collins, center Travis Frederick, right guard Zack Martin and right tackle Doug Free may be the team's best ever. Certainly the pedigree is there. Smith, Frederick and Martin are all first-round picks and Collins probably would have been if not for some off-field issues that kept him from being drafted. Even after the Cowboys finished 4-12 last season, the national website Pro Football Focus named the team's offensive line the best in the league for the second straight year.

"It's one of the best units that I have ever been around in football in terms of how close they are to each other and how hard they work," head coach Jason Garrett told Todd Archer of ESPN.com. "From the time they spend together in the weight room, to doing their drill work on the field, time they spend after practice together working on their fundamentals, time they spend together, it's a really close-knit group that pride themselves on being the hardest-working unit on the team, the hardest-working unit in the league.

"So they are very much grounded in trying to get better each and every day. They have a lot of great character guys, great personal character guys, great football character guys. So when you bring younger players in, they kind of understand what the culture is at that position group right away. So we're fortunate to have them. They can be the heartbeat of our football team."

The Cowboys' plan for the foreseeable future is simple, old school football, with rookie Ezekiel Elliot running behind what could be one of the greatest lines in NFL history. Whether it actually lives up to the hype will very likely depend on whether the Cowboys can get back to another Super Bowl … or two … or three.

Championship Games

THE ICE BOWL
Green Bay 21, Dallas 17
December 31, 1967 • Green Bay, Wisconsin

As the late, great Frank Luksa liked to tell the story, he was flat on his back in a ditch, just a short walk from Lambeau Field, when he began to understand that this day might be unlike any other in the history of the National Football League.

Not that Frank, who was in Green Bay, Wisconsin, on New Year's Eve, 1967, at the behest of the *Fort Worth Star-Telegram*, was especially concerned about the historical implications of that day's NFL championship showdown between the Dallas Cowboys and the Green Bay Packers at that particular moment. He was much more fretful, he would ruminate over a second (or maybe third) tumbler of amber liquid in years to come, about simply getting out of the ditch before he froze in place and his body was completely covered over by a passing snowplow.

Luksa, who went on to essay his clever and witty prose for the *Dallas Times Herald* and *Dallas Morning News* in later years, had thought he might save a few minutes by getting off the media bus, which was log-jammed in pre-game traffic, and walking the last few blocks to Lambeau's press box. He'd taken about three steps when his feet went out from under him on the ice-slick sidewalk and he went down flat on his back, portable typewriter and all, and slid into the ditch alongside.

The lanky sports writer, who grew up in Georgetown, Texas, climbed warily to his feet, made a futile attempt to brush the ice and snow off his clothes, and hurried to Lambeau's press gate, barely pausing to wonder why no one was there to check his credential, or to even say "boo," for that matter. It wasn't until he'd found his seat, reached for the paper cup full of coffee that he'd just poured and found it already slushy with ice, that Luksa began to realize that something really was dreadfully amiss.

"And I remember that I kept thinking, I'm inside, thank God," Luksa told Mike Shropshire for his 1997 book *The Ice Bowl*. "And I wondered how those poor devils out in the stadium seats and down on the field were ever going to survive."

Luksa, the rest of the Texas and national media assembled in iconic Lambeau Field that New Year's Eve afternoon, and more than 50,000 shivering fans – one elderly fan actually died of exposure – were about to witness arguably the most memorable game in NFL history. It was, depending on the temperature gauge being checked, somewhere in the neighborhood of 15-degrees below zero with a piercing arctic wind that made it feel like 70-below down on the field and in the stands.

Hell had indeed frozen over. The Ice Bowl was about to cement its place – in a block of frozen ice, mind you – in the psyche of American sports culture forevermore.

Just one year and one day earlier, Dec. 30, 1966, the Cowboys had the football at the Green Bay two-yard line late in the fourth quarter, trailing by seven. The Cowboys needed a touchdown against the fading Packers to force overtime in front of a raucous Cotton Bowl crowd.

"The Cowboys had all the momentum in the world there at the end and with all that incredible crowd noise, if the game had gone into overtime, well…" Paul Hornung had told Shropshire, writing for the *Fort Worth Press*, after the game.

But the Cowboys didn't score. Instead, caught in the grasp of Green Bay linebacker Dave Robinson, quarterback Don Meredith sidearmed a desperation pass into the end zone, where a grateful Tom Brown intercepted. The pick clinched a 34-27 victory for the Packers and sent them into the first-ever NFL-AFL championship game against the Kansas City Chiefs.

The Cowboys had been a young – only one player over 30 – and inexperienced team before that 1966 game but a year later, they headed to Green Bay for another championship showdown, confident that this time they were better than the aging Pack. Vegas wasn't so sure, having installed the Packers as 6 ½ point favorites at home.

Nor was the weather a major concern as the Cowboys worked out at Lambeau Field in balmy 18-degree windless temperatures the day before the game. Green Bay coach Vince Lombardi had even taken Cowboys general manager Tex Schramm and visiting reporters deep under the stadium to proudly show off his $80,000 turf heating system, that would ostensibly keep the field pliable and playable in freezing temperatures.

What Lombardi, Schramm and players from both teams didn't know was that an arctic front was barreling down from Canada so fast it had fooled the weather forecasters, who didn't think it would arrive in full strength until Monday. NFL officials, in fact, when told late Saturday that game time temperatures might be as low as 5 degrees, thought seriously about postponing the game for 24 hours until they were assured it would likely be even worse on Monday.

Just after midnight, the arctic blast began rolling into Green Bay. It got worse far faster than anyone could have dreamed.

Cowboys' players, in fact, were sure they must still be dreaming when wakeup calls at their Appleton, Wisconsin, hotel, 35 miles outside of Green Bay, cheerily told them, "It's 7 o'clock and 14 degrees.... below zero."

Bob Lilly's face turned white when roommate George Andrie said, "Watch this...." And threw a glass of water against the inside of the window. It froze instantly on contact.

The Cowboys were so unprepared for this kind of weather, Schramm spent the morning on the phone, trying to find a sporting goods store or hardware store that would open on a Sunday morning and sell as many pairs of gloves as they could find.

Back at Lambeau, Lombardi's pride and joy, the heating system under the field, was already beginning to fail. It wasn't equipped to deal with cold like that. The field was beginning to freeze, but not like an iced over pond, Packers' fullback Chuck Mercein told Shropshire. It was more like "a stucco wall laid horizontal," Mercein said, "The actual surface of the ground was rough and pointy, with thousands of little clods of dirt and clumps of mud already freezing solid to the turf. And the field was already getting hard. It was dreadful."

Still, this was part of the Packers' aura. This was their turf, their territory. Their weather. Packers weather. They would not show that it affected them at all. It was their psychological advantage and they would put it to good use.

On the opposite side of the field, the Cowboys were simply trying to find ways to keep warm, cutting holes in stockings to try and make facemasks. Wide receiver Bob Hayes spent almost the entire game with his hands stuck down in the front of his pants and Packers' defenders quickly realized that when he approached the line of scrimmage that way, he wasn't going to be involved in the play. For many of the Cowboys' players, it wasn't football that was on their minds; it was sheer survival.

Hayes, in fact, caught a sideline pass for 10 yards on the Cowboys' first play from scrimmage and was essentially taken out of the game – not by Tom Landry, not by the Packers' defense, but by the weather – after that, contributing only six more yards the rest of the way. The man who had meant so much to the Cowboys' offense all season, who had totaled 281 yards in receptions and returns in the playoff victory over Cleveland a week earlier, was basically a non-factor in the most important game in Cowboys' history to that point. The cold and frozen field conditions had effectively erased the one sure advantage the Cowboys had: their overall team speed.

The deteriorating conditions, in fact, made any kind of downfield passing attack difficult, at best, and impossible at worst, but somehow Packers' quarterback Bart Starr connected with Boyd Dowler on two touchdown passes in the first half. The Cowboys had countered when George Andrie scooped up a Starr fumble after a Willie Townes sack and rumbled seven yards into the end zone and with a Danny Villanueva field goal. The Cowboys only trailed 14-10 and it was a worried Lombardi that led the Packers into the locker room at halftime.

After two quarters, the middle of the field had seen enough action and had suffered the gouging cleats of 275-pound behemoths that there was at least some small traction available. Not so along the sidelines, which were as slick as a fresh Zambonied ice rink.

In the stands, the fans hunkered down in sleeping bags, wrapped their legs in plastic trash bags and guzzled whiskey straight from flasks they kept tucked deep inside their parkas, for fear they too would freeze. Their collective breath rose up into the air above Lambeau like the steaming, vaporous exhalation of some huge, ravenous animal.

This was history in the making. Sane people would have scurried for home and a soft recliner and blanket in front of the fireplace. Not these fans. They would stay through the bitter cold, no matter the cost. This was a day they knew they would someday tell their grandchildren about.

Alicia Landry and Marty Schramm always watched road games from the stands while their husbands were at work. They were prepared for cold weather, but Texas cold, not this ridiculous deep freeze, this arctic blast straight from the North Pole. They would say later that only the generosity of some of the Packers' fans, who gave them plastic bags to wrap around their legs, kept them from freezing to death right there in the Lambeau stands.

For the first time in the game, the Cowboys strung first downs back-to-back early in the third quarter, the second on a 14-yard pass from Meredith to Frank Clarke, who had replaced the listless Hayes. The Cowboys' drive, however, died at the Packers' 13 when linebacker Lee Roy Caffey jarred the football loose from Meredith and Herb Adderley recovered.

The Packers still led 17-14 at the beginning of the fourth quarter and by then, the field conditions weren't conducive to the one advantage that the Cowboys had over the Packers coming into the game: their speed. Instead, the treacherous footing turned it into a game of short passes from Bart Starr to his backs floating out of the backfield, Mercein and Donny Anderson, the Texas Tech All-American from Stinnett in the Texas Panhandle. Time and again Anderson and Mercein gouged the Cowboys by drifting into the flat, taking a pass and then making the Cowboys' skidding linebackers miss on the icy field.

"I kept my hands warm by sticking them in (guard) Gale Gillingham's armpit," Anderson said later. "After a while I quit noticing the weather."

Or, apparently, the odor. Not that anyone was sweating on the field that day.

The Cowboys countered Anderson and Mercein with the gliding

Dan Reeves, who seemed to have an innate ability to skim over the ice-coated turf. His success running against the Packers' defense set up Reeves' halfback option pass to Lance Rentzel for a 50-yard touchdown and the Cowboys' first lead of the day at 17-14 on the first play of the fourth quarter.

The game would come down to Green Bay's final possession, starting 68 yards away with 4:45 left on the clock.

"It all came down to this drive," Starr told Shropshire. "We all realized what had to be done."

The Packers met the moment as if they'd been there before. No panic. No desperation. No fear. Just single-minded resolve. Get the ball down the field. Score. Win the game. Period.

The big men on both sides were wearing down. Beyond that, they were having more difficulty on the deteriorating field. They could barely stand, much less move laterally. And the offensive backs had the advantage, Anderson said, because they knew what they were going to do, giving them a split-second before the defenders could react and gain traction.

Anderson caught a six-yard swing pass. Mercein rambled seven yards for a first down at the 38. Starr hit Dowler across the middle for 13 yards and a first down at the Dallas 42. But then the Cowboys sniffed out the famed Packer sweep and Townes stuffed Anderson for a nine-yard loss.

Anderson noticed that linebacker Chuck Howley was playing off him a bit to help out in pass defense and told Starr he was open. He caught short passes for 12 and nine yards to pull the Packers out of a second-and-19 hole. Thirty yards to go.

Mercein made a nice snare on another Starr swing pass, ran through attempted tackles by Howley and Cornell Green for a huge 19-yard gain, getting out of bounds to stop the clock at the Dallas 11. The Packers ate up eight of those 11 yards by faking their patented Packer Sweep and sending Mercein through the hole vacated by Bob Lilly, who pulled with Packer guard Gillingham.

Lombardi would label it a "brilliant" call by Starr, taking advantage of a player who had been brutalizing the Packers inside all day. Anderson plunged into the line for two yards for a first down at the one as the clock slipped under a minute and kept ticking.

On first down, Anderson bucked into the line again, was buried under a pile of players and looked down to see the goal line under his nose. He thought he'd scored but the officials placed the ball just outside the end zone. Second down. Again the handoff went to Anderson, who stutter-stepped and slipped on the ice. Third down and a foot to go, clock at 19 seconds, 18, 17, 16 …

At 13 seconds, Starr called Green Bay's last timeout and trotted over to confer with Lombardi in front of the Packer bench. The Packers could go ahead and try a game-tying field goal. They could attempt a pass and if it was incomplete, then kick the field goal. Or they could go for it on third down.

Starr told Lombardi he thought he could score on a quarterback sneak behind center Ken Bowman and guard Jerry Kramer. Starr told Shropshire that Lombardi said simply, "Do it and let's get the hell out of here."

The play was Brown right, 31-wedge. Snap count was one. That play, however, was not the designation for a quarterback sneak. It calls for a dive play by the fullback between the center and right guard. The blocking assignment, however, is the same.

At the line of scrimmage, the Cowboys' defensive linemen pawed at the ground with their feet, trying to dig out a hole for traction. Because it was just third down, the Cowboys defense and even the announcers in the TV booth expected a rollout pass.

Mercein was thrilled, thinking he was going to get the chance to score the game-winning touchdown. He was shocked when he looked up to take the handoff and Starr was digging in and falling across the goal line behind Kramer's block on Jethro Pugh.

Anderson said afterward he and his Packers' teammates sat in front of their lockers, thawing out, and realizing that they very likely had just played in the greatest football game of all time.

It was, in fact, an incredible game-winning drive in deplorable, impossible conditions. With hands frozen and as senseless as hunks of concrete, there had not been a fumble. With feet numb and as dead as bricks, there had not been a slip down or a critical stumble. Even facing a second-and-19 had not deterred the Packers.

Nor could Pugh be faulted for Starr's fateful sneak that mercifully ended the anguish of that long afternoon. He was simply pushed backward across the ice and was helpless to do anything about it.

The Packers were heading to the warm sunshine of Miami and the first Super Bowl. The Cowboys trudged silently to the warmth of a long plane ride home. They would futilely try to dull the sting of frost-bitten fingers and toes and an even worse ache blossoming in their hearts with an unceasing flow of whiskey and beer as their plane flew into the darkness and headed south to Texas.

The two franchises were also figuratively headed in different directions. The Green Bay Packers were soon to embark on a quarter century stumble through an NFL wasteland. The Cowboys were nearing a turning point that would send them to five Super Bowls in the '70s, a journey that would validate them as America's Team.

Tex Schramm would say that the legend of America's Team started that day in Green Bay, because of the admiration the Cowboys earned from the nation's sporting public, even in defeat. Maybe he's right. He usually was.

What we know for sure is that what happened that afternoon in the polar vortex of Lambeau Field will live in the annals of the National Football League forever.

It truly was the greatest game ever played.

SUPER BOWL V
Baltimore 16, Dallas 13
January 18, 1971 • Miami

Before there was "America's Team," there was "Next Year's Champions." Strangely, they were basically one and the same team, just at different stages of their NFL lives. Before the Dallas Cowboys could become one, they had to first endure being the other.

After five straight playoff appearances, starting in 1966, and three trips to the championship game, the Cowboys finally made it to the newly-christened Super Bowl after winning the NFC title in 1970, only to be robbed by a combination of witchcraft, voodoo and pure dumb luck on the part of the Baltimore Colts.

The 16-13 loss on Jim O'Brien's 32-yard field goal with five seconds to play was a bitter pill for the Cowboys, who essentially dominated the game but saw every break go the other way. They also knew it was frustrating validation for the pundits who had already begun labeling them, "Next Year's Champions."

It would be another year before they could shake that not so flattering nickname and start replacing it with one that would instead infuriate every other team in the league.

Super Bowl V itself was far from aesthetically pleasing, no matter who the fans were rooting for, as the Cowboys and Colts combined for 11 turnovers. That stat alone prompted reporters and columnists to nickname it – take your pick – "The Blunder Bowl," or "The Blooper Bowl."

Seven of those turnovers came courtesy of the winning team, more evidence that the Colts couldn't lose for trying on this particular Sunday afternoon. Even the eventual hero O'Brien wasn't immune to his team's sloppy antics, previously missing a field goal and having an extra point kick blocked before nailing the game-winner as time expired.

Rather than take advantage of Baltimore's generosity, the Cowboys attempted to match the Colts' ineptitude with four turnovers of their own, including a pair of critical fourth-quarter interceptions from quarterback Craig Morton. Just for grins and to even things up even further, the Cowboys pitched in 10 penalties for a whopping 133 yards, still a Super Bowl record more than four decades later.

"And to think, television was worried that situation comedy was dead," longtime scribe Tex Maule wrote in *Sports Illustrated*. "The teams bumbled through a laugher of a Super Bowl, but in the end the joke was on the Cowboys who made the biggest mistake of all – losing."

Even President Richard Nixon chimed in with his critique the day after the game.

"I sure hope I don't make that many mistakes," quipped Nixon, who was about 3 ½ years away from making perhaps the biggest mistake any U.S. President had made since Lincoln decided to go to the theater instead of the bowling alley.

Cowboys' coach Tom Landry bristled at the criticism, blaming the turnovers more on the ferocious hitting in the game rather than the two teams playing fast and loose with the football.

"I haven't been around many games where the players hit harder," Landry told reporters afterward. "Sometimes people watch a game and see turnovers and talk about how sloppy the play was. The mistakes in that game weren't invented, at least not by the people who made them. Most were forced."

There was some truth to Landry's postgame defense. The Cowboys came into the game with the league's fourth-ranked defense. "Doomsday" boasted Bob Lilly and George Andrie up front, Lee Roy Jordan and Chuck Howley at linebackers and Mel Renfro and Herb Adderley in the secondary. Baltimore had its own headhunters, among them fierce defensive tackle Bubba Smith and physical linebackers Mike Curtis and Ted "The Mad Stork" Hendricks.

The game's MVP was Howley, who had two interceptions. Howley remains the only player from the losing team to ever win a Super Bowl MVP trophy.

A pair of Mike Clark field goals gave the Cowboys the early 6-0 lead but even then there was a feeling that they would pay for not converting those opportunities into touchdowns. Fate, luck or just bad karma asserted itself in the second quarter when Johnny Unitas, destined to have his day abbreviated by a torn rib cartilage after a hit by Andrie, called a pass for Eddie Hinton over the middle.

Unitas' bullet caromed off Hinton's hands, sailed high over the out-stretched arms of Renfro and came down cradled against the chest of tight end John Mackey, who loped 75 yards for the touchdown. No one has ever explained what a tight end was doing that far downfield in the first place.

Under NFL rules at that time, two offensive players couldn't touch a pass in succession, so it was an incompletion, right? Not according to the officials, who ruled that Renfro had touched the ball after Hinton and before it got to Mackey. Did he?

Not even Renfro knows for sure.

"I had no sensation of touching the ball," Renfro told Peter Golenbock for his 1997 book, *Cowboys Have Always Been My Heroes*. "That was the hand I have no feeling in three fingers. If it hit me, it had to have gone off the finger next to the thumb (and) I have no feeling in that finger."

Even then, safety Charley Waters might have been able to tackle Mackey if he wasn't hopping up and down, complaining to the official about the lack of a flag on the tipped pass from Hinton to Mackey.

It was 6-6 after the Cowboys blocked O'Brien's PAT.

The Cowboys counter-punched in the same quarter when Unitas had to scramble on third-and-10 and Jordan forced a fumble that Jethro Pugh recovered at the Colts' 28. It took just three plays for the Cowboys to cover the distance. Duane Thomas picked up four on a burst over the right side, Dan Reeves went for 17 on a pass from Morton and then Thomas took a swing pass seven yards for the touchdown.

The Cowboys were up 13-6 at halftime and immediately threatened to blow the game open when Baltimore's Jim Duncan fumbled the second half kickoff. Dallas recovered at the Colts' 31. It took just five plays for Dallas to reach the two.

Morton stuffed the ball into Thomas' belly and Dallas guard John Niland would swear later he heard an official say, "He's over, he's over!" At the same time, Curtis reached in and yanked the ball loose. Cowboys' center Dave Manders fell on it just inches outside the goalline.

Colts' tackle Billy Ray Smith began jumping up and down, screaming, "Our ball! Our ball!" and pointing toward the opposite goal. Referee Jack Fette looked at Smith – not Manders – and signaled that the Colts had recovered, even as Manders was handing the ball to the ref.

"I know (Manders) recovered it," Niland told Golenbock. "I was right there, on the ground next to him. That was the turning point of the game. If we had made that touchdown we would have been up 20-6 and it would have been almost impossible for Baltimore to come back."

Niland is probably right. Remember, the still dangerous Unitas had been knocked out of the game and replaced by veteran backup Earl Morrall.

Where was instant replay when the Cowboys needed it? Oh yeah, Jerry Jones had yet to arrive to overhaul the NFL's front office rules and procedures.

The Cowboys saved their worst mistakes for last in this game. Midway through the fourth quarter Morton's pass intended for Walt Garrison bounced off his hands, was intercepted by Baltimore's Rick Volk and returned 30 yards to the Dallas 3.

The Colts said thank you and punched in the game-tying touchdown.

Two possessions later, the sore-armed Morton (why wasn't Roger Staubach playing?) again threw a tipped pass, this one intended for Reeves, and Curtis picked it off, returning it to the Dallas 28 with 59 seconds to play. Two running plays later, O'Brien trotted on to kick the first game-winning field goal in Super Bowl history.

As the final second ticked off, a frustrated Lilly heaved his helmet 40 yards down the field, another Super Bowl record that has never been broken.

To this day the Cowboys who were there can't figure out how they lost that game.

Almost a decade later, Golenbock wrote, Niland was having dinner in a Dallas restaurant when he spotted Billy Ray Smith at a table across the room.

"I yelled over to him, 'Hey, Billy Ray, you still wearing my ring?' He knew exactly what I was talking about," Niland said. "He raised his hand and showed me his Super Bowl ring."

The Cowboys would have to wait another long year to have one of their own to wave around.

SUPER BOWL VI
Dallas 24, Miami 3
January 16, 1972 • New Orleans

Maybe it was because the Cowboys had come so close for so many years, so much so that they'd been branded with the not-so-flattering nickname "Next Year's Champions," that when they finally reached the mountaintop in Super Bowl VI in New Orleans they still didn't really get the credit they deserved. Instead of saying "Wow!" America's sporting public, led by the national media, seemed to say instead, "Hey, it's about time you got here."

In a sense the wags were right. The Cowboys had come so close for the six previous years – even losing Super Bowl V to Baltimore on a field goal with five seconds left – that when they finally beat down the Miami Dolphins 24-3 in their second straight appearance in the big game, the feeling for the Cowboys themselves was more one of relief than exultation.

"I feel like I've walked uphill the last six years and just reached the top," star defensive tackle Bob Lilly sighed afterward.

It was Lilly who had encapsulated the Cowboys' six years of "almost" exactly one year earlier when he'd heaved his helmet some 40 yards downfield in frustration as the final second ticked off the clock in Miami. This time, he walked off the field at Tulane Stadium knowing that the Cowboys had just completely dominated the AFC champions. They are still the only defensive unit in 50 Super Bowls to not allow a touchdown.

Fittingly, it was Lilly who made the play that most vividly illustrated the Cowboys' dominance, crashing through Miami's offensive line and relentlessly pursuing Dolphins' quarterback Bob Griese for an incredible 29-yard loss on the final play of the first quarter. Already leading 3-0 at the time, the Cowboys outscored the Dolphins 21-3 the rest of the way.

Griese had reacted exactly as the Cowboys had wanted him to as they drew up their game plan the week before the game. Head coach Tom Landry had studied the career of the Dolphins' quarterback. He knew Griese could be cool and calm – and deadly – if allowed to stand freely in the pocket and pick his targets. But if the Cowboys could put pressure on him … different story.

"Coach Landry said, 'Griese's a very difficult quarterback,' " defensive tackle Jethro Pugh told *The Sporting News* for a story on previous Super Bowls in January of 2012. "We want to make him go back to his old ways, because he was a scrambler, and all of a sudden he was a pure pocket passer. The thing that was stressed to the defensive line, make him go back to his old ways."

On third-and-nine, knowing the Dolphins had to pass, Cowboys' defensive coordinator Ernie Stautner had signaled from the sideline for Lilly and defensive end George Andrie to do a "limbo," Lilly looping outside of Andrie. Lilly immediately broke through into the backfield as Griese began to quickly retreat. Meanwhile, left defensive end Larry Cole also sprang free and it was Cole who seemed as if he would get to Griese first.

Griese had first looked left for his primary receiver, Paul Warfield, but safety Cliff Harris had him covered. By then, he had to pull the ball down to try and escape Cole, who made the mistake of leaving his feet in hopes of blocking the pass.

If Cole hadn't jumped, he probably would have sacked Griese then and there. Instead, the chase continued. Remember that scene from the movie *Rocky II*, when Burgess Meredith put Sylvester Stallone in a pen with a chicken and told him to catch it? In this one, Griese was the chicken, darting this way and that, and Lilly and Cole were the pursuers, relentless, implacable, desperate. Would Griese have the split-second it would take to find an open receiver, or even to just dump the ball?

"My biggest thing was making sure he was to my inside, just keep him in the pocket, or in the middle of the field," Cole told TSN. "Have you been to the rodeo? It was like herding cattle. Corral him, keep him in the middle. That's what it felt like."

Finally, 29 yards back down the field into Miami territory, Lilly reached out and snaked his left arm around Griese's waist and then mercifully dragged the exhausted Dolphins' quarterback down. There was a feeling that Griese, given his choice, would have preferred to just stay there for the rest of the afternoon. It didn't get much better for the Dolphins the rest of the way.

The Cowboys' defense would hold the Dolphins to 185 total yards of offense and pressured them into three turnovers. The Dolphins' running game with Larry Csonka and Jim Kiick, who had carried Miami into the Super Bowl, was a non-factor against the Dallas defense. Doomsday surrendered a total of only 18 points throughout the entire playoffs, second only among 49 other Super Bowl winning teams to the 1985 Chicago Bears. Another irony: the man who coached that Bears team was Mike Ditka, who caught a seven-yard touchdown pass from Roger Staubach to put Super Bowl VI on ice.

The Cowboys were equally dominating offensively, executing Landry's game plan to perfection. The strategy was to take advantage of the aggressiveness of Dolphins' middle linebacker Nick Buoniconti with counter plays, which worked beautifully. The Cowboys gouged the Miami defense for a then-Super Bowl record 252 rushing yards. Duane Thomas, the "Silent Sphinx," picked up 95 yards on 19 carries and fullback Walt Garrison another 74 on 14 totes. There was no letup when Calvin Hill spelled Thomas at running back.

The running game was so successful, quarterback Roger Staubach barely worked up a sweat, passing only 19 times and completing a dozen for 119 yards and twin 7-yard scoring tosses (to Ditka and Lance Alworth). Still, Staubach was named the game's MVP, mostly because the media wasn't sure Thomas would even speak afterwards.

There's an argument to be made that the 1971 Cowboys might have been the strongest Dallas team ever, or at least right there with the 1977 and 1992 versions. Lilly, Ditka and Staubach were three of nine Hall of Famers who played on that '71 team, along with Alworth, Bob Hayes, Rayfield Wright, Forrest Gregg, Mel Renfro and Herb Adderley. Of course, coaches Tom Landry and Ernie Stautner (who made it as a player) and Dallas GM Tex Schramm are also enshrined at Canton.

Dallas, in fact, is the only franchise that can claim that its Super Bowl-winning quarterback (Staubach), tight end (Ditka) and both wide receivers (Hayes and Alworth) are in the Hall of Fame, as are both starting cornerbacks, (Renfro and Adderley). None of that was on the Cowboys' minds that day in New Orleans, however. They were simply happy to have finally shed that dreadful moniker, "Next Year's Champions."

"It was like the monkey off of your back," defensive tackle Jethro Pugh said. "We finally did it. Winning is not all that great. It's good, but it's not all that great. You win because you don't want to lose, because if you lose, you just feel awful. You win because you don't want to go through the agony. It's like a final exam. The main thing is, you don't want to flunk it."

This time, the Cowboys definitely didn't. Next year had finally arrived.

SUPER BOWL X
Pittsburgh 21, Dallas 17
January 18, 1976 • Miami

If you can name every one of Dallas' "Dirty Dozen" rookies who shockingly made the team out of training camp and fueled the team's success in 1975 and beyond, you truly are a diehard fan. The rookies nicknamed themselves based on the 1967 movie of the same name. The movie, featuring an ensemble cast that included Lee Marvin, Clint Walker, Telly Savalas and former NFL great Jim Brown, tells the story of a group of U.S. Army misfits who penetrate deep into German-occupied territory to attempt a highly dangerous covert mission.

The Cowboys' rookies may have overlooked the fact that in the movie, most of the "good guys" die in the end, but it was mission accomplished anyway, which almost, but not quite, summed up the Cowboys' own quest that would take them all the way to Super Bowl X. To continue with the movie theme, but in another era, it was there that the Cowboys would come up against the black and gold "Evil Empire," also known as the Pittsburgh Steelers. The Cowboys, at that time the first wild card team to ever advance to the Super Bowl, were in reality the not-quite-ready for prime time players. The Steelers, conversely, were the Darth Vaders of the NFL, a distinction that was well-earned.

"The first one, in 1975 against Pittsburgh, we were a wild card team; we weren't expected to do much," Roger Staubach said of the Cowboys' two Super Bowl matchups with the Steelers in the '70s. "We were a little better prepared a few years later."

Indeed, after the 1971 season and their dominating victory over Miami in Super Bowl VI, the Cowboys twice fell just short of a return trip to the big game, losing the 1972 NFC Championship Game 26-3 at Washington. The 1973 season also ended abruptly in the championship game with a 27-10 defeat to Minnesota. It almost looked like "Next Year's Champions" were back, except that the 1974 team couldn't even live up to that nickname. The Cowboys slipped to 8-6 and failed to make the playoffs for the first time since 1965.

But the team was in transition and there would be better days ahead. The change began when head coach Tom Landry finally settled on Roger Staubach as his quarterback over Craig Morton in the second half of the '71 season. By that time, Staubach had already made it known to the Cowboys that if he wasn't going to have an opportunity to start in Dallas, it might be better if they would just trade him. That wasn't going to happen, of course.

Landry finally announced that Staubach would be the Cowboys' starter. Morton settled in as his backup for a couple of years and then was traded to the New York Giants in late October of the '74 season. A strong-armed gunslinger of a quarterback named Clint Longley, who claimed to be a great nephew of wild west gunfighter Bill Longley, was drafted out of Abilene Christian and joined the team as a rookie in 1974. Longley, in a less public way, would become to Staubach what Robin Ventura was to Nolan Ryan, playing his own small role in the legend of "Captain America."

Other major changes were shaping the face of the team as well. Defensive end George Andrie, Bob Lilly's longtime partner on the right side of the defensive line, hung 'em up after the '72 season. All-Pro and Super Bowl MVP linebacker Chuck Howley retired a year later. Cornerback Herb Adderley ('72) and safety Cornell Green ('74) were gone. Lilly himself, "Mr. Cowboy," would also leave after the '74 season. Middle linebacker Lee Roy Jordan would hang on through 1976, but his best years were behind him. "Doomsday" simply had to be rebuilt and that's what Tex Schramm, Gil Brandt and Tom Landry set out to do before the '75 season.

On the offensive side, guard John Niland was traded to Philadelphia after the '74 season and lasted only one more year in the league. Center Dave Manders said he'd had enough in '74 as well. A troubled Bob Hayes was traded to San Francisco after '74, and running back Calvin Hill signed with the World Football League, then wound up with the Washington Redskins. He retired after four seasons in Cleveland as mostly a third-down back. Walt Garrison hadn't planned to retire yet, but a devastating knee injury during a rodeo in Bozeman, MT, after the '74 season made the decision for him.

The Cowboys were a team in flux as they looked ahead to the '75 season. They had to figure out how to replace the most dominant defensive player in the league in Lilly at right tackle, they had to find a deep threat to replace Hayes, and a running back to step in for the departed Hill. In other words, '75 was shaping up as a total rebuilding year for the Cowboys. They had struggled to post an 8-6 record the year before and things didn't look as if they would get much better in '75.

Schramm, however, had as big an aversion to "rebuilding" then as Jerry Jones does now. It was up to the Cowboys' brain trust to pull a rabbit out of the hat and somehow make the team instant contenders again. The basic infrastructure was still in place, especially with Staubach at quarterback and in the midst of a Hall of Fame career, but there were lots of holes to fill. The extra first-round pick the Cowboys received from the Giants would certainly help.

What the Cowboys didn't know, as they pondered the '75 draft scheduled for Jan. 28-29 at the New York Hilton, was that they were about to hit the equivalent of the powerball lottery. It would be a jackpot of such proportions, it would catapult them all the way to their third Super Bowl and is regarded today as not only the best draft class in franchise history, but one of the best in the history of the NFL. Eleven members of that draft class and one undrafted free agent would make the Cowboys' opening day roster. The "Dirty Dozen" was born.

The Cowboys would begin the overhaul of "Doomsday" by taking Maryland's Randy White, a future Hall of Famer, with the second overall pick in the draft. This was the draft pick they'd obtained from the Giants for Morton. The Giants obligingly posted a pitiful 2-12 ledger in 1974, meaning the Cowboys turned the trade into gold, taking White right after Atlanta picked quarterback Steve Bartkowski with the first overall pick.

The Cowboys wouldn't know it for a couple of years – they initially tried to make a linebacker out of White – but they had discovered the one player who could replace Lilly. Nicknamed "The Manster," – half man, half monster – White became the rock the Cowboys' defense of the late '70s-early '80s would be built upon.

Their second first-rounder, their own pick, was the 18th overall and it was another Gil Brandt special. The Cowboys selected linebacker Thomas Henderson out of tiny Langston University, 35 miles north of Oklahoma City. Henderson, before he buried himself in white powder, was a dynamic, athletic defender with the kind of speed linebackers simply didn't possess. There was literally nothing on the field he couldn't stop, including himself when it came to cocaine.

Linebacker Bob Breunig (third round, Arizona State) gave the Cowboys a long-term replacement for Jordan. Randy Hughes (fourth round, Oklahoma) was a nice fit at safety. Roland Woolsey (sixth round, Boise State) added depth to the secondary. The Cowboys' defense had the new blood it needed. Interestingly, the Cowboys also selected linebacker Mike Hegman (seventh round) that year but a dispute over his eligibility kept him from joining the team until the 1976 season. Just as well. He might have ruined the nickname in '75 (instead of "Dirty Dozen" it might have been "Baker's Dozen").

On offense, Burton Lawless (second round, Florida), Pat Donovan (fourth round, Stanford), Kyle Davis (fifth round, Oklahoma) and Herb Scott (13th round, Virginia Union) helped reconstruct the offensive line. Scott Laidlaw (14th-round, Stanford) immediately stepped in for Garrison. Mitch Hoopes (eighth round, Arizona) replaced Marv Bateman at punter. Percy Howard, a basketball player out of Austin Peay who had never played organized football, stuck as an undrafted free agent wide receiver. He would play just the one season and make one catch – a touchdown in Super Bowl X.

"Tom didn't like to start rookies, but that year we didn't have much choice," Lee Roy Jordan told Peter Golenbock for his book, *Cowboys Have Always Been My Heroes*. "We had to use these guys. Those rookies renewed our enthusiasm after being out of the playoffs. We came back with a real committed attitude."

After a lackluster 2-4 pre-season, the Cowboys opened the regular season with an 18-7 upset of the Los Angeles Rams and won their first four games before dropping a 19-17 heartbreaker at home to Green Bay. They bounced back to nip Philadelphia 20-17 on the road, then lost two in a row to Washington and Kansas City. At 5-3, the season could have gone either way, but the Cowboys closed it out by winning five of their last six games to finish at 10-4 and grab the wild card berth in the playoffs.

The Cowboys were distinct underdogs as they headed for Minnesota and the divisional playoff matchup with the Vikings. It would produce one of the most remarkable comebacks in Dallas Cowboys' history, with Roger Staubach hitting Drew Pearson with a 50-yard touchdown pass with 24 seconds left for a 17-14 victory.

If the historic "Hail Mary" pass was the signature play of Drew Pearson's career, another Pearson would follow it up a week later with his own career game in a shocking 37-7 upset of the heavily-favored Rams in the NFC Championship Game.

The Cowboys had astutely signed cagey running back Preston Pearson just before the '75 season began after the Steelers surprisingly cut him at the end of training camp. Pearson had been the team's player representative and had walked the picket lines during the aborted players strike. He believes to this day that he was cut because his union activities rubbed head coach Chuck Noll the wrong way.

"Chuck Noll decided they could do without me," Pearson said for this book. "I'd had a confrontation with him, but I was representing an entire team of players. I didn't like Chuck Noll for a long time after that. In the long run, I was happy to be coming to Dallas."

The Cowboys, likewise, were happy to have him. Pearson was a good runner, an outstanding blocker and an absolute revelation as a pass receiver coming out of the backfield. Pearson rushed for 509 yards and helped Robert Newhouse, the Cowboys' main running threat in '75, pile up a career-high 930 yards. Pearson also finished fourth in receiving that season with 27 catches for another 351 yards.

Tom Landry saw in Pearson a complement not only to Newhouse, but an opportunity to use him as a receiver out of the backfield and as the first real slot receiver in the NFL. Pearson was the perfect foil for the Rams' over-aggressive defensive line and the Cowboys hurt them time after time with quick screen passes and shovel passes to Pearson who would sneak in behind the L.A. pass rushers.

"The Rams had two very good defensive ends in Fred Dryer and Jack Youngblood, both very good pass rushers," Pearson recalled. "Tom wanted to attack them with the running game and take away their pass rushing abilities. The one play we worked on all week was the shovel pass. The other play I scored on was the screen pass. We executed both of those plays to perfection."

In fact, as Staubach himself pointed out afterwards, there wasn't much the Cowboys did that day that wasn't perfect. The Cowboys hit the Rams hard and often. Staubach threw for four touchdowns, three to Preston Pearson. The Rams were down 34-0 before they even knew what hit them.

"It was total devastation," Pearson noted. "I had one of those games a running back – any running back – can only dream about."

Defensively, the Rams replaced starting quarterback James Harris with Ron Jaworski, but nothing seemed to make a difference. Running back Lawrence McCutcheon, who had pounded the Cardinals for over 200 yards a week earlier, was held to 11 yards on 10 carries by the ferocious Cowboys' defense.

The Cowboys and their "Dirty Dozen" rookies were headed to the Super Bowl for a matchup with the black and gold bad boys of the NFL, the 12-2 Pittsburgh Steelers and their "Steel Curtain" defense. For Preston Pearson, the scenario couldn't have played out any better. If there was one team he wanted to beat, it was the Steelers.

"I was geeked up, as they say," Pearson recalled. "The whole week I was planning on showing them they got rid of the wrong guy. I wanted to show Joe Greene, L.C. Greenwood, Jack Hamm, all those guys I was friends with, that their coach made a mistake.

"Looking back, I may have been too geeked up. I got out there and couldn't catch my breath. You get in games like that, you have to learn and know how to breathe. It took me awhile to understand that."

It was a Super Bowl of contrasting styles. The Cowboys were known for their flash and dash. Their reputation nationally was as a finesse team, not as a team of slobberknockers like the Steelers. Landry knew that the Steelers would try to intimidate his young team, draw them into response-penalties, so he warned them repeatedly during Super Bowl week not to retaliate when the Steelers resorted to roughhouse tactics.

Pearson believes that strategy backfired on the Cowboys. When the Cowboys didn't fight back, the Steelers only grew bolder and more aggressive, taking more and more liberties.

"When a bully comes after you repeatedly, there's only one way to get 'em off of you; you better get right back in his face," Pearson said. "Show 'em you're not going anywhere. I do believe it backfired on us."

The Steelers cornerbacks, allowed to belt receivers around virtually all the way down the field, broke wide receiver Golden Richards' ribs. Steelers' linebacker Jack Lambert picked Cliff Harris up bodily and tried to pile drive him into the ground on a special teams play, Pearson said.

THE DIRTY DOZEN
- DT/LB Randy White
- LB Thomas Henderson
- LB Bob Breunig
- OT Pat Donovan
- G Herb Scott
- P Mitch Hoopes
- S Randy Hughes
- WR Percy Howard
- FB Scott Laidlaw
- G Burton Lawless
- C Kyle Davis
- S Roland Woolsey

"I had words with Jack," Pearson said, and a couple of other Dallas players took verbal exception as well. "Then Tom yelled at us when we came off the field, 'No fighting!' So we let them intimidate us."

Staubach's own temper flared when he saw Lambert deliberately try to kick Pearson in the groin and the Cowboys' quarterback got in the big Steeler linebacker's face.

"I couldn't believe one of our big linemen didn't get into it with them," Staubach said. "I think they were the most penalized team in the league that season and they didn't have a single penalty called against them in that game. They absolutely won the war of intimidation."

It wasn't as if the Cowboys couldn't have held their own in a brawl, Pearson noted.

"Hey, when I've got Randy White, Ed Jones, Harvey Martin, Pat Donovan on my side, why do I need to back off?" he said. "To me, that was just the wrong strategy."

Pacifists or not, the young Cowboys were still clinging to a 10-7 lead at the beginning of the fourth quarter. But the relentless Steelers blocked a punt for a safety and turned the ensuing Cowboys' free kick into a 36-yard Roy Gerela field goal, giving the Steelers their first lead of the game at 12-10. When Mike Wagner intercepted Staubach on the first play after the kickoff and returned it to the Dallas seven, the Cowboys' defense stiffened, but Gerela nailed an 18-yarder.

It was Lynn Swann's remarkable day receiving – a Super Bowl-record 161-yards, capped by a 64-yard fourth-quarter touchdown catch – that ultimately separated the two teams.

Staubach's 34-yard touchdown pass to Percy Howard – amazingly the only pass he ever caught as a Cowboy – sliced the Steelers' lead to 21-17. The Cowboys had a final last gasp chance to win the game when Staubach threw another one into the end zone for Howard, a former basketball star at Austin Peay, as the final seconds ticked away, but Howard was pulled down by a Steelers' defensive back, no flags flew, and this time there was no "Hail Mary" rescue for the Cowboys.

The Steelers had won Round 1. The rematch would be even better.

SUPER BOWL XII
Dallas 27, Denver 10
January 15, 1978 • New Orleans

The late, great Harvey Martin said it best years later in talking to Peter Golenbock for his epic book *Cowboys Have Always Been My Heroes*. "One player, I moaned to myself, just one running back, and we'd be the best damn team God ever gave breath to."

Martin was talking about the prayer he said after the Cowboys' disappointing 14-12 loss to the Los Angeles Rams in the divisional playoff round following an 11-3 regular season run in 1976. The loss blocked the Cowboys from a potential second straight Super Bowl.

From Harvey's lips, to God's ears.

Twelve months after that letdown against the Rams, the Cowboys had their running back, were back in the big game and were absolutely "the best damn team God ever gave breath to." At least in 1977 anyway.

The disappointing and abrupt end to the '76 season jolted the Cowboys, especially quarterback Roger Staubach, who took much of the blame on his own shoulders. The season really hadn't started out poorly for Staubach. First, at training camp, he literally chased backup quarterback Clint Longley out of town; then he took on the rest of the NFL, almost singled-handedly at times.

Oh, he could still rely on that terrific Cowboys' defense that was continuing to grow into its own, but offensively there was Staubach and Drew Pearson and ... well, there was Staubach and Drew Pearson and occasionally Billy Joe Dupree. But when Staubach tried to play with a broken hand in the second half of the season, even the passing game went south.

The lack of a running game, something to take the heat off Staubach, was killing the Cowboys. Robert Newhouse and Preston Pearson were both battling injuries. Third-year back Doug Dennison would lead the team in rushing with a mere 542 yards. Martin was right as he looked ahead to 1977: the Cowboys desperately needed a primo running back if they were ever going to fulfill their immense promise.

Tex Schramm, who sometimes seemed to think he was God, or at least his first lieutenant, saw the answer to the Cowboys' problem in a smallish, 5-11, 190-pound tailback from the same Pennsylvania steel mill country that had once produced a rugged tight end named Mike Ditka. Not that Tony Dorsett was one of those unheard of gems the Cowboys seemed to find regularly at some small college. Dorsett had just won the Heisman Trophy at the University of Pittsburgh, where he was a three-time All-American and the first college player ever to run for over 6,000 yards.

So how in the world could a team that had just been to the Super Bowl a year earlier and finished 11-3 in '76 have a shot at drafting a player with Dorsett's lustrous credentials? Because the shrewd Schramm and his partner in crime, Gil Brandt, hoodwinked a very-obliging John Thompson, the Seattle Seahawks' general manager. The Seahawks, who at the time didn't really like ponying up big money for rookie talent, liked the idea of taking the Cowboys' No. 1 pick and three No. 2s instead. With those picks, the Seahawks could rebuild their team with four prime players instead of one.

The Cowboys needed a third partner in the deal, too. The trade with Seattle was contingent on Tampa Bay, which had the No. 1 overall pick, taking running back Ricky Bell from USC. Schramm and Brandt felt confident that's what the Buccaneers would do and they were right. History says that Schramm not only picked Seattle's pocket, but he got the best of two big running backs as well.

It's debatable whether Schramm's trade or Jimmy Johnson's 1990 swap of Herschel Walker to Minnesota for a passel of draft picks was the greatest heist in Cowboys' history. Both would lead directly to Super Bowls.

Dorsett's extraordinary ability was obvious to everyone, but Tom Landry being Tom Landry, he wasn't going to just hand his precocious rookie the starting job as soon as the team plane landed at Thousand Oaks, California, for training camp. Dorsett would have to earn his way into the starting lineup while understudying Preston Pearson.

In the second game of the season, Dorsett carried the ball just seven times, but scored two touchdowns. In a trouncing of Tampa Bay in the third game, Dorsett averaged 7.2 yards a romp on 10 carries. In Game 4, a 30-24 victory over St. Louis, Dorsett ran crazy, gaining 141 yards on just 14 carries. He scored twice, once on a 77-yard gallop that showed his game-breaking ability.

"Tony was just an incredible runner," Staubach said. "He made a huge difference in our team that year."

With rookie Tony Hill also contributing, the Cowboys' offense was hitting on all cylinders. Everyone knew that Dorsett should be starting ... everyone, that is, but Landry, who continued to bring his star back along slowly.

Dorsett wouldn't get his first NFL start until the season's 10th game, ironically against Pittsburgh. He comported himself well, rushing for 73 yards on 17 carries. Dorsett saved his real coming-out party for two games later against Philadelphia, however, erupting for a then club record 206 yards on 23 carries, including one remarkable 84-yard touchdown.

"Just like when they drafted, him" a sour Eagles' coach Dick Vermeil growled afterward. "He's the best in the country."

Despite carrying just 21 times in the first three games, Dorsett finished the regular season with a rookie club record 1,007 yards rushing, earning the NFL's Offensive Rookie of the Year Award.

The 12-2 Cowboys, led by the newest version of their Doomsday Defense, easily disposed of Chicago (37-7) and Minnesota (23-6) in the playoffs, to coast into Super Bowl XII against their old quarterback Craig Morton and the AFC champion Denver Broncos in New Orleans. Ironically, the Cowboys had just beaten the Broncos 14-6 in the regular season finale.

Morton, despite his success in Denver, didn't scare the Cowboys' defenders. In his half dozen years at the helm of the New York Giants, Morton had never beaten his former team. Harvey Martin and Ed

"Too Tall" Jones were all but salivating at the thought of the virtually immobile Morton, 34, standing in the pocket. Randy White, the story goes, sharpened his teeth with a file.

The Cowboys knew they couldn't afford to give Morton time to pick his targets. Given time, he was still a highly accurate quarterback. The key to beating Morton – and thus the Broncos – was to put pressure on him, to blitz, to create havoc in and around the Denver quarterback, to make him fear for his life.

When Landry explained this to Martin, White and company, it was like taking the leash off a platoon of trained Dobermans. Somebody was going to bleed. That somebody was the ill-fated Morton.

The Cowboys would win 27-10 despite an offense that fumbled three times in the first five minutes. Efren Herrera would miss three field goals. Landry, perhaps spooked by Denver's "Orange Crush" defense, unnecessarily pulled out just about every trick and gadget play in the Cowboys' playbook. None of it mattered. The Broncos sniffed out the Cowboys' fullback option pass and Robert Newhouse still completed a 29-yard touchdown pass to Golden Richards. Butch Johnson would make an incredible diving catch in the end zone for a touchdown.

Most of all, however, the Cowboys simply dismembered the hapless Morton, who was harried into four first half interceptions, half of Denver's eight turnovers. The Broncos were held to a mere 64 yards passing. Morton completed just 4 of 15 passes for 39 yards. He and backup Norris Weese were sacked a combined four times.

Writers at the game voted to give the MVP award to the entire Dallas defense but the NFL wouldn't allow it. The writers settled for splitting it between Harvey Martin and Randy White, unprecedented in Super Bowl history.

Morton, naturally, was portrayed as the fall guy for the Broncos, but Staubach never bought into that scenario. He always respected and liked his former teammate.

"Our defense just totally dominated the game," Staubach told Golenbock. "They could have had Jim Thorpe at quarterback for Denver and he would have been in trouble. So it wasn't Craig Morton's fault. Craig Morton didn't have a shot in that game."

It also wasn't Morton's fault, Staubach told me, that he ran into arguably the greatest Cowboys' team of all-time in the ultimate game.

"I think the '77 team might have been our greatest team," Staubach said. "It was similar to the '71 team, but when we got Tony Hill and Dorsett, we became a great team. We were just so balanced offensively, and I thought we had the best defense in the league."

Winning was becoming a habit for the Cowboys. In some ways, that took some of the glitter off the victory in Super Bowl XII. They had been good enough, for long enough, that winning was something they simply expected to do.

And they weren't finished winning yet.

SUPER BOWL XIII
Pittsburgh 35, Dallas 31
January, 21, 1979 • Miami

The stakes are always high for a Super Bowl, but this time there was added drama: Super Bowl XIII would determine the "Team of the Decade" and the first team to win three Super Bowls. The game has often been called the best Super Bowl in history.

The Cowboys came in as defending Super Bowl champions after having destroyed Denver 27-10 a year earlier and with a score to settle against the Steelers, who had won a rough and tumble Super Bowl X against the Cowboys, 21-17. This time, the Cowboys were sure, would be different. This time they had a future Hall of Famer in Tony Dorsett at running back and a deep threat in Tony Hill to pair with Drew Pearson. This time the Cowboys wouldn't allow the Steelers to intimidate them.

"We were as good if not better that second game," Preston Pearson said. "The first one (in '75) we were young, snot-nosed kids, a team with a dozen rookies. We weren't expected to be there. When we lost that first one, guys just went home, saying, 'Well, we got there. We can get better.' Fortunately, we did and we did get back.

"When we went up against them the second time, we were a very good team. Randy (White) had settled in at defensive tackle, Harvey Martin was a monster. Ed Jones was in the prime of his career. He'd had a monster game against Denver in Super Bowl XII."

And still the Cowboys couldn't find a way to beat the Steelers.

Too many mistakes. Too many turnovers. Too many phantom penalties. Tom Landry knew going in that the Cowboys would have to play a near-perfect game to win and that didn't even come close to happening. Looking back almost 40 years later, Roger Staubach can only shake his head at what might have been.

"We had a really good team," Staubach said. "Our offense was great, but Pittsburgh was really good, too. The team that made the mistakes would lose the game and we had a few things happen that hurt us."

Perhaps the one that stung the most came in the third quarter, Cowboys trailing 21-14 facing a third-and-one at Pittsburgh's 11-yard line. Landry called for a three tight end-set, which he hoped would make the Steelers believe the Cowboys planned to run the ball. Tight end Billy Joe Dupree was the primary target. The fullback would swing out to the flat as an outlet receiver. Tight end Jackie Smith, the veteran picked up from St. Louis early in the season, would work toward the back of the end zone.

It was designed as a goal-line play, and the Cowboys had been practicing it all week from the one or two-yard line, not 10 yards further out. Mel Blount covered DuPree. Jack Lambert blitzed up the middle but running back Scott Laidlaw stood him up with a textbook block. Smith hit the end zone wide open. Under pressure, Staubach had to release the ball before Smith even turned, so he took a little off, leaving the pass a shade lower than he wanted.

Smith's feet skidded on the turf as he turned and began to fall backward, just as the ball slipped through his hands, hit him in the chest and bounced harmlessly away.

On NFL replays available on YouTube today, fans can still hear Verne Lundquist's shocked call of the play.

"Dropped! In the end zone, Jackie Smith, wide open. ... Oh, bless his heart he has to be the sickest man in America!"

No sicker than the millions of Cowboys' fans watching on TV back home, though.

"I don't remember much about it except I dropped it," Smith said in the postgame lockerroom. Though he was headed to the Hall of Fame, it was the last play of Smith's illustrious career.

"You just feel like you let a lot of people down," he said. "You're so disappointed in yourself. You can't redo it, so I don't know what to tell you. As the ball was coming, I was trying to get down to catch it against my chest. I guess I just wasn't in the right position."

Staubach and other Cowboys felt so badly for Smith that none would point fingers in his direction afterward. Staubach blamed himself for not zipping the ball into Smith, instead of lobbing it.

"The thing was he hadn't really run that play," Staubach told Peter Golenbock for his book, *Cowboys Have Always Been My Heroes*. "If he would have stopped at the goal line, he would have been standing there, waiting. It would have been real easy to hit him and he would have caught it.

"The play was perfect, a great call, a great play if Pittsburgh blitzed and they loved to blitz deep in their territory, so it worked like a charm. But Jackie was surprised and the ball hit him in the chest and he couldn't catch it."

Equally damaging was a play late in the third quarter when Steelers' quarterback Terry Bradshaw, who passed for a then-Super Bowl record 318 yards and four touchdowns, threw one up for grabs. Benny Barnes, running behind the ultra-talented Lynn Swann, had good coverage, but Swann pushed him, Barnes lost his balance and both players fell over each other. The official closest to the play, back judge Pat Knight, waved his arms signaling an incompletion. But from across the field, a flag came flying from the hand of field judge Fred Swearingen. Barnes was called for pass interference.

Years later, Staubach didn't hold back his feelings, calling it "the worst call in the history of football." Even commissioner Pete Rozelle would later admit he thought it was a bad call. Too late for the Cowboys. The 33-yard penalty set up Franco Harris' 22-yard touchdown run with just over seven minutes left in the fourth quarter.

Then the Cowboys made yet another fatal mistake. Roy Gerela shanked a short kickoff into the arms of Randy White, who should have simply fallen down on the ball. Instead White, wearing a cast on one arm, tried to run with it and fumbled it back to the Steelers. Bradshaw capitalized with a quick 18-yard scoring strike to Swann and the Steelers led, 35-17 with 6:51 left in the game.

The Cowboys were reeling, but with Staubach still on his feet, far from dead. Staubach led the Cowboys on an 89-yard march, capped by a seven-yard TD pass to DuPree, but the drive ate up much of the remaining time. The Cowboys kept fighting. Dallas recovered an onside kick and Staubach hit Butch Johnson for a five-yard TD to bring the Cowboys back within four with 22 seconds to play. That was all they had left. The Steelers denied Staubach another chance at a dramatic comeback when Rocky Bleier recovered Rafael Septien's next onside kick.

"I thought we were the better team," Preston Pearson said. "We probably should have won the game except for some mistakes in execution. We were just as physical. We didn't let them intimidate us. Our game plan was pretty darn good."

As badly as the loss hurt at the time, Staubach can look back now with some admiration for what the Cowboys accomplished, not just in battling back in that game, but in the decade of the '70s.

"I've always appreciated the good things," Staubach said. "We were the winningest team of the '70s. We won a couple of Super Bowls. I have a lot of respect for the Steelers. We were playing arguably one of the best teams in the history of the NFL. They were on a roll. We didn't lose to a bunch of weaklings. We lost, but it could have gone either way."

The Steelers went to four Super Bowls in the '70s and won them all. After beating the Cowboys in Super Bowl XIII to become the first three-time Super Bowl winner, they bumped the bar higher the next year by also beating the Rams 31-19 in Super Bowl XIV. Their won-loss record for the '70s, including postseason, was 117-48.

The Cowboys went to five Super Bowls in the '70s and won two. Their combined regular season and playoff record was 121-49. As Staubach said, the Cowboys were "the winningest team" of the '70s.

But "Team of the Decade?" No getting around it, Cowboys fans, give the Steelers credit. They won twice as many Super Bowls in the '70s and they defeated the Cowboys head to head in the ultimate game on two different occasions. By almost any measure, the "Team of the Decade" wore black and gold.

For all those reasons, the loss in Super Bowl XIII was particularly devastating to the Cowboys. Landry himself was shaken.

"This was the culmination of nine years when we had been to five Super Bowls," he told reporters in the aftermath. "We could have been the first team to win three Super Bowls (instead of the Steelers) and it would have been a great climax to an era."

Tex Schramm was equally broken-hearted but pragmatic at the same time. "It's hell to lose," he said. "But we've been here before and we'll be back."

He was both precisely right and fatefully wrong. The Cowboys would definitely be back in the big game, three more times in fact, but it would be 14 long years before the Cowboys' star made another appearance in the Super Bowl and when it did, neither Schramm, nor Landry, would be part of it.

End of an era indeed.

"THE CATCH"
San Francisco 28, Dallas 27
January 10, 1982 • San Francisco

There are a few games that have achieved iconic status in NFL history and, perhaps not so surprisingly, the Cowboys have at least a handful on their résumé. Unfortunately for Cowboys fans, some of those games tend to bring bittersweet memories.

Two immediately come to mind: The Ice Bowl game at Green Bay's Lambeau Field to decide the 1967 NFL championship, and "The Catch" game in San Francisco for the NFC championship and the right to go to the Super Bowl following the '81 season.

Though they came 14 years apart, those two games have one thing in common: The Cowboys lost both of them on nail-biting, gut-wrenching plays at the end of the game.

Which one hurt the most? We could debate that until hell – or Lambeau Field – freezes over. Let's just agree that both losses were gut shots that devastated the Cowboys because in each game they played so well, came so close, and still lost. In both games, the Packers and 49ers made the plays at the end; the Cowboys did not.

Bart Starr's one-yard quarterback sneak for the game-winning touchdown in the Ice Bowl seemed almost inevitable. At that point on that frozen field, the Cowboys needed a miracle to keep the Packers out of the end zone and they didn't get it. In San Francisco 14 years later, Dwight Clark's soaring catch at the back of the end zone was far more startling, perhaps because it looked as if 49ers quarterback Joe Montana had, in desperation, thrown the ball far too high for human consumption. This time, it was the 49ers who needed the miracle.

For a split second, hope soared in the breasts of Cowboys' fans everywhere. Then, as if he had catapulted himself from a trampoline, Clark levitated into the air above Dallas' Everson Walls, reaching as high as his arms would stretch, his fingertips straining for the impossible, his back arching, and then, somehow, the ball was in his hands, and he was coming down – he couldn't still be in bounds, could he?!?!?! – and then there he was, tiptoeing just inside the end line, holding the ball aloft, and the 49ers had scored with inside a minute to play.

Just writing those words re-opens that horrendous wound for Cowboys fans. It still oozes blood today and likely always will. It hurts to pick at that scab.

It was an incredibly pivotal game in the history of both the Dallas and San Francisco franchises. The young 49ers would go on to upset Cincinnati 26-21 in the Super Bowl, the first of four they would win in the decade as they became the team of the '80s. The Cowboys were in the middle of reaching three straight NFC title games and losing each one (to Philadelphia, San Francisco and Washington).

The Cowboys didn't realize it, but they had reached the apex of their two decades of success and the sun was about to set on Tex Schramm, Tom Landry and an unparalleled era of NFL excellence.

What might have happened had Clark not found a way to climb the ladder and make "The Catch" in that game? Would the Cowboys have gone to win a third Super Bowl for Schramm and Landry, beating the Bengals as the 49ers did? One likes to think so.

Might Landry, with almost a quarter of a century of coaching the Cowboys under his belt, have decided to go out on top and retire at that point? Unlikely. The Cowboys were still having too much success. Landry wasn't one to quit at any time, much less while the gravy was still flowing.

But might another Super Bowl victory have sparked the necessary energy for the Cowboys to avoid, or at least delay, the coming slide that marked the end of an era in the late '80s? Perhaps, but again, maybe not. Father Time is inexorable and at the same time that key Cowboys' players were growing older, the edge the franchise had held in scouting, drafting and signing players was rapidly disappearing.

At the very least, a victory that day in San Francisco would most likely have changed the course of quarterback Danny White's career, giving him the shot at being a Super Bowl-winning quarterback that he deserved but never had. White had paid his dues as backup to Roger Staubach before taking over as the Cowboys' starter after Roger the Dodger decided that five concussions suffered during the '79 season put him over the head injury limit.

Staubach was 38. It was tempting to stay because he knew the Cowboys still had a "very good team" and he enjoyed playing with Drew Pearson, Tony Dorsett and the rest of his teammates. But he also knew it was time and that White was more than ready.

With White at the helm for his second full year as the starter, the Cowboys reeled off four relatively easy victories to begin the '81 season. They lost two in a row on the road, 20-17 at St. Louis and, ominously, 45-14 at San Francisco. But they quickly regrouped for another four-game winning streak.

That streak was snapped by a 27-24 loss at Detroit, but the Cowboys clinched another NFC East Division flag with yet another four-game winning streak before closing out the season with a meaningless 13-10 overtime loss at the New York Giants.

They were primed for the playoffs, destroying Tampa Bay 38-0 at Texas Stadium in the divisional round, setting up the rematch with the 49ers at Candlestick Park.

White had passed for over 3,000 yards and 22 touchdowns during the regular season. Dorsett was second in the league in rushing with 1,646 yards and Ron Springs added another 625 on the ground. White spread the ball among all his receivers. Tony Hill and Springs each had 46 catches and Hill averaged 20.7 yards per reception. Pearson caught another 38 for 614 yards. Butch Johnson came off the bench often enough to snare 25 passes, five for touchdowns.

Despite the early season wipeout at the 49ers' hands, the Cowboys weren't worried about the return trip to Candlestick. The defense had keyed the destruction of the Bucs, intercepting quarterback Doug Williams four times, returning three for touchdowns, forcing him into a pair of intentional grounding penalties and sacking him four times. Tampa Bay managed all of 22 yards rushing. The Cowboys were ready for Montana and the 49ers.

True to form, it was the defense that was giving the 49ers fits in the title game, intercepting Montana three times and recovering three fumbles on the way to a 27-21 lead. The Cowboys might have put the game away late in the fourth quarter, but White just missed Doug Donley on a pass that would have put them in field goal range. Another three points would have put the 49ers two scores down with little time left.

Ultimately, it came down to Montana and company taking over at the San Francisco 11 with 4:54 to go, needing a touchdown to win. Strangely, the Cowboys came out in their nickel defense, which played right into the 49ers' hands. Head coach Bill Walsh had already told Montana that the 49ers would have to march the ball down the field, settling for quick runs and short passes.

"We knew we couldn't get it in big chunks," Walsh said after the game. "We had to methodically pick them apart."

Montana, as he did so often in the clutch in his career, executed the plan perfectly, patching together a 13-play drive that brought the 49ers to a third-and-four play from the Dallas six-yard line. The longest play of the drive had been a 14-yard reverse by receiver Freddie Solomon.

"It was a long way," Clark agreed, "but we had to get it a little bit at a time."

In the huddle, Montana called for "Red right tight, sprint option," with Solomon as his primary receiver. Montana was already worried that he might have blown the 49ers' best chance at a victory when he'd over-thrown Solomon two plays earlier from the 12.

"He could have walked into the end zone, he was so open on that play, and I threw it three yards over his head," Montana remembered years later.

As Montana rolled out of the pocket to the right on the third down play, he was still looking for Solomon, but Freddie had fallen down. So Montana scanned quickly for his secondary receiver and spotted Clark, loping across the back of the end zone, covered by Walls.

"We had never thrown the ball to Dwight on that play," Montana said. "He was supposed to set a pick for Freddie, who was down. (Clark) didn't think it was coming to him, but he saw the play was still going so he finished his route like he was supposed to, but had never done before. It just took his slow butt a long time to get there. He did make a nice catch."

There are Cowboy fans who still believe Montana was simply trying to throw the ball away to avoid the sack – Too Tall Jones was bearing down on him – and give the 49ers another chance on fourth down. Not so, Montana insists.

"Early in camp, Bill Walsh made us practice that throw," Montana said. "We thought he was nuts because we never used that play. Then, in the biggest game of our lives, we pull it out.

"I didn't try to throw it that high. When I let go of it, I thought it would be high, but not that high. But you have to take into account that I was throwing it over Too Tall."

Clark wasn't at all sure that he could get high enough to get to the ball.

"As I ran my route, I looked back and saw the ball coming," he said years later. "I thought, 'Damn, that's high!' I just went up and got it, made a play. I talked to Everson Walls later and he said he thought the ball was going out of bounds and he relaxed. He said when he felt me going up, he thought, 'Oh, my goodness!' ... or something like that."

"The Catch" stands as one of the single-most exceptional plays in NFL history, but the Cowboys still almost rendered it a moot point. Trailing 28-27 with 51 seconds left, Danny White hit Drew Pearson over the middle and for a moment, it appeared as if the elusive and fleet receiver might break away and score.

"I thought I was gone," Pearson said afterward. "I got caught from behind, but I never saw the guy. He was able to grab my jersey."

That play, Montana said, was what really "saved the game."

Pearson was dragged down by Eric Wright, who snagged Pearson by the jersey, then the shoulder pads, a play that very well might have drawn a flag for a horse collar tackle under today's rules. The Cowboys needed another 20 yards or so to set up a potential game-winning field goal by Rafael Septien. But on the next play White retreated. Looking for Tony Hill, he held the ball too long and was eventually hit and fumbled. San Francisco recovered. Game over.

For the 49ers and their fans, "The Catch," stands as a linch-pin moment in their ascendency to the NFL throne as the best team of the '80s. For the NFL, it is one of those iconic plays that will live forever in league history.

For the Cowboys and their fans, it simply lives in infamy, as a bad memory and a reminder of what might have been.

Try not to pick at the scab.

SUPER BOWL XXVII
Dallas 52, Buffalo 17
January 31, 1993 • Pasadena, California

Did it start on the night of Feb. 25, 1989, with "The Saturday Night Massacre," when Jerry Jones sat in front of dozens of television cameras and hundreds of notepads and promised that he would be in charge of everything, including "socks and jocks?"

Or did it really begin when Jones and Jimmy Johnson made Troy Aikman the first overall pick in the 1989 draft two months later on April 13?

Some may argue that it actually kicked off on October 12 that year when Jimmy Johnson gleefully announced that the Cowboys had traded their premier player, running back Herschel Walker, to the Minnesota Vikings for a first-round draft pick in 1992 and what sounded to the assembled media like the proverbial handful of pinto beans and an as yet unnamed bovine, a deal that was panned by virtually every local pundit and "expert." It was a trade that has since been labeled "The Great Train Robbery" – in Dallas' favor.

Then again, maybe the start of it all was when Johnson and Jones turned one of the half dozen or so draft picks they received in that deal into the 17th overall selection in the 1990 draft and tapped a smallish running back out of the University of Florida – a kid named Emmitt Smith, who would go on to become the NFL's all-time leading rusher.

Or could it have begun earlier than all of these things, when Tex Schramm, Gil Brandt and Tom Landry had the foresight to draft a mouthy wide receiver out of the University of Florida named Michael Irvin?

Fortunately, we don't have to choose from among all these myriad potential starting points for a team that would win three Super Bowls in a four-year span in the early to mid-1990s. All were crucial and almost certainly, the Dallas Cowboys' triumphant march to the pinnacle of NFL success would not have happened without each of those events – and dozens of others – taking place just as they did.

The facts are these: Somehow, in the NFL of the early '90s, before salary caps and free agency as we know it today, Jerry Jones and Jimmy Johnson were able to inherit a team coming off a 3-13 season in 1988, a team that hadn't had a winning season since 1985, dismantle it to the tune of a 1-15 record in '89, then reconstruct it into a Super Bowl champion by 1992. Essentially, in three short years, the new regime built a team from the bottom up that would win three of four Super Bowls in the mid-'90s.

In the NFL, that's called a dynasty.

And it all happened so fast, fueled by that Cowboys' swindle of a trade with Minnesota that landed a plethora of high draft picks, a commodity Johnson and Jones had quickly recognized as the key to their rebuilding effort. That deal had helped the Cowboys to add players like Emmitt Smith, Russell Maryland, Kevin Smith and Isaac Holt, among others. All would play key roles in one or more of the Cowboys' three Super Bowl championships.

From 1-15 in '89, to 7-9 in '90 and then 11-5 and a playoff win in '91: just like that, the Cowboys were on the doorstep of their first Super Bowl run in two decades. In his second year in the league, Emmitt Smith had led the league in rushing, Michael Irvin topped the NFL in receiving yardage and Jay Novacek led all tight ends with 59 catches.

A 38-6 blowout loss to Detroit in the second round of the playoffs in '91 emphasized the one weakness Johnson had already recognized in his defense: one-on-one pass coverage, especially against teams employing a run-and-shoot style offense that spread the field. The Cowboys addressed that problem in the off-season, picking up both Kevin Smith and Darren Woodson in the draft, inserting Kenny Gant into the nickel package and, the piece de resistance, trading for defensive end Charles Haley at the end of training camp. Nothing helps a pass defense more than an elite pass rusher in a quarterback's face.

Finally, the Cowboys also traded for strong safety Thomas Everett from Pittsburgh just before the '92 season began. Jones and Johnson had aggressively shored up the team's biggest weakness. The stage for Super Bowl success was set.

Part of the reason things came together so quickly for the Cowboys was the atmosphere created by Johnson and his assistants. If Johnson had been a holy terror in 1989 as he discarded players he knew couldn't measure up and wouldn't play for him, by the early '90s he was making his players feel like part of a family with a common goal.

"Chemistry is more than getting along on the surface," Johnson wrote in his 1993 book, *Turning the Thing Around*, about the reconstruction of the Cowboys and their first Super Bowl appearance since the '70s. "Chemistry is detailed, minute, indeed molecular. The second variable is also a cliché, 'attitude.' But we take it far beyond the rah-rah, gung-ho stages, high into the psychology of the self-fulfilling prophecy."

Johnson and his coaches essentially changed the culture of the Cowboys of the '80s and convinced them that if they listened, if they did as they were told, if they accepted the coaching they were getting, they would not only win, they would win it all. The players willingly bought into the message. Why wouldn't they? Johnson gave them little choice. It was buy in, or ship out.

"We worked hard, all of us, but we were not in a working environment," soon-to-be popular fullback Daryl "Moose" Johnston explained. "It didn't feel like work and if you find that atmosphere on a football team, you feel like you're blessed. Everybody had a defined role, embraced that role and did their best to excel in that role.

"We had a hodge-podge of guys who meshed into an unbelievable unit: offensive line, great running back, great quarterback, great receivers. The thing about The Triplets (Aikman, Smith, Irvin) that doesn't get talked about enough, the one area where they don't get enough credit, is that all three of them only wanted to win.

"Troy was driven only by winning games. He wasn't driven by anything but that. It was never about the numbers and Troy was what made that thing click. Michael was our heart and soul. Emmitt was the engine that wouldn't quit. There were no egos. They knew their legacy would be defined by winning championships."

Jones and Johnson knew their long-term plan might be developing a little ahead of schedule but it's not likely that anyone, coaches or players, went into the '92 season expecting it to end in Super Bowl XXVII. Or that their team would post the biggest blowout in Super Bowl history, pounding the hapless Buffalo Bills 52-17.

Yet, it was Johnson, channeling his inner Kreskin, who told both his players and the media (to reinforce his message to the players, of course) before the season even started: "The best game we will play will be the last game of the year."

Not even Nostradamus was that good.

The Cowboys started the '92 season by reeling off three straight victories. Emmitt Smith pounded the defending world champion Redskins for 140 yards in a season-opening 23-10 victory that Johnson had spent the entire off-season pointing toward. Troy Aikman riddled the Giants' secondary with a 22-for-35 day for 238 yards and two touchdowns and Michael Irvin caught 9 for 73 yards and a TD in a 34-28 win at New York and then Smith rushed for 112 yards and Aikman threw three TD passes in a 31-20 beating of Phoenix back home.

After the bye week, the Cowboys ran into an emotionally charged Philadelphia team, still mourning the off-season death of defensive tackle Jerome Brown in a car accident, and were hammered 31-7 at Veterans Stadium. The Eagles, Johnson would note later, were the most ferocious team in the league that season, but they would stay on an emotional roller-coaster. The Cowboys would catch them in one of their dips the next time they met.

The sobering loss to the Eagles might have been just what the young Cowboys needed to bring them back into focus after the bye-week. They responded with a five-game winning streak before dropping a 27-23 decision to the Rams at Texas Stadium when Tony Zendejas kicked a pair of fourth-quarter field goals to erase a 23-21 Dallas lead.

The Cowboys then won five of their last six, the only loss a 20-17 decision at Washington when the Redskins recovered an Aikman fumble in the end zone (Johnson still argues it should have been ruled an incomplete pass), to roll into the playoffs against Eastern Division rival Philadelphia. The two teams had split their regular season games but the Eagles were no match this time and the Cowboys, behind Aikman (2 TD passes) and Smith (114 and a TD) romped 34-10.

Aikman (24-34, 322 and 2 TDs) outdueled counterpart Steve Young (25-35, 313, 1 TD, 2 INTs) and the 49ers in the NFC championship game at Candlestick Park and the Cowboys cashed their ticket to their first Super Bowl since the '70s with a 30-20 triumph. It was in that postgame lockerroom that Jimmy Johnson stood up on a chair and screamed his famous, "How 'bout them Cowboys?" line.

Since preparation is basically Johnson's middle name, it was a given that the Cowboys would be ready for the Bills, who had been to the Super Bowl twice previously and lost both times. In a way, Johnson had been preparing for this moment all of his coaching life. At the University of Miami, getting the Hurricanes ready for national championships, Jimmy had picked the brain of the great Dolphins' coach Don Shula about how he prepared his team for Super Bowls. He had also had long conversations with Redskins' coach Joe Gibbs and Giants' coach Bill Parcells on the same subject. No detail, regardless of how minor, would be left unaddressed. During a week full of distractions, Johnson would keep the Cowboys focused on the task ahead.

"I was 100 percent sure we were going to win that game," Johnson wrote. "I had as much confidence in winning that game as any game that I have coached. We held a royal flush. It was just a matter of dropping the cards."

And boy, did the Cowboys drop the cards….like an anvil, right on the Bills' noggins.

Johnson's game plan stressed patience, anticipating Buffalo's turnover weakness to eventually begin showing itself. The Bills had capitalized on a blocked punt to take an early 7-0 lead, but the Cowboys struck back when James Washington intercepted a Jim Kelly pass, the first of a record nine Buffalo turnovers, and Aikman hit Jay Novacek cutting across the middle for a 23-yard catch-and-run touchdown.

On the Bills' first play from scrimmage after the TD, Kelly was hit by Charles Haley at his own 2-yard line. Jimmie Jones caught Kelly's fumble in mid-air and easily strolled into the end zone to give the Cowboys a 14-7 lead. The rout was on.

Aikman would throw four touchdown passes, two to Michael Irvin. Emmitt Smith rushed for 105 yards. The defense turned the nine turnovers into 35 points. The Cowboys' complete domination, in front of 98,374 fans, turned the Rose Bowl into a maelstrom of noise and celebration.

Aikman was almost perfect, hitting 22 of 30 passes for 273 yards and the four scores, earning game MVP honors.

"It's as great a feeling as I've ever had in my life," Aikman, said afterward. "I wish every player could experience it."

Irvin, of course, concurred.

"I can't sit here, I promise you, and put into words how this feels," the Cowboys' star wide receiver said in the clamor of the postgame interview room. "You dream about this moment. You dream about what it would be like. It's such a dream. Actually, it's a fantasy."

As explosive as the offense was, there wasn't a soul in the stadium who didn't recognize that it had been the Cowboys' defense, led by Haley, linebacker Kenny Norton and safety Thomas Everett (two interceptions) that set everything up.

"A lot of people forget how good our defense was, not just in that game but all season," fullback Daryl Johnston said for this book. "Our offense got all the attention but our defense was No. 1 in the NFL. They got no credit, but they never complained and were the best in the league."

As Johnson had predicted, the last game his team played in the 1992-93 season was its best.

"Understand this," Johnson said in his postgame address to his players. "As good as you feel right now, you must understand that the love and support you have for each other, the commitment you made, is what got you here. Never forget that."

Just 36 months after finishing 1-15, the new-regime Dallas Cowboys had climbed to the top of the NFL, winning their first Super Bowl since 1978. But the journey wasn't finished. There were still mountains to be conquered and miles to go before it would all shockingly fall apart.

SUPER BOWL XXVIII
Dallas 30, Buffalo 13
January 30, 1994 • Atlanta, Georgia

Jerry Jones knew Emmitt Smith could play ball. It's why the Cowboys had traded up in the 1990 draft to select the Florida dynamo with the 17th-overall pick. What Jones was about to learn after joyously placing his first Super Bowl trophy in his office in January of 1993, was that Smith could play hardball, too.

Besides being a great football player – after all, he'd just claimed two NFL rushing titles in '91 and '92 – Emmitt was a businessman who understood that professional football was a business. This was no Michael Irvin, who had caved in his own holdout a year earlier because he simply couldn't abide the idea that the Cowboys might play without him.

Emmitt wanted what he believed he deserved and he was willing to do whatever it took to get it, even if that meant holding out at the beginning of the '93 season. And what Smith wanted wasn't even close to what Jerry Jones appeared willing to pay. In 1992, while wrapping up a two-season ledger that included 3,276 yards rushing, two NFL rushing titles, 30 touchdowns and a Super Bowl championship, Smith had made $465,000. Chump change was how he looked at it, especially after his Buffalo counterpart Thurman Thomas, star running back on the team the Cowboys had just dismantled in Pasadena, signed a new four-year deal for $13.5 million.

When Smith's agent declared that Emmitt was worth more than Thomas, there was no argument from Cowboys' fans or the media. Smith said he wanted $17 million for four years. Jones had countered with an offer of just $9 million, leaving an astonishing and seemingly unsurmountable $8 million gap.

Jones contended he had almost no wiggle room because of the new NFL salary cap that would slam into place in 1994. "If he has to miss a few games," Jones told reporters, "so be it."

In Dallas-Fort Worth, Cowboys fans rumbled ominously, especially after the Cowboys opened the season with a disappointing 35-16 loss at Washington and came home to lose 13-10 to Buffalo, the same team they'd just demolished by 38 points in Super Bowl XXVII. To that point, no team had ever lost its first two games of the season and gone on to the Super Bowl.

Jimmy Johnson's impatience and resentment of Jones (he didn't like it that the media occasionally gave Jerry some of the credit for the team's turnaround) had already surfaced in a Skip Bayless *Sports Illustrated* article after the '92 season when Jimmy was quoted as saying, "My girlfriend knows more football than Jerry." Now, Johnson, along with many of the players, were livid that Jones might be in the process of blowing the season by being tight-fisted with Emmitt.

In fact, there was an underlying hint that the Cowboys players might not have given their best effort against the Bills when SI's Peter King quoted an unnamed Cowboys' player as saying, "As crazy as it sounds, we knew the only way we could get our team back was to lose.

We weren't trying to lose, but we knew if we won a game, Jerry would figure we could get along without Emmitt. And we knew we're not the Dallas Cowboys without Emmitt."

Charles Haley was explosive in the postgame locker room after the Bills' loss, flinging his helmet against the wall and screaming "We're never going to win with this rookie running back!" as he walked past Derrick Lassic, the first-year back from Alabama who was trying his best to replace the league's best runner but had fumbled twice in the game.

The pressure on Jones to cut a deal was becoming immense and he upped his offer to $13.6 million for four years. Smith had publicly come down to $15.1 million. The problem was that the two weren't actually talking to each other. It finally took *Fort Worth Star-Telegram* Cowboys beat writer Mike Fisher to relay to Jones that Smith had told him he would take the $13.6 million – $100,000 more than Thomas got from the Bills – if Jones would just call and make the offer official.

Did a reporter actually save the Cowboys' season? That's probably overstating it. After all, Jones had finally arrived at a number that would satisfy Smith. It just took a little communication to get it done. At the very least, though, Fisher had helped to finally get it kick-started in the right direction.

Naturally, his teammates welcomed Smith back with open arms and immediately reeled off a seven-game winning streak. Smith averaged 106.5 yards per game and scored seven touchdowns in those seven victories, including a massive 30-carry, 237-yard game in a 23-10 romp over the Eagles. Smith's performance broke Tony Dorsett's club record of 206 yards (DeMarco Murray topped Smith with a 253-yard game against St. Louis as a rookie in 2011).

Everything was hunky-dory until the Cowboys stumbled in a 27-14 loss at Atlanta, followed by a fluke loss to Miami in a snow and ice covered Texas Stadium on Thanksgiving Day. Defensive tackle Leon Lett had gained infamy in the previous Super Bowl when he celebrated too early as he carried the football toward the end zone after a fumble recovery, only to have Don Beebe slap it out of his hand just before Lett reached the goal line. Considering it was a Cowboys' rout, it didn't matter anyway. Let one-upped himself on Thanksgiving Day after Jimmie Jones blocked the Dolphins' 41-yard field-goal attempt with Dallas leading 14-13 and only 15 seconds to play. All Dallas had to do was let the ball roll dead, then run out the clock for a victory. Instead, Lett came slipping and sliding into the ball, like some out of control giant bear on ice skates. The Dolphins recovered at the 1 and kicked an easy field goal to win, 16-14.

Flukes aside, the Cowboys were not to be deterred. They didn't lose another game all season. The finale at New York furnished Smith with an opportunity for his finest hour in a game the Cowboys needed to win for the NFC East title and home field advantage throughout the playoffs. Smith separated his shoulder at the end of a 46-yard gallop near the end of the first half and his availability in the second half was doubtful. In the Cowboys' lockerroom at halftime, he wept from the pain, but insisted he would play.

"I'd always heard about playing with pain," said Smith, whose career was amazingly injury-free. "I wanted to show I could do it, too."

Trainers taped his arm to his side down to the elbow and added extra pads to his shoulder.

The Cowboys led 13-0 at the half but the Giants cut it to 13-10 by the fourth quarter and David Treadwell's fourth quarter field goal tied it up and sent the game into overtime. Smith, despite the injury, put together a remarkable game, carrying 32 times for 168 yards and catching another 10 passes for 62 yards and a touchdown. The numbers represented the heaviest workload in franchise history.

"I don't know if it was my best game," Smith said, "but I knew how important it was."

In overtime, Smith touched the ball on nine of 11 plays to set up Eddie Murray's game-winning field goal.

"After the game, I remember Emmitt was bent over in the training room," Michael Irvin said later. "I was just thanking him for the game. We were both crying."

Smith wrapped up a third-straight NFL rushing title and won his first MVP. Interestingly, the vote was taken before that final game.

Smith would spend the night in a Dallas hospital, hooked up to IVs and pain-killers. The injury was diagnosed as a Grade 1 separation, the least degree, but if the Cowboys had lost and had to play the next week, it would have almost certainly have been without Emmitt.

Instead, the victory earned the Cowboys a week off before taking on Green Bay in the first round. Smith was limited to 13 carries for 60 yards but Troy Aikman skewered the Packers' defense by completing 28 of 35 passes for 302 yards and three touchdowns. Next up: the NFC championship game and the always challenging San Francisco 49ers.

On the Thursday night before the game, Jimmy Johnson added some spice to the contest when he spontaneously called into Randy Galloway's sports talk radio show on WBAP/820-AM. It didn't hurt that Jimmy had been relaxing with a few Heinekens on ice. "We will win the ballgame," Johnson predicted, "and you can put it in three-inch headlines. We will beat their rear end and go on to the Super Bowl. That's my personal opinion."

As usual, Johnson was right on the money. With Aikman playing an almost perfect first half – 14-of-18, 177 yards, 2 TDs – the Cowboys jumped out to a 28-7 halftime lead. Aikman was knocked out of the game with a concussion on the second play of the second half, but Bernie Kosar, Johnson's old quarterback at the University of Miami, stepped in to hit Alvin Harper with a 42-yard touchdown pass. Smith had a wonderful game, carrying 23 times for 88 yards and a touchdown and nabbing seven passes for another 85 yards and another TD.

Super Bowl XXVIII in Atlanta's Georgia Dome would pit the same antagonists as the previous Super Bowl. The NFL could only hope that it wouldn't also produce an equally disastrous runaway or TV sets might be clicking off by halftime all across America.

NFL officials got just what they wanted. The Bills, making their fourth straight Super Bowl appearance, were ready for the defending Super Bowl champs. They had the better offense, shut down the turnovers that plagued them a year earlier in Pasadena and kept defensive pressure on the Cowboys, holding them to a pair of field goals.

If only the game had ended at halftime.

The 13-6 lead Buffalo nursed at halftime blew up in a hurry. It took less than a minute into the second half to tie the score when James Washington snatched up a Thurman Thomas fumble and scampered 46 yards for the Cowboys' first touchdown. It was the first salvo in a run of 24 unanswered points.

Once the game was tied, the Cowboys felt confident in simply running it down the Bills' throats. Emmitt Smith carried on seven of eight plays for 61 yards of a 64-yard scoring drive in the third quarter. He capped the drive with a 15-yard run.

Emmitt plunged into the end zone on a fourth-and-one play early in the fourth quarter and Eddie Murray's 20-yard field goal with 2:50 left put the Bills to bed once and for all.

Smith, who had rushed for 108 yards a year earlier, tacked up 132 this time and earned MVP honors. He joined Miami's Larry Csonka as one of only two backs to post back-to-back 100-yard rushing games in the Super Bowl. In fact, Smith hit the trifecta in '93-'94, winning league MVP honors, a rushing title and the Super Bowl MVP trophy. How close, we have to wonder, did the Cowboys come to missing out on this Super Bowl victory because of, take your pick: a) Smith's holdout or, b) Jones' stubbornness in not giving him what he was worth at the beginning?

Better question: Could Jones have lived with himself if the impasse in negotiations had ultimately cost the Cowboys a trip back to the Super Bowl? Happily, for Jerry and for the fans, we never had to find out.

Smith had proven that he was worth every penny of that contract, if not more. The future looked even brighter than it ever had before for the Dallas Cowboys.

"You can't ask for anything more," Smith said after the game "Before every game, all we talk about is turnovers and touchdowns. That's what we got here.

"For me, there is a lot of room for growth and for the team to grow. This has been a great year for all of us. Everybody back in Dallas has a lot to cheer about and they're going to be cheering for a long time. I promise you."

Yes, there would be more cheering, but not quite like expected. It was a promise, it turns out, that even Emmitt couldn't keep. The chaos and turmoil ahead would be completely out of his control.

SUPER BOWL XXX
Dallas 27, Pittsburgh 17
January 28, 1996 • Tempe, Arizona

Ah, yes, Super Bowl Triple X: The perfect designation for the Dallas Cowboys' 1995 season from hell. That it would come to an end in Tempe, Arizona, with Jerry Jones and Barry Switzer hoisting the Cowboys' third Super Bowl trophy in four years, makes it all the more astounding, all the more poignant, all the more mystifying. It speaks mostly to how incredibly talented those Cowboys' teams of the mid-'90s truly were. It also begs the question: how did something that went so wrong, so fast, end up with yet another wild Cowboys' celebration in the desert? There are no easy answers to that question, only what-ifs, and what might-have-beens.

As a personal sub-plot, Super Bowl XXX would also provide a career journalistic highlight as well as stand as a character-tester for me. Somehow, though, it was the Cowboys who captured all the headlines and glory. Imagine that. I was simply relieved that the Cowboys won the game and no one burned my house down back in Texas. More on that later.

To fully appreciate what the Cowboys accomplished with their Neil O'Donnell gift-wrapped 27-17 victory over the Pittsburgh Steelers, it is necessary to rewind back to a year earlier, 1994, and Switzer's first year as Cowboys' coach. It is important to remember that not every player in the Cowboys' organization was unhappy at Jimmy Johnson's shocking departure. Sure, they appreciated his ability to wring every ounce of sweat and tears from them. They respected his drive to win and make them winners, too, but there was also a sense of relief knowing that things were going to be a little more relaxed around Valley Ranch with the easy-going Switzer in charge. Switzer, the players knew and would see firsthand, liked to party and have a good time as much or more than they did.

In a way, what was about to hit Valley Ranch was the same kind of organizational culture shock that the hard-driving, in-your-face Johnson had brought with him when he replaced Tom Landry, who certainly had his own rigid, but mostly hands-off, professional style. For the Cowboys players, the party was just getting started. Johnson had no problem jumping on players for showing up late to practice or meetings; stars, subs, clipboard-holders, didn't matter. Switzer shrugged and looked the other way. Johnson tolerated no on-field horsing around or frivolity during practice. Switzer sometimes joined in himself. Johnson could stare down a player who might not show up at his best physically. Switzer, no hypocrite, shared hangover stories with them. Switzer hated and refused to set team curfews, because, Lord knows, he darn sure wasn't going to adhere to one himself.

It was as if pop had just handed the keys to the brand new Porsche to 16-year-old Billy Bob Jr., fresh out of military school.

"Jimmy was tough. It was a challenging time but there was tremendous success," fullback Daryl "Moose" Johnston said in an interview for this book. "Jimmy held everybody accountable. You were expected to perform at a certain level. He prepared you and on Sunday, you had all the confidence in the world that you would be able to get the job done.

"Barry ruled with a looser hand. We needed that discipline and structure that Jimmy provided. Barry felt we were men and could navigate things on our own."

Wrong. Switzer's philosophy was that he was dealing with grown men, professionals, and he left it to them to police themselves. History tells us how well that worked out. Given more and more rope, the Cowboys players would gradually do what came naturally: string themselves up.

"When Jimmy left, Jerry called me into his office and asked me what I thought of Switzer and I was all for the hire," quarterback Troy Aikman told me. "The guy I played for my two years at Oklahoma was a motivated and driven football coach. That's not who we got when he came to Dallas.

"I don't blame him for that necessarily because times had changed and I think the mandate for him was really just to drive the bus. Again, I think it points out that there was a lack of respect for what Jimmy did to get our team prepared on a weekly basis."

Jones, in other words, never fully appreciated what Johnson had accomplished or even the role of the head coach in the NFL.

"It's hard to win in this league," Aikman said. "I've said in college you can win a fair number of games with just great coaching and you can win with just great talent, but in the NFL you have to have both. One just isn't going to get it done. I don't think there was enough respect for what went into getting a team prepared and I suppose Jerry said that himself when he said that any of 500 coaches could win a Super Bowl with that team.

"I think decisions started being made to make people comfortable, rather than what was best for our team. There's a price for winning and sometimes that's hurt feelings, and egos get affected. The second half of my career I thought we were being put together to make people comfortable instead of necessarily to win."

All of this unrest and uncertainty boiled beneath the surface throughout the '94 season after Switzer arrived. The team that had just won two straight Super Bowls was still mostly intact but key coaches had been hired away. Still, the prevailing thought in the media was that maybe even Switzer couldn't screw this up. Certainly the problems boiling beneath the surface weren't obvious to the public, who watched the Cowboys surge to another 12-4 season and bury Green Bay 35-9 in the divisional playoff round.

As usual, though, the road to the Super Bowl wound through San Francisco, which is where the Cowboys found themselves for the NFC championship game on January 15, 1995. It would become one of the Cowboys' most memorable games, one of their proudest moments, and that it ended in a hugely disappointing 38-28 loss takes none of the luster off what Aikman considers perhaps his personal finest hour.

An interception and two fumbles turned into a 21-0 49ers lead in the first quarter. The Cowboys furiously battled back and ultimately out-gained the 49ers 451 yards to 294. Aikman passed for a then NFC championship game record 390 yards. Michael Irvin caught 11 passes for a record 192. All afternoon it seemed as if the Cowboys were on the verge of a miraculous comeback. But they could never quite get those first 21 points back. Switzer was so irate at the lack of a flag on then-49ers' cornerback Deion Sanders for interfering with Irvin late in the game, he drew a critical 15-yard unsportsmanlike conduct penalty.

Aikman was so proud of the way he and his teammates battled that day at Candlestick Park, he chose a photo of himself walking off the field after the game, his jersey muddied and sweat-stained, for the cover of the invitation to his post-Hall of Fame induction party at Canton, Ohio.

At that point of his career, Aikman couldn't have been sure he would ever have another chance at a Super Bowl. He certainly had no idea he would get that opportunity just a year later, thanks to his own resilience and the Cowboys' ability to somehow get things done on the field while near-chaos reigned behind the scenes.

"Barry gets a lot of blame, but we were losing players, losing coaches, and it was a no-win situation when he came in," Johnston said. "It wasn't going to end well. (Because of) the greatness of Barry Switzer, both things happened. We did win another championship, but things started to fall apart under his watch."

The problems weren't all that obvious throughout the '95 regular season, with the Cowboys winning eight of their first nine games. They were 10-2 heading into December, a critical month as the NFC East race came down to the wire. No Super Bowl team in the last 25 years had ever lost more than one game in December.

By now, the subterranean fault lines beneath the team had spread so far, so wide that they would even eventually affect the one position that the Cowboys – or any NFL team, for that matter – could least afford: quarterback. It began with Aikman feeling that he was being forced into playing the demanding Jimmy Johnson role because the new head coach wouldn't. During an early December practice, Aikman scolded wide receiver Kevin Williams for not focusing on a sideline route during what would become a 24-17 loss to Washington on December 3. Williams barked back and their disagreement blew up into a full-scale shouting match, continuing on the sideline.

Aikman would apologize to Williams later, but the exchange had been so heated and Williams so upset, the almost immediate and unfounded rumor was that he had crossed the line and used the "n-word," something Aikman insisted never happened. It certainly didn't fit the character of the Aikman everyone knew. Aikman felt sure that defensive line coach John Blake, a Switzer friend from OU, was behind the whispers of racism. In fact, Blake had gone to Switzer to voice concern that Aikman seemed to come down harder on some of the black players. Finally fed up with the constant behind-the-scenes whispers, rumors and melodrama, Aikman asked Switzer for the opportunity to address the entire team to settle the issue once and for all. Switzer said he didn't want to do that.

For an incensed Aikman, it was the last straw. He needed the head coach's support and didn't feel he was getting it. Even as the Cowboys clawed their way toward their third Super Bowl in four years, the team's starting quarterback vowed not to speak to the head coach again.

December had started out badly with the loss at home to the Redskins. It didn't get any better with a 20-17 defeat at the hands of the Eagles in Philadelphia a week later when Aikman, his focus obviously shattered by the turbulence at Valley Ranch, struggled badly in the wind at a miserably cold Veterans Stadium. Rodney Peete led the Eagles back from a 17-6 halftime deficit to a victory that threatened to decimate the shaken Cowboys.

This was the game in which Switzer would be publicly skewered for twice calling for a running play dubbed "load left" when the Cowboys faced a fourth-and-one foot at their own 20-yard line in a game tied 17-all. That's right, at their own 20-yard line! After Emmitt Smith, running behind Mark Tuinei, Nate Newton and Daryl Johnston, came up short the first time, the Cowboys got a reprieve when the ref blew his whistle signaling the two-minute warning. Punt now into a vicious wind and play for overtime, right? Nope. Stubbornly, Switzer called the same play, with the same result, again.

"They deserve to lose," a disgusted John Madden grumbled on the national TV telecast. Four plays later, the Eagles took their gift 42-yard field goal and a 20-17 victory. The loss, coupled with a 49ers' victory, gave San Francisco the edge for home field advantage and allowed the Eagles to close to within one game in the NFC East.

Interestingly, the Cowboys' players to a man supported Switzer's decision. Aikman flatly said he didn't think it was the wrong call. The media, both local and national, totally disagreed. A headline in the *New York Post* even labeled Switzer, "Bozo the Coach."

Remember, the Cowboys' soap opera starring Aikman and Switzer was playing out totally behind the scenes, out of the eyes of the media and fans. Over the final weeks of the season, bits and pieces of the story would occasionally surface, but reporters couldn't quite nail down exactly what was going on or why the big chill had settled over Valley Ranch. Aikman quelled some of the digging by telling a few favored reporters he would sit down and tell them the whole story when the season was over.

What was obvious was that the Cowboys were in deep trouble if they couldn't win their final two games of the season, at home against the New York Giants and on the road at Phoenix against the Cardinals. In their seven combined Super Bowl seasons, Tom Landry and Jimmy Johnson's teams had gone 26-2 in their final four games of the season. Switzer's team was now 0-2 and cracking. Even with the 5-9 New York Giants coming to Texas Stadium, Cowboys' fans had every reason to be nervous.

So if I told you that the Giants unleashed buffalo-sized running back Rodney Hampton for 187 yards rushing on 34 carries, that the Giants converted nine of 15 third-down opportunities, that New York owned the clock, 33:05-to-26:55, that Aikman went 3-of-9 for 66 yards in the first half and that he threw a critical interception with the Giants leading 20-18 and only 3½ minutes left in the game, I could probably convince you that Cowboys lost this game and never really went to Super Bowl XXX, right? Who said numbers don't lie? Somehow the Cowboys defense held the Giants to a three-and-out when it mattered most. Then Aikman, with key passes to – guess who? – Kevin Williams, led the Cowboys down the field from their own 25 and Chris Boniol pulled out the unlikely 21-20 victory with his fifth field goal of the game, a 35-yarder.

On the same day, the 49ers held on for a 37-30 win over the Minnesota Vikings. To get the critical first-round bye and home field advantage in the playoffs, the Cowboys would have to win their finale at Arizona on Christmas Day and pray that the 9-6 Atlanta Falcons could somehow upset the 11-4 49ers on Christmas Eve. Somehow, even for a team disintegrating from the inside out, the fates aligned perfectly.

"We needed something positive to happen," Daryl Johnston said. "I think people forget the dynamics at that time, what was happening in the NFL. We couldn't beat San Francisco. San Francisco couldn't beat Green Bay and Green Bay couldn't beat us. When we were flying out to Arizona, Atlanta upset San Francisco that day. So if we won, we got home field. It meant San Francisco would have to host Green Bay. Everything came out to benefit us.

"Green Bay had really struggled in Dallas in the playoffs. We're on the plane and something happened (Atlanta's victory) that nobody expected. With a win (Christmas) night, we're right back in it. Like everything, there was a little bit of luck involved."

Or was it simply a really nice Christmas gift from Ol' St. Nick?

Give the Cowboys credit, they didn't waste the opportunity. Full of confidence and rekindled hope, they went out and destroyed Buddy Ryan's desperate 4-11 Cardinals, 37-13. Aikman hooked up with his new BFF Kevin Williams nine times for 203 yards and a pair of touchdowns.

Santa Claus had one more surprise for the Cowboys, too. Back at Switzer U, the Sooners had decided that a year of Howard Schnellenberger and his 5-5-1 record was enough. The OU faithful all but held candlelight vigils in hopes that Switzer would return. If Cowboys' fans had known what was going on at Valley Ranch, they might have done the same. But Switzer wasn't about to turn the clock back at Oklahoma. Instead, emerging as one of the leading candidates for the OU job was none other than Cowboys' assistant John Blake. It seems highly likely that Switzer had a great deal to do with OU's ultimate decision to hire Blake, both because it was a great job for his old friend and because it might help settle things down inside Valley Ranch. Thus, the Cowboys graciously assured Blake he could go ahead and get started in his new job and they'd somehow manage to muddle along in the playoffs without him.

With a full week to prepare and playing at home, fueled by the Packers' 27-17 pounding of the 49ers a day earlier, the Cowboys crunched the Eagles 30-11. Aikman was 17-of-24 for 253 yards and a touchdown. The rekindled Kevin Williams caught six passes for 124 yards. Emmitt Smith carried 21 times for 99 yards and a TD. No doubt, there were more than a few "load lefts" mixed in that day.

The NFC championship game broke just as Johnston thought it would. Trailing the Packers 27-24 entering the final quarter at Texas Stadium, Aikman led the Cowboys on a 14-play, 90-yard march, capped by Smith's 5-yard touchdown run. Aikman completed 6-of-7 passes during the drive.

Larry Brown's interception of Brett Favre and a 36-yard Aikman-to-Michael Irvin pass set up Smith's 16-yard run to cap the scoring and insure a 38-27 Cowboys' victory. Against all odds and despite all of the sub-plots and intrigue at Valley Ranch, the Cowboys were headed back to their third Super Bowl in four years.

As Terrell Owens would say some years down the road, "grab your popcorn," and find a seat, the real show was about to get started.

Having been to Super Bowls in Pasadena and Atlanta, most of the Cowboys' players knew what to expect and how to make the most of Super Bowl week, especially now that the rigid and demanding Jimmy Johnson wouldn't be here to ride herd on his crew. Under the loose and care-free Switzer, the attitude was, anything goes.

Super Bowl week thus began with a cavalcade of 11 stretch limos, each rented by a Cowboys' player from the Dallas company First Impressions, tooling into the long driveway at Phoenix's posh desert resort, The Buttes, Cowboy headquarters for the week. It was as if The Academy Awards had come to the desert. The only thing missing was the red carpet. The Buttes, a gorgeous, sprawling, multiple-wing hotel carved into the red sandstone cliffs that surround the city, would have been happy to supply that, too, if Jerry Jones had asked.

If anyone suggested that perhaps the Cowboys were going a little bit over the top this time around, the players indignantly noted that the limos would help them avoid DUIs, a defense that would have appalled Johnson because it suggested they planned on doing a lot of drinking during the week.

In fact, one of the biggest early stories was whether Jones and the Cowboys could somehow find a way to circumvent Phoenix's 1 a.m. last call ordinance on the night after the game. Jerry, who had thrown massive postgame parties that lasted into the wee hours of the morning following the team's last two Super Bowl appearances, was determined that this would be his best ever. The fact that Jerry was already referring to it as the team's "victory party" only made the Cowboys seem that much more arrogant.

Jones would eventually strike an agreement that would allow him to pitch the world's largest heated party tent on a parking lot a quarter mile down the hill from the hotel. Officials could legally look the other way, because now it was a private party. The party, said to have a $250,000 price tag, would rock loudly until after 4 a.m.

But let's not get ahead of ourselves. For the journalists there, it was an interesting week. On Tuesday, Wednesday and Thursday of Super Bowl week, players from both teams meet the media for an hour a day at hotel venues, where they sit at individual tables in large ballrooms and hold court. On Tuesday morning during the Cowboys' hour at Media Day at Sun Devil Stadium, Aikman made vague allusions to the team's internal problems without elaborating to reporters, most of whom had no idea what he was talking about. Some of us, however, were finally getting a peek at the underbelly of the team's dysfunctional situation.

A week earlier when the *Fort Worth Star-Telegram*'s team of Super Bowl columnists and reporters met for a strategy and planning meeting, I had stressed that we needed to finally get to the bottom of this story that was looming like the Titanic iceberg just beneath the surface. Understand, it is extremely difficult to break news stories at the Super Bowl. There's rarely a chance for one-on-one interviews or conversations. But every sports journalist hopes to have the opportunity.

To that end, I had landed a one-on-one interview with Jerry Jones in his hotel suite on Tuesday night. That hour-long recorded chat would play a key part in the column I would write for Thursday morning's paper. I had also made it a point to "accidentally" run into players close to Aikman at the hotel early in the week. Some of them had been extremely helpful for background or off the record. Putting the information I gathered there together with the interview with Jones, I finally felt like I had enough to go with the story.

As luck would have it, late Wednesday afternoon, having written my column, I ran into Aikman sitting alone in one of the many atrium entrances around the resort, waiting for a ride. I told him what I'd written and asked him to confirm whether it was essentially correct. He said it was and gave me a quote I could use as well.

The story broke in Thursday morning's edition of the *Star-Telegram*. The lead – the first paragraph – read: "The Cowboys will attempt to win their third Super Bowl in four years Sunday with a coach and a quarterback who are barely speaking and an owner who is convinced that a victory against the Steelers is the panacea for that trouble relationship. He's dead wrong."

Aikman was quoted, saying, "The idea that one game, one victory, would change the way I feel about this season – no, that's not going to happen."

I also wrote, "Aikman, on more than one occasion the past few weeks, has called this season 'the most difficult of my career.' ... The internal strife is at the root of the problem between Switzer and Aikman. Friends of the quarterback say the two haven't spoken more than a few words to each other since mid-season (it was actually since November). That's when reports got back to Aikman that defensive line coach John Blake ... complained to Switzer that Aikman regularly seemed to single out black players as targets for his occasional angry outbursts. The quarterback was furious and took pains to ask other players and coaches whether they had a problem with his approach."

I had quoted Switzer, too. "I respect him (Aikman). If he wants to respect me is not important ... I don't go around asking him."

If he had, it's doubtful Aikman would have responded anyway. Earlier in the week the two had found themselves on the same elevator at The Buttes. They stared straight ahead and neither spoke.

The time frame was off in the story – the problems started near the first of December, not at mid-season – but the rest was essentially correct.

The story hit like a bombshell with word filtering around – remember, this was before the world had been taken over by the Internet – just about the time the Cowboys were showing up for their final mandatory media session of the week. They would only have to deal with the questions and fallout for 45 minutes or so.

For the players this was old news. For them, the issue had been settled when Aikman and Williams talked things out and when Blake departed. They spent the hour denying that Aikman was a racist. Michael Irvin was especially passionate in the defense of his quarterback and friend.

"I don't know what John Blake said," Irvin declared to a host of reporters. "I am as black as anybody you could ever see. I am as black as they come. And I know this man (Aikman) loves me."

Switzer was under siege a few yards away as reporters barraged him with questions about his relationship with Aikman.

"We are committed to winning," he said. "That's all that's important. I'm not going to drink R.C. Colas or double-date with him, but that's not important."

Meanwhile, Aikman was trying his best to keep things under control.

"The players on this team know it has been discussed, it has been resolved and that is all that matters," Aikman told the clamoring reporters. "There are a number of things being written about this week regarding my relationship with Barry. I don't think anybody pays any attention to it within our organization or locker room."

When the Cowboys players and coaches were finally able to beat a hasty retreat, I found myself wishing I could go with them. I was immediately surrounded by 20 or so reporter friends, begging for more information. Most had not even had a chance to see the column yet. About the only thing I could offer was to tell them to find the story and read it.

My phone rang at 6:30 the next morning. It was The Ticket's (KTCK) morning show boys, Craig Miller and George Dunham. They were doing their show in an outside alcove at The Buttes and asked if I would come out and pop on with them to discuss my column.

Overnight a cold front had hit Phoenix and it was freezing outside. The radio hosts were bundled up in quilts and had an extra one for me. Most of the callers were irate that I would dare to potentially upset the Cowboys players with such a report practically on the eve of the Super Bowl. Didn't I want them to win? I tried to explain that this wasn't breaking news for the players, but no one was really listening.

Then Jerry Jones joined the party by phone. Jerry promptly began denying pretty much everything he'd told me in our interview and pooh-poohing the story, saying things weren't nearly as bad between Aikman and Switzer as I'd suggested. I could only shake my head in frustration.

That night on ESPN, Chris Berman and other network anchors dismissed the story, essentially saying they'd seen no problems when they were around the Cowboys so there must be nothing to it. This, despite Aikman's confirmation in front of dozens of reporters earlier that day.

"(The allusion to racism) had been dealt with earlier in the season because I dealt with it right away," Aikman said for this book "I went right to the bottom of it and said I'm going to find out who said what.

"It came back to an assistant coach (Blake) who was basically trying to protect his turf. There was no validity to it whatsoever. It was created and manufactured by someone trying to disparage me because of what I thought we needed to do. I confronted it right away, went to the people who supposedly had been affected, and everyone knew it was bullshit."

That's pretty much how Cowboys' fans back in Texas felt about it, too. A local TV station sent a crew to the managing editor's office at the newspaper in downtown Fort Worth to interview her about the column. Letters to the editor were basically calling for my head (not the first time and not the last). If I'd never rooted for the Cowboys to win before (and I had, quietly of course) I would be on Sunday. I didn't want to think about how bad things might get if they lost.

I don't remember if I ever mailed that "Thank You" card to Neil O'Donnell. I certainly intended to do that. If you didn't get it, Neil, please accept my eternal gratitude. It was a bad day for you, but a very good one for the Cowboys and a huge relief for me to think that maybe the homestead wouldn't be torched after all.

The Cowboys led just 13-7 in the third quarter when O'Donnell had his first brain-dead moment. His pass down the right side wasn't even close to a Steelers' receiver. In fact, the only uniform in the same ZIP code was Larry Brown. He gratefully intercepted the ball, rambled to the Steelers' 18 and in just two plays, the Cowboys led 20-7.

Then it got hairy. A Pittsburgh field goal sliced it to 20-10 with 11:20 left in the game. Onside kick, right? Everyone in the stadium and millions watching at home knew what was coming, but still the Steelers recovered the onside kick. Nine plays and 52 yards later, after Bam Morris' one-yard touchdown plunge, it was 20-17 and sweat was beginning to trickle down the back of my neck.

It turned into a deluge when Aikman was sacked and the Cowboys had to give the Steelers the ball back with 4:15 to play. But on second-and-10 at their own 36, O'Donnell rode to the rescue one more time. Facing a Cowboys' blitz, a panicked O'Donnell whistled a pass into the flat for his safety receiver. Except he wasn't there. Larry

Brown, that man about town, was in the right place at the right time once again. The ball buried itself in Brown's midsection. He yanked it out of his belly button and scampered to the Pittsburgh 6-yard line. Two plays later, Emmitt Smith bolted in from four yards out to seal the Cowboys' 27-17 victory and their third Lombardi Trophy in four years. No word on whether Brown, named Super Bowl MVP, sent his own thank-you card to O'Donnell.

For all the turmoil, all the intrigue, all the chaos throughout the season, there were Switzer and Jerry Jones on the dais at Sun Devil Stadium, taking turns shaking the Lombardi Trophy over their heads while Switzer shouted, "We did it! We did it! We did it!"

Indeed, somehow they had.

The postgame player interviews were vastly unlike those following the team's victories at the Rose Bowl and the Georgia Dome. This time, the prevailing attitude from most was one of simple relief, not just that they'd won, but also that the long, divisive season was finally over.

Somehow, Switzer and Aikman would find a way to co-exist for another two seasons, but the quarterback's concerns that the lack of structure and discipline would have a price were validated. Michael Irvin's drug and legal troubles would begin to play out in the media in '96. The infamous Valley Ranch "White House," where many of the Cowboys players partied, was outed. Hollywood Henderson's cocaine addiction was splashed across the papers.

Then, in the 1996 divisional playoff round at Carolina, Irvin suffered a dislocated shoulder and the Cowboys were routed 26-17. The next season, they fell to 6-10 and out of the playoffs. Switzer was fired, but not soon enough for Aikman. The Cowboys had begun their long swoon toward mediocrity. After the 2000 season, only 33 years old but victimized by 10 concussions and persistent back pain, Aikman retired.

"I think everybody has their little things they deal with in life," Aikman said. "When it's you, you tend to view it a little differently than when it's somebody else. That (1995) was not an enjoyable season for me. Each year got a little bit tougher after '93.

"It became clearer to me that we weren't making good decisions for the betterment of our team. It would have been nice to have been with an organization late in my career that was really on top of things. As good as it was in the first half it was just as bad on the back end. I don't let those tough times overshadow the front end. I was fortunate to be with the Cowboys in those early years."

Like all Cowboys' fans, Aikman can't help but wonder what might have been if … if Johnson had stayed around … if Jerry had hired a coach other than Switzer … if, if, if.

And like all the rest of us, he will never know.

The Breakup

More than two decades later it is still inconceivable to those who lived through it, even witnessed it firsthand, that Jerry Jones and Jimmy Johnson couldn't co-exist long enough to win a Super Bowl ring for every finger. There's a scene in the classic movie *Scarface* after Florida drug kingpin Tony Montana has just pulled a coup and murdered his boss to take over the business himself when a neon-sign-carrying blimp passes over his Miami mansion with the message, "The World Is Yours."

That's pretty much where Jones and Johnson were after the 1993 season when the Dallas Cowboys had just trampled the Buffalo Bills – again – to win their second straight Super Bowl. Troy Aikman was on a star path few NFL quarterbacks ever tread. Emmitt Smith was simply the best at his craft and was just coming into his own. Michael Irvin, Jay Novacek, Alvin Harper, that incredible Cowboys' defense. This was the right moment in time, the right place for the Cowboys to build an unchallenged NFL dynasty. The world was their oyster, complete with a giant pearl in the middle of it.

And then Jerry and Jimmy spit it out.

It wasn't enough for Jerry Jones and Jimmy Johnson. Not even Texas Stadium was big enough to contain their out-of-control egos. Jerry wanted Jimmy to at least acknowledge his presence in the draft room, maybe even act like Jerry was making a contribution there, no matter how fraudulent that might be. Jimmy wanted Jerry to just go away and write checks, leave the football completely to him. Jerry, no Clint Murchison, hadn't paid $140 million for the Dallas Cowboys to be told to get lost by the coach he'd hired. The squabble turned from off-season soap opera into a full-fledged divorce tragedy.

Meanwhile, nobody seemed to care about the "kids," also known as the players, who were shell-shocked that their owner and their head coach, at the pinnacle of team success, would be so stupid, so careless, so selfish, that they would even consider breaking up a winning partnership that meant so much to the players, the community, even the entire state of Texas.

"It's very disappointing because I can honestly say that our team during those years was a really unselfish group and yet Jimmy and Jerry couldn't get along because they couldn't agree on who should get the credit," Troy Aikman told me. "Believe me, that wasn't going on among the players. That's the most disappointing thing to me."

It's important to understand that these two former University of Arkansas roommates were never particularly close friends despite how the media had initially portrayed them. It just made for a nice little story angle. As Johnson wrote in his book *Turning the Thing Around*, he learned more about Jerry and what he was about in the 10 or 11 days before the announcement that Jones had bought the Cowboys than he had in the previous 28 years he'd known him. They had roomed together on Friday nights before Razorback games, both on the road and in Fayetteville, because the rooming list was drawn up alphabetically.

"How well do you get to know a guy on a few Friday nights in the Holiday Inns of Waco, or Fort Worth, or Austin?" Jimmy wrote. "Not very. You get off the plane, board the bus, ride to the hotel, pick up your room key, throw your things in the room, go to the team dinner, then into team meetings, then to the room to make curfew. Maybe you lie there on your beds talking about the opponents for a few minutes, or bitch a little about how hard practice has gone all week, but that's about it. Lights out. Jerry and I spent a total of about 30 such nights together in our lives. Then we'd gone out into the world, rarely to see each other over the next 24 years."

Neither had thought they would pursue football after college. Jones was headed for the insurance and oil and gas business. Johnson's plan was to become an industrial psychologist. The plan was derailed when he spent three months as an interim coach at Louisiana Tech and was hooked. Fate had brought the two former college teammates back together again with the Dallas Cowboys.

Even before the end of the '93 season, Jones and Johnson, two demanding and high-ego personalities, were already getting under each other's skin. Johnson, who wanted to be Tom Landry and Tex Schramm all rolled into one, hated what he labeled Jerry's pretense of being a football guy. Jerry resented his head coach's resistance to the owner's need to be a part of everything. They had bonded together over their singular drive to win, first at Arkansas and now in Dallas. But once that was attained, the relationship foundered.

As David Magee wrote in his book with Jones, *Playing to Win, Jerry Jones and the Dallas Cowboys*, "Jones was a family man, a hugger and backslapper who enjoyed big gatherings and up-close-and-personal warmth." Johnson, on the other hand, shunned parties and multiple personal relationships. He liked to celebrate big moments with his coaches, the men who helped him attain success, but preferred time alone on his boat in the Florida Keys. Jerry was and is a party animal. He likes having people of like mind around him. Jimmy is the lone wolf.

The conflict, it seems, was inevitable. During the '93 season Johnson had already fired a warning shot by alluding to his intrigue with a potential coach/general manager gig in Jacksonville. Jones attempted to shrug the barb off as a joke, but was clearly bothered by it.

The rest reads like a bad Hollywood script. Another party, this one at Disney's Pleasure Island during the NFL's spring meetings in Orlando following the '93 Super Bowl championship season. Johnson sat at a table with two of his former assistants, Dave Wannstedt and Norv Turner, along with former Cowboys' personnel chief Bob Ackles, whom Jones had fired a year earlier in order to replace him with son Stephen. Jones was in a celebratory mood. He felt a rapport that men share when they've accomplished something together. Jerry had already had several cocktails when he walked up to the table and lifted a toast to them for their part in helping the Cowboys raise two Super Bowl trophies. The response from those at the table was muted, at best. Johnson, by never saying a word, made his boss feel like what he hated being most of all – an outsider.

Jerry knows a snub when it slaps him in the face. According to author Peter Golenbock, he angrily snapped at Johnson, "You can go back to your fucking party now," and stalked off. For all intents and purposes, their relationship ended then and there. The rest would just be details.

Later, back at the Hyatt Regency Hotel, Jones repaired to the bar and sought solace with his favorite painkiller du jour. He was not bashful as he ranted to friends about the slight he'd just received from Johnson. "I should have fired him and brought in Barry Switzer," Jones fumed loudly. "There are 500 coaches who could have won the Super Bowl with our team." It was Jones' calculated answer to Jimmy's earlier insult in a *Sports Illustrated* article that his girlfriend knew more about football than Jerry did.

The Hyatt bar was filled with fans, NFL employees, and at least four reporters, some from Dallas. The newspaper headlines the next day proved that none of them were deaf.

I was in Port Charlotte, south of Sarasota on Florida's west coast, at Rangers' spring training when the story broke in the next morning's papers. Before mid-morning, I was in the car, headed to Orlando. That night, I found myself alone with Jerry in his suite at the Hyatt Regency, trying to figure out if he had really meant what he said. Did he really intend to fire Johnson, who had partnered with him to win the last two Super Bowls? Was there still a way to back out of this? Could both men save face and continue what had been a very lucrative arrangement?

Jerry said he wasn't sure. Nor did he seem overly concerned about it. He was still smarting from the snub the night before. OK, I said, but you can't be serious about hiring Switzer, the same coach who had prevailed over a University of Oklahoma program that had been riddled with scandal and left in disgrace, right? That was just a way to goad Jimmy, wasn't it?

"Why not?" Jerry shot back. "He's a great coach."

That's when I knew that the Cowboys were in serious trouble.

Switzer would inherit a remarkable Cowboys' team and take it to the NFC championship game in San Francisco after the '94 season, where the Cowboys played one of their greatest games ever and still lost. A year later, the Cowboys, on sheer talent alone, survived a chaotic, controversy-filled season to battle their way to Super Bowl XXX, where they somehow beat the hated Pittsburgh Steelers 27-17. Even now, players look back at that season and wonder how they did it.

"We were walking off the field after winning the Super Bowl and (assistant coach) Joe Brodsky came up to me and said, 'That was the greatest achievement I have ever seen. You won despite the coaching,'" Darryl Johnston said. "There were a lot of challenges at the back end of the season. We were not a team that was in synch at that time."

The Cowboys won three Super Bowls in four years, but the question everyone asks, even more than two decades later, is this: How many more Super Bowls might they have won if Johnson had remained as head coach?

It's a question with no simple or easy answer. The NFL was changing, implementing a salary cap and expanding free agency. Cowboys' team success meant that Johnson's top lieutenants, like Wannstedt and Turner, were leaving for their own head coaching jobs.

"My answer to that (question) has always been that I don't know if we would have won any more," Aikman told me. "My gut says we likely would have. But when you get into that, it takes away from how hard it is to win a Super Bowl.

"I think we would have been really good for a long period of time. We would have been right there, knocking on the door year after year, the way New England has been in the hunt, year after year, since (Tom) Brady and (Bill) Belichick arrived, that's how we would have been. I'm really disappointed that we couldn't keep that group together."

Like Aikman, Daryl Johnston says there is no definitive answer possible because of all the circumstances involved.

"It was kind of the perfect storm," Johnston said. "It wasn't just Jimmy leaving. We weren't just losing some of our players to free agency; we were losing (assistant) coaches, too, people who had made a huge difference for us.

"How many could we have won? If we could have kept the whole group together....some of us say four, some say five. If our coaching staff stays the same as in '92-'93, the sky's the limit. Even with free agency, it would still have been a unique franchise."

Back in Dallas after the NFL meetings in Orlando, Jimmy and Jerry did get together to see if there was a way to patch things up, but neither had their hearts in it. Jimmy ultimately settled on a $2 million buyout of the last five years of his 10-year contract. Jerry, as he'd promised, hired Barry Switzer.

"Gunsmoke" days had arrived in Dallas. Not surprisingly, within two years the franchise was adrift in controversy and scandal.

Keeping Up With The Joneses

First things first: Yes, Jerry Jones has said it before and he'll say it again: if he had it to do over again, he would have handled Tom Landry's firing much differently. Not that the deed wouldn't have been done. Landry's epic 29-year run as Cowboys' head coach was doomed with the sale. But not the way it happened, not when it happened, not how it happened.

Secondly, because it's perhaps the most asked question he gets from media and fans whenever he grants in-depth interviews about his tenure as Cowboys' owner, given another chance, he also would have tried harder to make peace with Jimmy Johnson and keep him around as Cowboys coach for another year or three. Now, Jerry being a little less hard-line with Johnson might not have changed anything. It takes two to do the Texas two-step and, at the time, Jerry and Jimmy were stepping all over each other's toes. But on his end, Jones wishes he'd tried harder, been more tolerant, more understanding, more forgiving. Like the rest of Cowboys Nation, he can't help but wonder what might have happened with the Cowboys if he and Jimmy could have somehow put their differences aside for another year or three.

"I look back at my own experiences, my own mistakes, and obviously there are plenty of those," Jones said. "I second-guess all the ones that I can point directly to that didn't turn out right. There are some I wish I had a chance to do over again."

One of those is the way Jones' ownership began, with his handling of the Landry firing and how it left such a bitter taste with fans, some of whom still haven't forgiven him. If it's any consolation, he doesn't blame them. He's not sure he has forgiven himself either.

"I'll go back to Day One," Jones said. "I got in a big hurry to switch staffs when I bought the team. I got in a big hurry to bring Jimmy in and make the change with Coach Landry. I got in a big hurry to do that because we were trying to get – and I'm not blaming anybody – but the college staffs were being put together and Jimmy really wanted to bring (Dave) Wannstedt and his Miami college staff to Dallas. If we didn't get it done real quick, we were running out of the time to be able to have flexibility because coaches were making commitments at the college level.

"When I announced the purchase, it was too fast to come behind that, that quick, with a coaching change of Coach Landry. It was just too fast. Not necessarily fast by the year, I'm not going that far. We should have announced the purchase of the team and then the coaching change later, whether it be weeks, months, whatever, but not the same night. Too fast."

In retrospect, Jones admits he also should have let former owner Bum Bright handle the distasteful job of firing Landry. Bright wanted to do it. At the time, Jones felt it was his responsibility.

"Contrary to appearances, I had such respect for Coach Landry and for those coaches. Not just coaches, those coaches," Jones said. "(Making the change at that time) created a perception that I didn't (respect them), when in fact, it was just the opposite.

"When you look at the times, and how bad the financial times were in the country, to come in and make that financial commitment, you shouldn't necessarily have been Darth Vader (to Cowboys fans). I mean, you shouldn't have been. But I helped that along."

Five years later, Jones stumbled over his ego again, this time when he couldn't, or wouldn't, find common ground with former college roommate Johnson, despite the fact the two had just won back-to-back Super Bowls together. Both were stubborn. Neither would back down.

"If I had it to do over again, I would have been more tolerant (regarding) my reasons for changing Jimmy," Jones admitted. "I would have been more tolerant of anything I did that influenced that decision. I'm not saying I totally influenced the decision at all. There were two of us. But my part of it. And that's not because we didn't have success (after Jimmy) because I view the success that we had with

Barry (Switzer) as very successful. That was a harder job than people give him credit for.

"If I had (splitting with Jimmy) to do over again, I would have accepted that role of, 'Let's see how much we can make this work out.' The concerns I had, and the acute situation we were in, I was afraid it would blow up during the year."

In the first year post-Jimmy, the Cowboys lost to San Francisco in the NFC championship game in 1994, then capped a tumultuous 1995 season with a win in Super Bowl XXX against Pittsburgh in Tempe, Ariz. But were there more Super Bowls to be won if Johnson had stayed? That's a question that haunts Cowboys fans, but not necessarily Jones.

"We had a heck of a team the next year and really by rights, you'd have to say we were the best or right there at the best, in the NFL," Jones pointed out. "So we didn't leave that year on the table. You can say, well, you should have won it, but that's cutting hairs. We won it the next year (1995).

"Jimmy was never, ever, ever going to be a 10-year guy. He was never going to be a 15-year guy. He was never going to be a Coach Landry for the next 29 years. He was never that. He would never have been that."

Cowboys players like Troy Aikman, however, contend that the decline in discipline under Switzer helped lead to the team's gradual demise as an NFL power at the time. Jones isn't so sure.

"The real question is, 'Did we have issues when we won three out of four Super Bowls?' Not, 'Did they start after that?' " Jones said. "The answer is, Yes, we had issues, by the fact that some of the same people were here. For the most part, the discipline issues were products of the same individuals.

"You can say that Jimmy kept them in check and I would submit to you that success brings those challenges out in you. I would submit that the (discipline) challenges on this team were not the reason we didn't compete (after '95), because we competed for three more Super bowls. I think it was a diminishing talent base. I think Barry did a heck of a job. The nature of some of the issues that were coming, if Jimmy had stayed, would have been detracting as well."

After a shaky 10-6 season and a wild card win in '96, the Cowboys went 12 straight seasons without winning another playoff game. It wasn't the discipline issues off the field (Michael Irvin, Erik Williams, the "White House"), as scandalous as they may have been, that hurt the Cowboys nearly as much as the lack of discipline on the practice field, which bled over into the games. That was a direct reflection on Switzer, who was the exact opposite of Johnson in disciplinary approach.

Jones learns things about himself, about his team, about others, when he looks back, and he does it often. But he'd much rather look ahead. He likes to envision where the league, where the Cowboys, will be in five years, in 10, in 20, even far beyond that point where Jerry Jones himself will be directly involved.

From the very first moment, almost three decades ago, when Jones purchased the Cowboys from Bright in February of 1989, he knew it would be a family enterprise. Even so, that it has evolved to the point where virtually every member of his immediate family – wife Gene and their three and children, with even grandchildren working on their "internships" – might have at least mildly surprised Jones. It has become so much more than just a family business. It is a family lifestyle and as far as Jones can look into the future, he sees the Jones family imprint all over the Cowboys for decades to come and maybe even longer. There is, he says, no end in sight, so if fans are waiting for Jerry to finally give up and ride off into the sunset, this ain't Roy Rogers and Trigger, folks. A septuagenarian, Jones has already established a plan of succession as far as his family's management of the Cowboys is concerned.

"We've written our book together," Jones said. "This isn't the way grandpa used to do it; this isn't the way daddy did it. This was us, doing it together, when we didn't know how to do it. This is the way we've learned and evolved over a 30-year period of time. The succession is in place, and it will be seamless."

It is gratifying to Jones to know that in his three children – Stephen, Charlotte and Jerry Jr. – and his nine grandchildren – he has a built-in work force, a human resource director's dream team, if you will.

"We have the talent, the passion and the incentive," Jones said. "We will not have to call on an unknown (read: non-family) person. We don't have to. It's in place on a week's notice. It's in place on a year's notice. Everything is structured around my family and their successors."

Not that Jones plans on stepping down from his position as owner/president/general manager any time soon, mind you. It's just that he is mindful of his age and that time is the one big fullback that simply can't be stopped at the goal line. When The Big Guy scores and time runs out, there is no overtime period in the offing, no chance for one last Hail Mary.

"I obviously see the gravity of things, gravity being age," Jones conceded. "I know these are precious years ahead. I have an attitude of when I look to the future of the Cowboys I'm particularly excited about what we have in place with our management, with Stephen and Charlotte and Jerry (Jr.). And of course guys like (senior director of pro and college personnel) Will McClay and with Jason Garrett."

With almost three decades of his ownership and management style on record, it is absolutely fair to judge Jones on what he and the Cowboys have accomplished as well as what they haven't. The bottom line: There were three Super Bowl championships in the first seven years; a paltry three playoff wins and no Super Bowl appearances in the next 21. That 20-plus-year drought has frustrated Jones and Cowboys fans alike, yet somehow the Cowboys brand – Charlotte Jones' department within the Jones family hierarchy – may be more popular than ever. The Cowboys were the most popular team on Twitter in 2015 and, though he dropped out of the top five in the second half (out of sight, out of mind), Tony Romo was the most tweeted about player in the league halfway through that season. An annual Harris poll came out in October 2015, naming the Cowboys the most popular team in the NFL for the seventh time in eight seasons (they'd temporarily dropped out of the top spot in 2014 after a six-year run). Even better for the Jones' bottom line, Forbes magazine announced that the Cowboys topped all NFL teams with a value of $4 billion, thanks to the cash cow that is AT&T Stadium and the Jones family's marketing genius.

All of that is well and good but it's not really what the fans want to hear and it's not what Jones wants most of all either. He wants to win. He wants another Super Bowl before the paramedics haul him out of The Star at Frisco, site of the Cowboys' spectacular headquarters and practice facility, which opened in August 2016. While his track record as a prognosticator is suspect, at best, Jones firmly believes he will see his Cowboys back in the Super Bowl sooner rather than later.

"We've had some bad luck," Jones said. "A lot of people would say you've had bad management relative to football. We've had bad luck. We have knocked on the door three or four times. Certainly if you look at the Giants and you look at the couple of Super Bowl wins they've had, we really should have been in it two or three, maybe four times, over the last 10 or 15 years.

"We'll get ours. I think it will swing for us. I really believe that. I believe so strongly in that. We're going to keep firing at 'em. Here's where I'm coming from: I can sleep like a baby knowing we're going to get our Super Bowls. It may be catch-up time. It may be in a bunch, like when we came in and got three out of four, but we're going to get our Super Bowls. I really believe that."

By most accounts, the Cowboys have already constructed the best offensive line in the league. With the fourth overall pick in the 2016 draft, they added top-ranked running back Ezekiel Elliott out of Ohio State. Almost as an after-thought, they spent a fourth-round pick on Mississippi State quarterback Dak Prescott, hoping he might eventually develop into an NFL quarterback. Heading into the 2016 season, they confidently believed that their success or failure over at least the next two or three seasons would ride on Romo's health. After all, the NFL is a quarterbacks' league. With a good one, anything can happen.

Turns out, they were absolutely right, but for all the wrong reasons.

Finish The Fight

No doubt Kyle Brister, a high school classmate with a special connection to Dak Prescott, closely followed his friend's 2016 season in the NFL.

"I'm sure that kid is still talking about how the quarterback of the Dallas Cowboys carried him off the field one night in Haughton, La.," Jason Brotherton, the former football coach at the town's high school, told me.

"Dak got the whole team together behind the bench and they decided they would carry Kyle off the field on their shoulders," Brotherton went on.

Brister was autistic and the team manager, who was about to move to Texas with his family.

"You know, kids that age aren't supposed to think of things like that. But that's who Dak was at an early age and obviously still is today."

Prescott has shown, again and again, that he is not your typical athletic standout.

Years from now, when most of the individual heroics, the touchdowns, the amazing catches, have faded from memory, there are two indelible images from the Cowboys' 2016 season that may live in the minds of the team's fans forever.

One was a "I-can't-believe-he-just-did-that" moment when Cowboys' rookie running back Ezekiel Elliott pranced deeply into the end zone after a touchdown, leaped into an oversized Salvation Army red kettle, then mischievously peeked out like a playful genie in a bottle.

The other was a simple but totally unexpected act of common

courtesy. Early in the season, rookie Prescott was caught on national TV in the middle of a game tossing a wadded-up Gatorade cup at a trash can. He missed – a rarity in and of itself on that day and in this magical season – and normally, that would be the end of it. The cup, we all expected, would lay there on the turf until an equipment manager – like Kyle Brister was at Haughton – threw it away during postgame cleanup. But Prescott wearily hoisted himself from the bench, sauntered over and picked up his litter, then deposited it properly, a "Don't Mess with Texas" approach that evoked an outpouring of amazed admiration from around the country.

Each incident, each in its own way, gave us distinct insight into who these fresh new Cowboys are and why they captured the hearts of fans so quickly. Sure, talent helped, but so did the personalities of these two young stars who took Texas and the NFL by storm in their first seasons in the league.

From the very start they were the ying and yang of the Cowboys, the peanut butter and jelly, the bacon and eggs. In the locker room they played off each other like Abbott and Costello. On the field, they were Butch and Sundance, a lethal combination of intelligence, finesse, speed and power that would carry the Cowboys to a franchise record-tying 13 regular season victories and into the postseason for only the second time in the last eight years.

No wonder they were easily 1-2 in NFL Offensive Rookie of the Year Award voting, with Prescott garnering 28 of 50 first place votes and Elliott snagging 21-of-50. Naturally, they both went on stage to accept at the awards ceremony, with Prescott graciously asking for a knife "so we can cut this (trophy) in half."

That the Cowboys' season ended far too soon in a shootout with Aaron Rodgers and the archrival Green Bay Packers in a divisional showdown at AT&T Stadium on Jan. 15, 2017, left an aching Cowboys Nation panting for more. As even Jerry Jones would concede, there was no moral victory in the Cowboys' 34-31 loss to the Packers on Mason Crosby's 51-yard field goal as time expired. But there is hope, personified in the accomplishments of Prescott and Elliott, of wide receivers Dez Bryant and Cole Beasley and in an offensive line that re-established itself as the best in the business. There are a multitude of reasons to believe that the Cowboys will be back on that postseason stage again, and sooner rather than later.

This is a franchise that, more than two decades after its last appearance in the ultimate game, still measures success by Super Bowl appearances and by Vince Lombardi trophies. That can lead to massive and regular disappointment, but it also can result in the highest of highs.

How did this happen? How did the Cowboys go from a dismal 4-12 to a miraculous 13-3 in just 12 months? And with a rookie quarterback who was the 135th overall player taken in the April draft? Elliott, we can at least get our minds around. He was the fourth overall pick out of collegiate powerhouse Ohio State. The Cowboys and the rest of the NFL expected him to be great and he was.

But the NFL is a quarterbacks' league – never more evident than in watching Mr. Rodgers and Atlanta's Matt Ryan dominate the NFL neighborhood in 2016 – and seven other college quarterbacks were taken before the Cowboys almost reluctantly selected Mississippi State's Prescott in the fourth round. The Cowboys had even made last-ditch efforts to trade up to acquire either Paxton Lynch, who went to Denver, or Connor Cook, selected instead by Oakland. Prescott all but fell into their laps, whether they had their minds originally set on him or not.

Prescott's selection, ostensibly as a project quarterback while Tony Romo closed out the final years of his NFL career and young Kellen Moore tried again to prove he could be a capable NFL backup, was just the first example of magic dust sprinkled on the Cowboys in 2016. Call it serendipity or whatever, many other pieces would also fall into place, all coming together to light a fire under Cowboys Nation like none that we've seen since the days of The Triplets in the 1990s. There's ample evidence, in fact, to believe that Dak, Zeke and Dez Bryant are absolutely the New Triplets and despite the loss, their performances on the Big Stage, the divisional playoff loss to the Packers, illustrate why that's so.

Prescott completed 24 of 38 passes for 302 yards and three touchdown in that narrow loss to the Pack. He scored a game-tying two-point conversion on a critical quarterback draw. In the game's final 17 minutes and 19 seconds, he hit 13 of 17 passes for 143 yards and two TDs, twice bringing the Cowboys back to tie the score. Elliott, despite getting just 10 carries in the first half after the Cowboys fell behind 21-3, finished with 125 yards on 22 carries. They leaned on him heavily in the fourth quarter, when he carried the load to twice tie it up. Bryant was brilliant with nine catches for 132 yards and two touchdowns.

Former Cowboys' fullback Daryl Johnston, owner of three Super Bowl rings, can see definite similarities between the champs of the '90s and today's Cowboys.

"The Cowboys had that run in the '70s (five Super Bowls in nine years) and we had ours in the '90s (three in four years)," Johnston noted. "Maybe this is the run that starts in 2016."

There's no argument that, Rodgers' performances aside, no one player can make a team great. Remember, even Hall of Fame-bound Troy Aikman was 0-11 as a starter in his rookie season in 1989. But there's also no doubt that it all starts at quarterback and that the Cowboys' "discovery" of Dak Prescott was the key turning point in 2016.

How did NFL scouts miss so badly on Prescott, even after he threw 29 touchdown passes with just five interceptions in his final season at Mississippi State and had the third longest streak of completions (288) without an interception in SEC history? Maybe they didn't remember that when he'd come home from his high school practices at Haughton he'd sometimes confess to his mom that he'd thrown an interception that day. Peggy Prescott, who died of colon cancer in 2013, would innocently but pointedly ask, "Why are you practicing that?"

Or maybe they didn't realize that he is so focused on avoiding turnovers that he won't even toss the ball to a defensive teammate in warmups. "Some of them try to get me to do it," Prescott told reporters. "The best I'll do is maybe rolling it to them on the ground."

What the Cowboys, who had drafted just two quarterbacks in the previous 15 years (Quincy Carter, 2001; Stephen Moore, 2009), did know for sure was that of the seven quarterbacks they invited to Valley Ranch for pre-draft visits, a list that included Carson Wentz, Jared Goff, Lynch and Cook, they identified Prescott as having the highest football IQ among that group.

Obviously, they were still unsure about his physical ability or they wouldn't have been trying so hard to snare someone else.

Before the draft, Prescott worked on shoring up his perceived weaknesses with private coach Tom Shaw in Orlando, where every snap was under center. They worked together on his timing, his footwork, his mechanics.

"The offense we ran at Mississippi State was nothing short of an NFL offense," Prescott said. "The only thing that was different is that we didn't go under center. I swear to you, in (pre-draft) visits, every play (teams) showed me, I could name it; we just called it something different (at Mississippi State)."

Playing his senior season behind a makeshift offensive line – Alabama sacked him nine times – Prescott was less spectacular than he was consistent. He often checked down to his third or fourth receiver in the flat. The results looked a whole lot like his first season with the Cowboys. His completion percentage jumped from 61.6 to 66.2 and he threw for 29 touchdowns with just five picks.

"I learned last year that you win at this position by knowledge," he said, "by being ahead of the defense mentally."

Prescott had committed early to Mississippi State and, frankly, other major colleges weren't exactly banging down his door until after he accounted for 60 TDs his senior season. Prescott, however, was simply not going to waver on his commitment to the Bulldogs. Having given his word, he was determined to keep it.

Once he arrived at Mississippi State, however, any reservations coaches had about his ability vanished. By his final season there, Prescott had been named All-SEC, was a nominee for the Heisman Trophy, Maxwell and Davey O'Brien awards, and set single-season school records for total offense, passing yards and passing TDs. The fact that he'd played in a spread offense and been arrested on suspicion of DUI (although later acquitted) just a month before the NFL draft likely knocked him down to the fourth round.

Cowboys quarterbacks coach Wade Wilson had few questions about Prescott's character after visiting him in Starkville before the draft. Wilson would later note that he left their blue-plate lunch at Restaurant Tyler with a bill too small to expense and a strong impression of the soon-to-be Cowboys' new quarterback.

"He has an aura and confidence about him," Wilson said. Neither had a premonition that that confidence would face its sternest test before the summer was out.

"To tell you we expected him to do what he did, I'd be lying to you," said Brotherton, who was an assistant coach while Prescott was at Haughton. "He was a lightly recruited high school quarterback who basically changed the whole program at Mississippi State. He loves it when the odds are against him. He feeds off that. Now it wouldn't surprise me if he winds up in the Hall of Fame. It's just an example of good things happening to good people."

It's the "good people" part, coupled with his amazing performance in 2016, that makes Prescott's story so compelling for Cowboys fans. They'd still love him based on that 13-3 record alone, but that he's someone they can admire for his humanity, his basic "goodness," makes it that much sweeter.

Brotherton still remembers the very last game of Prescott's senior season at Haughton. The Bucs had gone 10-0 in the regular season and won their first two playoff games before losing 49-41 to eventual state champion Franklinton. The coaches consoled their players, then retired to a nearby restaurant with their wives to rehash the game and the season. When they returned to the locker room to pack up almost two hours later, they were amazed at what they found.

"Dak is still in the locker room. playing catch with all of the coaches' kids, 6-, 7-, 8-year olds," Brotherton said. "Instead of leaving with his buddies, doing what other high school kids do, he was still there, entertaining these kids after maybe the toughest loss of his life. He is such a unique person in so many ways."

Head coach Rodney Guin, who retired from Haughton and then took a job as head coach at Calvary Baptist in Shreveport, became like a second father to Prescott. He remembers Dak as one of the most genuine people he's ever known.

"He treated everybody the same," Guin said. "He never put himself above anybody. His work ethic was unequaled in my experience. He always had tremendous confidence in what he could do. Nothing was too big for him.

"He also played with a bit of a chip on his shoulder. People doubted him and his goal was to prove them wrong. I don't think any of us realized he would one day play for the Dallas Cowboys, but we knew he was special. For him, it was always about the team. He didn't care if he threw for any yards as long as we won. He was never afraid if we fell behind. He always believed he could get things done in the end."

When the NFL draft rolled around in April of 2016, his high school coaches didn't know what to think or what to expect.

"As a coach who knows Dak and loves him, you just hope he gets drafted," Brotherton said. "Then you're hoping he just makes the team. Then you're hoping he'll wind up as the backup quarterback. Next thing, you look up and he's starting. I told my wife the week before the Cowboys played Cincinnati (fifth game of the season) that we needed to get to a game in Dallas while Dak was still starting."

He needn't have worried. Four weeks later, with the Cowboys sitting at 8-1 under Prescott, a healthy but disappointed Romo made his now famous concession speech. It put the exclamation mark on what the Cowboys' front office and coaches had clearly concluded: This was now Dak Prescott's team. Romo's concession speech simply made it official.

This paragraph was at the core of what Romo said that afternoon at Valley Ranch:

"You see football is a meritocracy. You aren't handed anything. You earn everything every single day, over and over again. You have to prove it. That's the way that the NFL, that's the way that football, works. A great example of this is Dak Prescott and what he's done. He's earned the right to be our quarterback. As hard as that is for me to say, he's earned that right. He's guided our team to an 8-1 record, and that's hard to do. If you think for a second that I don't want to be out there, then you've probably never felt the pure ecstasy of competing and winning. That hasn't left me. In fact, it may burn more now than ever."

By the time the off-season arrived, that flame apparently had guttered out. Instead of opting to continue his career with another team, Romo chose to retire from football and accept a job with CBS, working alongside Jim Nantz as the network's No. 1 analyst, replacing Nantz's longtime boothmate, former Giants quarterback Phil Simms.

If it appeared that Romo was lucky to have been offered such a golden parachute, he had nothing on Prescott, whose rising star was now soaring to virtually unprecedented heights. Three times in Prescott's football career, at three levels, the door to the starting quarterback position had been opened by injury.

First, as a sophomore at Haughton, Prescott stepped in when senior starter Matt Smith went down. Dak never looked back. The scenario would repeat itself at Mississippi State, when senior starter Tyler Russell was felled by injury during Prescott's sophomore season. He took the job and ran with it.

Finally, the Cowboys practically did all they could not to draft Prescott. After watching their backup quarterbacks go 1-11 following Romo's collar bone fractures in 2015, owner Jerry Jones was determined not to repeat that mistake. He tried to trade for a backup quarterback in the off-season, to no avail. He had no better luck finding one in free agency when first Colt McCoy, then Chase Daniel, signed for more money elsewhere.

That left only the draft. The Cowboys explored two first-round trades, attempting to get to Paxton Lynch after Jared Goff and Carson Wentz went 1-2 overall. Instead, the Broncos drafted Lynch with the 26th pick following a trade with the Seahawks. Later, Jones would admit that the Cowboys offered the No. 34 overall choice and the 67th choice to Seattle to move up for Lynch. Jones said Lynch had "the highest upside in the draft."

That left Cook, but the Raiders quickly traded ahead of the Cowboys to take him. Disappointed, the Cowboys drafted Oklahoma defensive end Charles Tapper with the next choice, No. 101 overall, and finally landed their quarterback – Prescott – with a compensatory pick at No. 135.

Clearly, they had no idea what they'd just done. "It was the perfect storm," quarterbacks coach Wade Wilson would say later.

It wasn't over, either. Prescott was still seen as a project, with Kellen Moore slated to return as Romo's backup. Fate would once again step in to assist Prescott. Moore fractured his right ankle in training camp practice on Aug. 2.

Prescott, to be candid, is not generally regarded as a great practice quarterback and immediately underscored that fact when he stepped in with the second unit, replacing Moore. He dropped his first snap.

"In my head I'm like, 'Did you really just do that?'" Prescott said afterward.

Just 23 days later, Romo started his first game since his second collar bone fracture the previous season, an exhibition game at Seattle. Only three plays into the game, Romo was chased down from behind by Seahawks defensive end Cliff Avril, who chopped him high on the shoulder pads and brought his full weight down on Romo from behind. Romo writhed on the ground in pain while Cowboys Nation collectively sucked in its breath. There would be a sigh of relief later when Romo was spotted on the sideline, lobbying to get back into the game, but it was short-lived. The next day the news from his MRI hit the team with a Dick Butkus-sized impact: Romo would miss six to 10 weeks with a compression fracture in his back.

The only quarterbacks still standing were a rookie named Dak Prescott and former practice-squad hopeful Jameill Showers.

"It was really crazy luck," Wilson admitted. "There are a lot of things that could have happened that didn't happen, to our betterment."

As Prescott had already proven in high school and again in college, once he got his hands on the starting job, there was no way he was letting it go, not even once Romo was finally healthy. The Cowboys signed veteran Mark Sanchez the week of the season opener as Prescott's backup and an insurance policy in case the rookie was simply overwhelmed by the speed of play in the NFL.

"At this level, in general, timing is everything," Sanchez told reporters of Prescott's sudden elevation to a job once held by such NFL princes as Don Meredith, Roger Staubach and Troy Aikman. "You've got to prepare yourself as best you can and then hope things fall into place, whether it's coaching, injuries, the team you're on, the talent around you, all that kind of stuff plays into it, and there's so many factors you can't control. But what he has controlled is everything he could."

Since 1978, when the NFL went to a 16-game schedule, there have been only 18 quarterbacks who have started all 16 games of their rookie seasons. The list includes future Pro Bowlers Peyton Manning, Matt Ryan, Joe Flacco, Cam Newton, Andrew Luck and Russell Wilson. Add Dak Prescott's name to that list.

Manning won three games as a rookie. Newton won six. Ryan, Flacco, Luck and Wilson all won 11 games. Ryan, Flacco, Luck and Wilson, plus Sanchez and Andy Dalton all took their teams to the playoffs as rookies. All went as wild-card entries. Prescott won an

NFL rookie-record-tying 13 games and put the Cowboys into the postseason as NFC East champions and the top seed in the NFC playoff bracket.

Wilson threw the fewest interceptions of any of the 16 previous 16-game rookie starters with 10. Prescott lowered that bar dramatically to four, stitching together streaks of 176 consecutive passes without an interception to start the season and another streak of 171 consecutive passes during the middle of the year. By comparison, Manning threw a rookie-record 28 interceptions in his three-win debut season. Hall of Famer Terry Bradshaw? He threw 24 interceptions on his way to five wins as a rookie. Troy Aikman went 0-11 as a rookie and was intercepted 18 times. Read into it what you will, but obviously Prescott played well beyond his years.

That doesn't mean that his playful streak doesn't still surface on a regular basis. Prescott and Elliott were having fun winning and enjoying themselves off the field as well. Prescott had to dodge spitballs that Elliott was shooting through a straw during an interview near the end of the regular season. Prescott retaliated the next day by filling Zeke's helmet with M&Ms.

For a franchise and a fandom wondering what the future would hold when Romo's fragile body simply couldn't hold up any longer, Prescott and Elliott have provided an amazing breath of fresh air and soaring optimism for the future of the Dallas Cowboys.

It was a storybook season for each of them and it wasn't all about what they did on the field. Prescott showed his attention to detail and focus when he passed up a late-night talk show invitation and overseas endorsement opportunities to spend the bye-week back home in Louisiana with his grandmother. Elliott partnered with the Texas SPCA to do $21 (matching his jersey number) adoption specials at the Dallas Animal Shelter and donated $2,100 himself. He personally brought each family their new pet. He bought his offensive linemen four-wheelers for Christmas.

Even as rookies, Elliott and Prescott were both heavy in the conversation for NFL MVP. They led five Cowboys into the Pro Bowl. Zeke was named NFL Rookie of the Year by the Pro Football Writers Association, but Dak won the overall NFL award. Both made the all-rookie team.

When the season ended, there was no more debate: With Romo gone, the Cowboys became Dak and Zeke's team. With new hope and renewed dreams, the Cowboys came a long way in 2016, but the journey had just begun.

Acknowledgements

The aim of this book was to give the reader – presumably many of them diehard Cowboys' fans – a primer on Dallas Cowboys franchise history by focusing on the personalities and players who have made them both great and dramatically interesting. It is not meant to be a definitive history of the team. Author Peter Golenbock produced that with his voluminous and highly detailed 1997 book, *Cowboys Have Always Been My Heroes: The Definitive Oral History of America's Team*. See, it says it's definitive right there in the title. And even though it has been upwards of two decades since Golenbock's tome was released, it's not as if he missed a lot of Cowboys' championships in this millennium.

Golenbock's 800-plus page book is one of the foundation pieces of research for this one. There have been scores of books written on the Cowboys over the years, by former players, coaches, owners, broadcasters and sports writers like me. I owe all of them a debt of thanks for providing a tremendous storehouse of information, stories and anecdotes, some of which have been repeated through the years, some of which you may be hearing for the first time.

Some deserve special mention, because I often leaned on their work in compiling this one. Special thanks to Jerry Jones and Jimmy Johnson. Also to former colleagues who plowed much of this ground before me, men like the late, great Frank Luksa, Carlton Stowers, Skip Bayless, Mike Fisher, Jean-Jacques Taylor, Denne Freeman, Jaime Aaron and Brad Sham. I had help from my amigo of nearly half a century, Randy Galloway, columnist-in-crime Gil LeBreton, fellow Jason D. Williams lover Dale Hansen, and Clarence Hill, the *Fort Worth*

Star-Telegram's Cowboys' beat writer, and Charean Williams, the paper's former NFL and Cowboys writer. Also, to Mark Ribowsky for his excellent work, *The Last Cowboy:A Life of Tom Landry*.

Thanks to all those I talked to or interviewed personally over the years and specifically for this book, including Troy Aikman, Daryl Johnston, Emmitt Smith, Roger Staubach, Preston Pearson, Drew Pearson, Bob Lilly, Nate Newton and many, many others. A project like this could not get done without the help of the Cowboys' great PR staff, so a tip of the Tom Landry fedora to Rich Dalrymple and Scott Agulnek, along with Jerry Jones' amazing executive assistant Marilyn Love.

Thanks also to my terrific editor, Tom Johanningmeier, and to my publisher Barry Shlachter for allowing me the opportunity to take on a project like this.

I went to work for the *Fort Worth Star-Telegram* in 1969, a died-in-the-wool, 23-year-old Cowboys' fan who had yet to learn that it wasn't cool for a sports writer to adore any team as much as I did the Cowboys. Just as well then that I wound up spending 11 years on the Texas Rangers beat in the '70s and '80s. I became a general sports columnist in 1987, just in time to get in on covering the last two years of Tom Landry's amazing 29-year run as Cowboys' head coach and the beginning of the Jerry Jones era and I was hip deep in Cowboys when they won their three Super Bowls in the '90s.

Thanks to Tex Schramm, Gil Brandt and Tom Landry for their combined genius in building a franchise like the Cowboys, setting a standard never before seen in the NFL.

Let me also acknowledge you, the fans. In more than half a century of covering sports, I've never seen a sports franchise capture the imagination of an entire nation as the Cowboys have for more than six decades. I realize it rubs a lot of people in New York, Washington, Philadelphia, San Francisco and elsewhere as raw as a saddle sore, but there's only one America's Team, and it's the Dallas Cowboys. Get over it and join the party.

Jim Reeves

Index

Accorsi, Ernie, 74, 77
Aikman, Troy, 36, 37, 38, 40, 41, 42, 43, 46, 47, 62-66, 67, 76, 83, 84, 85, 95, 96, 101, 106, 107, 146, 148, 149, 150, 155, 158-72, 175, 179
Anderson, Donny, 113-15
Andrie, George, 103, 111, 112, 118, 122, 126
Arkansas (University of), 18, 19, 34, 35, 39, 40
ArkLA (public utility), 19
Arkoma, 19
Avril, Cliff, 191

Baker, Bobby, 9
Baltimore Colts, 72, 117-120
Bell, Ricky, 73
Bielski, Dick, 89-90
Bradshaw, Terry, 64, 139
Brandt, Gil, 10, 21, 27-29, 53, 73, 78, 84, 102, 103, 126, 127, 133, 134, 146, 182
Bright, H.R. "Bum," 11-14, 20, 177
Briskin, Barney, 9
Brister, Kyle, 183-84
Brotherton, Jason, 183, 188-89
Brown, Larry, 108, 168

Bryant, Dez, 47, 86-88
Buffalo Bills, 66, 96, 146-56
Campo, Dave, 42-43
Carolina Panthers, 41, 169
Carter, Quincy, 43-44
Catch, The, 141-45
Chambers, Eugenia "Gene," 19
Clark, Dwight, 61, 141
Coaches, Campo, Dave, 42-43; Gailey, Chan, 41-42; Garrett, Jason, 46-48, 108, 179, 181; Johnson, Jimmy, 18, 21, 22, 23, 33-40, 42, 47, 62, 76, 77, 84, 87, 95, 101, 106, 134, 146, 149, 152, 155, 157, 160, 162, 164, 171-76; Landry, Tom, 8, 10, 11, 12, 14, 15, 17, 20-24, 30-33, 34, 35, 36, 47, 50-56, 59, 60, 71, 72, 75, 91, 92, 93, 98, 100-04, 106, 112, 113, 118, 121-23, 126, 129, 130, 134, 135, 137-40, 142, 146, 162; Parcells, Bill, 43, 45, 67, 94, 99, 150; Phillips, Wade, 45-46; Switzer, Barry, 39, 40-41, 42, 62, 63, 157-64, 166, 167, 169, 170, 174, 176
Cole, Larry, 122
Cook, Connor, 185, 186

Cosbie, Doug, 93, 95
Cowboys Have Always Been My Heroes: the Definitive Oral History of America's Team (Golenbock), 9, 21, 28, 32, 74, 119, 128, 132, 138

Dallas Morning News, 13, 14, 15, 21, 25, 35, 52, 92, 105, 109
Dallas Times-Herald, 50
Denver Broncos, 75, 93, 104, 132-36
Dial, Buddy, 51
Dirty Dozen, 125, 127-28, 130, 132
Ditka, Mike, 89, 91, 92, 123, 133
Donohue, Terry, 41
Dorsett, Tony, 73-76, 101, 103, 133, 134, 136, 137, 143, 153
DuPree, Billy Joe, 89, 91, 92-93, 94, 133, 138, 139

Elliott, Ezekeil, 182, 183-86, 192

Fort Worth Star-Telegram, 14, 15, 22, 43, 94, 99, 109, 153, 165

Gaechter, Mike, 28, 78
Gailey, Chan, 41-42
Galloway, Randy, 15, 17, 23, 34
Garrett, Jason, 46-48, 108, 179, 181
Garrison, Walt, 33, 53, 58, 59, 71, 120, 123, 126, 128
Gent, Pete, 28-29, 49
Goff, Jared, 186, 190
Golenbock, Peter, 9, 12, 21, 28, 32, 50, 51, 54, 60 62, 74, 119, 120, 128, 132, 136, 138, 173
Great Train Robbery, The, 38, 76, 146
Green, Cornell, 28, 72, 78, 103, 114, 126
Griese, Bob, 121
Guin, Rodney, 188

Hail to the Redskins, 8, 10
Haley, Charles, 107, 147, 150, 151, 153
Hansen, Dale, 15, 16
Haughton (La.) High, 183, 188
Hardin, Wayne, 54
Harper, Alvin, 40, 155, 171
Harris, Cliff, 28, 103, 106, 122, 130
Hayes, Bob, 28, 78-80, 91, 112, 126
Hill, Calvin, 71, 74, 123, 126
Houston Oilers, 32
Huff, Sam, 31
Hunt, Lamar, 53

Ice Bowl, 32, 52, 109-116
In Control (Henderson), 105
Irvin, Michael, 9, 37, 40, 41, 64, 83-86
  compared to Dez Bryant, 86, 88

Johnson, Jimmy, 18, 21, 22, 23, 33-40, 42, 47, 62, 76, 77, 84, 87, 95, 101, 106, 134, 146, 149, 152, 155, 157, 160, 162, 164, 171-76
Johnston, Daryl, 37, 151, 161, 162, 175, 186
Jones, Charlotte, 22, 180-81
Jones, Ed, 131, 137
Jones, Jerry, 12, 13, 14-23, 26, 33, 35, 43, 45, 46, 47, 62, 63, 77, 80, 83, 83, 87, 120, 127, 146, 151, 152, 157, 164, 165, 167, 169, 171-76, 177-82
Jones, Jerry Jr., 22, 180-81
Jones, Pat, 18
Jones, Stephen, 20, 22, 173, 180-81
Jordan, Lee Roy, 103, 105, 106, 118, 126, 128

Kansas City Chiefs, 53, 110
Kelly, Jim, 67, 150
Krause, Paul, 57, 82

Lacewell, Larry, 40, 181
LaFleur, David, 43
Lambeau Field, 109-116
Lambert, Jack, 91, 131, 138
Landry, Tom, 8, 10, 11, 12, 14, 15, 17, 20-24, 30-33, 34, 35, 36, 47, 50-56, 59, 60, 71, 72, 75, 91, 92, 93, 98, 100-04, 106, 112, 113, 118, 121-23, 126, 129, 130, 134, 135, 137-40, 142, 146, 162
Landry's Boys (Golenbock), 50, 54, 60, 72
Last Cowboy, The (Ribowsky), 29, 53
LeBaron, Eddie, 89-90
Lilly, Bob, 71, 102, 103, 104, 105, 106, 111, 114, 118, 120, 121, 122, 123, 126, 127
Lombardi, Vince, 31-32, 111
Longley, Clint, 59, 105, 126, 132
Los Angeles Rams, 17, 25, 27, 60, 74, 128, 129, 130, 132, 140, 149
Lynch, Paxton, 185, 186, 190
Lynn, Mike, 37, 77

Marshall, Corinne, 9
Marshall, George Preston, 9-10
Martin, Harvey, 104, 105, 131, 132, 135, 136, 337
Maryland, Russell, 38, 77, 108, 147
Meredith, Don, 49-53, 55, 66, 70 78, 90, 103, 110
Mia's Tex Mex, 21, 33, 35
Miami Dolphins, 73, 121-24
Miami (University of), 35, 36, 37, 42, 63, 84, 150, 155
Minnesota Vikings, 37, 42, 57, 71, 75, 77, 82, 125, 128, 134, 146, 147, 162
Monday Night Football, 53, 75
Montana, Joe, 61, 64, 94, 141, 143, 144, 145

Moore, Kellen, 185
Morton, Craig, 51, 52, 55, 56, 57, 117, 119, 120, 126, 127, 134-36
Murchison, Clint Jr., 8-11, 11-13, 49, 70, 171

Nelson, Sheffield, 19
New York Giants, 14, 31, 32, 46, 56, 57, 67, 73, 94, 126, 127, 135, 143, 149, 154, 162
NFC Championship (1982), see Catch, The
NFL Championship (1967), see Ice Bowl
NFL Hall of Fame, 17, 33, 28, 63, 65, 80, 81, 84, 85, 86, 102, 103, 104, 160
Novacek, Jay, 92, 93, 94, 95, 97

Oklahoma State University, 35, 62, 63, 87
Oklahoma (University of), 40, 62, 174

Parcells, Bill, 43, 45, 67, 94, 99, 150
Pearson, Drew, 28, 57, 61, 74, 75, 80-83, 92, 93, 101, 128, 129, 133, 137, 142, 145
Pearson, Preston, 57, 75, 82, 129, 130, 133, 134, 137, 139
Perkins, Don, 28, 49, 70-71, 89
Philadelphia Eagles, 128, 134, 142, 149, 161
Phillips, Wade, 45-46
Pittsburgh Steelers, 41, 51, 125-32, 137-40, 157-70
Prescott, Dak, 69, 183-93
Pugh, Jethro, 28, 103, 115, 119, 122
Reeves, Dan, 71, 113, 119
Renfro, Mel, 103, 106, 118, 123

Renfro, Ray, 56
Rhome, Jerry, 51, 55
Ribowksy, Mark, 29, 53
Ring of Honor, 25, 58, 70, 71, 75, 80, 83, 85, 97, 101, 102, 106
Romo, Tony, 44, 45, 47, 64, 66-69, 86, 99, 181, 182, 185, 189-93
Rozelle, Pete, 13, 25, 58, 73, 139

San Diego Chargers, 19, 20, 37
Saturday Night Massacre, The, 21, 33, 146
Schramm, Tex, 10, 12, 13, 20, 21, 23-29, 31, 32, 36, 53, 58, 70, 71, 72, 73, 78, 80, 84, 94, 111, 116, 123, 126, 127, 133, 134, 140, 142, 146,
Scott, Herb, 75, 132, 128
Sham, Brad, 26, 61, 83, 86
Shaw, Tom, 187
Shula, Don, 150
Simpson, Jessica, 45, 67
Smith, Emmitt, 37, 38, 40, 75, 76-77, 83, 146, 147, 149, 150, 151, 154, 156, 162, 169, 171
Smith, Kevin, 38, 77, 108, 147
Salomon Brothers, 20
St. Louis Rams, 16
Starr, Bart, 112, 113, 114, 115, 141
Staubach, Roger, 27, 33, 51, 53-59, 60-62, 64, 74, 76, 79, 80-83, 91, 92, 94, 104, 105, 120, 123, 125, 126-129, 131, 132, 133, 135, 136, 137-40, 141,
Stowers, Carlton, 25, 26, 27, 28, 29, 93
Super Bowl V, 55, 106, 117-20
Super Bowl VI, 11, 57, 73, 121-24
Super Bowl X, 125-132

Super Bowl XII, 61, 75, 93, 132-36
Super Bowl XIII, 137-40
Super Bowl XXVII, 65, 146-51
Super Bowl XXVIII, 151-56
Super Bowl XXX, 157-70
Switzer, Barry, 39, 40-41, 42, 62, 63, 157-64, 166, 167, 169, 170, 174

Tampa Bay Buccaneers, 73, 134, 143
Thomas, Duane, 37, 71-73, 74, 119, 123
Tolbert, Tony, 108
Turner, Norv, 38, 45, 65, 84, 173
Turning the Thing Around: Pulling America's Team Out of the Dumps and Myself Out of the Doghouse (Johnson), 36, 63, 76, 96, 148, 172

UCLA, 36, 41, 63, 76
Unitas, Johnny, 32, 118

Walker, Herschel, 37, 76, 134, 146
Walls, Everson, 141, 145
Walsh, Bill, 144
Wannstedt Dave, 38, 76, 173, 175, 183
Washington Redskins, 8-10, 72, 90, 98, 126, 149, 150
Wentz, Carson, 186, 190
"White House," 9, 40, 169, 185
White, Danny, 36, 59-62, 68, 75, 91, 94, 142-43, 145
White, Randy, 104, 105, 127, 131, 135, 139
Wilson, Wade, 187-88, 190-91
Witten, Jason, 68, 92, 93, 96, 98-100
Wright, Rayfield, 102, 103, 123

About the Author

Jim Reeves retired in 2009 after 40 years as an award-winning sports columnist/baseball writer at the *Fort Worth Star-Telegram*. After retirement, he spent a year writing columns for ESPN.com and is now a freelance journalist.

Reeves, an honorary media member of the Texas Baseball Hall of Fame and a finalist for the 2017 J.G. Taylor Spink Award and induction into the National Baseball Hall of Fame in Cooperstown, New York, was nominated for a Pulitzer Prize in 1987 for his coverage of the sale of the Texas Rangers to a group headed by future President George W. Bush. He was presented the TCU Schieffer School of Journalism national Ethics Award in 2007.

Reeves covered the Dallas Cowboys extensively during the 1990s, when they won three Super Bowls.